Praise For
Encouragement Every Day

Throughout much of my life journey, Nancy Rosenow has been by my side as colleague, mentor, friend, chosen sister. She has listened to me with open heart and mind, offered insights from her own experiences and perspective, and encouraged me to trust my own instincts and make value-driven choices. Rather than telling me what to do as opportunities and challenges presented themselves, Nancy has offered heart-grounded counsel. *Encouragement Every Day* brings Nancy's support and wisdom to all of us, helping us to be our best, most generous, powerful and wise selves.

—**Bonnie Neugebauer,** Global Impact Engineer
and Co-founder, World Forum Foundation

Ask any early learning educator or care provider, they likely have a handful of quotes or mantras that keep them anchored in their dedication to serving children and families. *Encouragement Every Day* by Nancy Rosenow provides uplifting (and necessary) quotes and reflections for those doing the most important work in the world: early care and education.

—**Nick Terrones,** Preschool Program Director,
Daybreak Star Preschool and author,
*A Can of Worms: Fearless
Conversations with Toddlers*

Each morning, as I reflect, inspired by Nancy's encouraging words, I see myself sitting in companionable silence with a dear old friend, savoring the warmth of robust creamy decaf, remembering lessons learned.

—**Holly Elissa Bruno,** bestselling author,
*Happiness is Running Through the Streets
to Find You*, international keynoter,
former Maine Assistant Attorney General

Encouragement EVERY DAY

Nancy Rosenow

Exchange Press

ISBN 978-0-942702-87-3
eISBN 978-0-942702-88-0

Printed in the United States.

© 2023 Nancy Rosenow

Editor: Erin Glenn
Book Design: Stacy Hawthorne
Cover Illustration: Modulo @ Adobe Stock

This book may not be reproduced in whole or in part by any means without written permission of the publisher.

For more information about other Exchange Press publications and resources for directors and teachers, contact:

Exchange Press
7700 A Street
Lincoln, NE 68510
(800) 221-2864 • ExchangePress.com

Dedication

My family and friends encourage me every day. There are many of you and for that I am grateful. I love you all. I trust you know who you are without a list, but there is one person I must acknowledge by name. My husband John is the most steadfast encourager I know. And one more thing. Being able to put this book together with my dear friends at Exchange Press and to work with my daughter, Stacy Hawthorne, as the book's designer, was an experience I will forever cherish.

This Book is For You — and Me

Hope is being able to see that there is light despite all of the darkness.

—Desmond Tutu

In an increasingly challenging world, we all need to hold on to hope. This book is meant to offer some. Here's how it came to be:

For five years, during the time I served as Publisher of Exchange Press, I curated a daily emailer for the early childhood community, called Exchange Every Day. I inherited this writing gig from Roger and Bonnie Neugebauer, who founded Exchange Press, and I enjoyed it immensely. When the global pandemic hit in March, 2020, I began using each Monday's emailer to send an encouraging message. When I announced my retirement at the end of 2021, many readers wrote to me and said they would miss that support. I realized I would miss writing it. I needed that positive boost as much, if not more, than the readers.

Toni Morrison said, *"If there's a book that you want to read, but it hasn't been written yet, then you must write it."* So I am. I've written each day's encouragement as if I'm speaking to myself, but of course, it is meant for you just as much. Because I've written about what works for me, there will be some days when it may not hit the mark for you, and that's as it should be. Please use what works and adapt whatever doesn't. Feel free to read ahead, or look back on days that especially spoke to you. This is your encouragement to use as you please.

People who know me well tease me about how much I enjoy finding good quotes. So, it was a labor of love to search for 366 quotes I could use to begin each day's encouragement. I've always felt uplifted by other people's generosity in putting into words their discoveries about how to navigate our "one wild and precious life," as poet Mary Oliver describes it.

Desmond Tutu (1931–2021), South African bishop, human rights activist

I've tried to find quotes from many time periods and a variety of cultures. I've looked for diversity in life experiences as well. You'll notice that at the bottom of each page, I've included information about the author of each quote, including their nationality, and, if they are no longer living as of the printing of this book, the years of their birth and death. I've also provided a short biographical statement for each person, including those who are so well known that perhaps no description may have been needed.

Because I was an early childhood educator and administrator for most of my career, the first audience for this book is my fellow early care and education professionals. Even in the best of times, ours is a challenging profession. If these pages give you a lift before you begin your day, or after you've finished a long one, I'll be so glad. I believe with my whole heart that ours is also one of the most gratifying and important professions in the world.

But this book is also for everyone else. I've written it for anyone who gets up each day and does your best to navigate this crazy world with the most courage you can muster. Let's tackle the year together. I hope there will be days when you open a page and find serendipity — just what you needed. When that happens, I'll be smiling with you.

January

I love beginnings. If I were in charge of calendars, every day would be January 1.

—Jerry Spinelli

Jerry Spinelli, American writer of children's novels

JANUARY 1
Find My Authentic Self

Be yourself; everyone else is already taken.
—Oscar Wilde

Psychologist Carl Jung wrote, "The privilege of a lifetime is to become who you truly are." This first day of a new year is a good time to reflect on who I am beyond the standard descriptions of occupation, gender, age, and the other labels our world uses to define us. My answer will keep evolving, but over time I'll get closer to finding the core me, the one that doesn't change with circumstances.

One thing I've learned over my more than sixty years on earth is that I can always feel when I'm betraying that core me. If I'm agreeing to something I don't really believe, or acting in a way that doesn't feel right, I know I'm not being true to my authentic self. For those of us who have children or work with children in any way, I believe we can best support them in finding their authenticity by modeling our own. When I live my truth and embrace my unique way of being, especially when it might deviate from the norm, I am giving others permission to do the same.

Today I choose to trust myself by expressing what is authentically true for me. That doesn't mean I have to hit others over the head with my opinions, but I don't have to shrink from them either. I can express myself with conviction, while also giving grace for other points of view.

Today I am cultivating a sense of appreciation for the unshakable goodness I have deep within me, and cherishing my unique self just as I am right now, flaws and all.

Oscar Wilde (1854–1900), Irish poet and playwright

JANUARY 2

Enjoy Life Now

*You can't wait until life isn't hard anymore
before you decide to be happy.*

—Jane Marczewski

In his book, *Authentic Success*, Robert Holden, a British psychologist, author and broadcaster who works in the field of positive psychology and well-being, has written about what he calls "destination addiction." He defines it this way, "People who suffer from destination addiction believe that success is a destination. They are addicted to the idea that the future is where success is, happiness is." This obsession can lead us to believe that if only we had a different job, a different home, a different relationship, or moved to a new city, then we could be happy.

The reality is that if we can't define ourselves as happy until we've reached that mythical "perfect" destination, we will squander the joyful moments available to us right here, right now, in our less-than-perfect, messy, but nevertheless full-of-wonder lives.

Today I choose to celebrate moments of happiness, even if they are mixed in with challenges. Life is sweet right now, and I refuse to waste it.

Jane Marczewski (1990–2022), American singer-songwriter known professionally as Nightbirde

JANUARY 3

What Quality Will I Cultivate Today?

What you do makes a difference, and you have to decide what kind of difference you want to make.

—Jane Goodall

Every morning I open a small box filled with "quality cards" that list attributes such as courage, gentleness, strength, humility or creativity. On some days I pull a card at random and think about what that particular quality might mean for me. On other days I choose a quality that I want to cultivate. This simple exercise has been powerful. As Jane Goodall's quote reminds me, I get to decide how I'll make a difference with my life. I get to choose how I'll show up in the world each day. Focusing on how I want to BE, not just what I want to DO is a game-changer.

So today I am picking the quality of trust. I am going about my day trusting that I have the resources to deal with whatever comes along. And I trust that all is well, no matter what temporary challenges I face. I know I can learn from everything in some way.

Jane Goodall, English primatologist, anthropologist and writer

JANUARY 4

Gratitude Journal — My Way

When you arise in the morning, give thanks for the food and for the joy of living. If you see no reason for giving thanks, the fault lies only in yourself.

—Tecumseh

For a long time I resisted keeping a gratitude journal. It felt too close to forced positivity — even toxic positivity if I wasn't careful. I didn't want to have to pretend that all was well if it wasn't. But over the years I began to realize that expressing gratitude didn't mean that I also didn't feel pain. I began to realize I live in an AND world. Today I can experience gratitude AND discomfort. One doesn't preclude the other.

So, I began to keep a daily gratitude journal. I experimented with blank-paged journals, and ones with writing prompts, until I found the kind that worked well for me. Now, this daily ritual comforts and sustains me, reminding me that it's ok to live an AND life. Perhaps the moments of pain really do make the times of joy even sweeter. Sometimes I write my gratitude for my challenges. I know they can teach me if I'm open to learning.

So, today I am beginning and ending with my gratitude journal, celebrating all the ANDS.

Tecumseh (1768–1813), Shawnee chief

JANUARY 5
Seek Out Inspiration

*Inspiration can come to us at any time
and from many sources.*

–Jim Rohn,
The Five Major Pieces to the Life Puzzle

Inspiration, like comfort, is so individual. What inspires me might not do much for someone else. So today I am going to reflect on my own preferences.

I know reading is an important source for me, so I frequent libraries often. Sometimes if I'm pretty sure I'm going to love a book, I'll decide to buy it. I do need to be careful, though, because it wouldn't take much for me to stuff every corner of living space with books.

The right kind of movie can certainly touch my imagination, as can an intriguing podcast.

Time in nature is always stirring, so I'm going to think carefully about places that move me the most.

According to the Merriam-Webster dictionary, some synonyms for inspiring are: breathtaking, electrifying, exciting, heart-stopping, intoxicating, mind-bending, rousing, and thrilling. It's worth asking myself what kinds of things help me feel that way.

Today I'm going to look for one activity that could provide new inspiration. I hope you might do the same.

Jim Rohn (1930–2009), American entrepreneur and author

JANUARY 6
Celebrate Everything I Can

It is important to recognize the small successes.

—Rafael Nadal

In my book, *Heart-Centered Teaching Inspired by Nature,* I told the story of my first-grade teacher who one day completely forgot the importance of celebrating everything, even small accomplishments. It was silent reading time and we were not supposed to bother our teacher unless we were having trouble. But something miraculous happened to me and I needed to share it with someone. I read the word nightingale. There was a beautiful picture of the bird in my book, and I was actually able to read the name of that magnificent creature. It was amazing to me. I shot my hand up, and when my teacher appeared, she scolded me for calling her over for something that wasn't a problem. At the time I simply didn't have the words to explain how much I longed for her to celebrate with me.

I wonder how many times I've missed the opportunity to celebrate with a child, or a colleague, or a friend, because I simply forgot that small successes NEED celebrating.

Today I am finding reasons to celebrate something — no matter how small. And if I find someone else to celebrate with, all the better.

Rafael Nadal, Spanish tennis player

JANUARY 7

My Wise Inner Voice

Practice listening to your intuition, your inner voice; ask questions; be curious; see what you see; hear what you hear; and then act upon what you know to be true. These intuitive powers were given to your soul at birth.

—Clarissa Pinkola Estés,
Women Who Run With the Wolves

One thing I know is that it's impossible to listen to my wise inner voice if I'm too busy drowning it out with criticism. Years ago at a workshop, I was invited to pay attention throughout the day to what I was saying to myself internally. To my dismay, I heard many "you should have done this," and "why did you do that?" internal dialogues. I was shocked at how often I told myself I'd done something wrong or that I should have done something differently.

In his book, *The Untethered Soul: The Journey Beyond Yourself*, Michael Singer writes:

"In case you haven't noticed, you have a mental dialogue going on inside your head that never stops...If you're smart, you'll take the time to step back, examine this voice and get to know it better." Singer's book encourages us to realize that there's nothing more important to developing a sense of peace in life than learning that we are "not the voice of the mind." We can take charge of our inner dialogue once we learn, as Singer says, that "the 'I' who is always talking inside will never be content."

Today I choose to take charge of the voice in my head, realizing that I can stop its constant criticism and discontent. Today I choose to tune into my inner wisdom, which is always encouraging and loving.

Clarissa Pinkola Estés, American writer and Jungian psychoanalyst

JANUARY 8

Just Keep Going

*Sometimes you climb out of bed in the morning
and you think, I'm not going to make it,
but you laugh inside – remembering all
the times you've felt that way.*

—Charles Bukowski

We all have times when we want to go back to bed, burrow under the covers and stay there for the next 24 hours. On most days that's usually not an option. To get myself going when I'd rather not, I play the "just do three things" game with myself. The rule is I only need to take three small steps, then I can stop for a minute. My first steps might be to wash my face, throw on a robe and get a cup of coffee or tea. It's amazing how much better I start to feel with just that minimal movement forward. After that, it's another three steps, pause, and then three more until I've kicked myself into gear and I'm in full swing for the day.

Later in the evening, after a "don't want to move" morning, I ask myself what caused the inertia. Did I need more sleep? Was I worried about something I needed to do later that day? Have I been pushing myself too hard, without enough time off for rest and regrouping? I try to take stock and make a plan to get myself more support – in whatever way I need it.

The "just three steps" technique is actually a pretty effective way to get unstuck in many situations. So today, if I find myself dragging my feet, I am going to remember that I just need to keep going. Even three small steps can actually give me a pretty big push forward.

Charles Bukowski (1920–1994), German-American poet,
novelist, and short story writer

JANUARY 9
Find What I Like

To be beautiful means to be yourself.

—Thich Nhat Hanh

Today I am going to make sure I spend as much time as I can doing things that bring me moments of joy. In her book, *Joyful: The Surprising Power of Ordinary Things to Create Extraordinary Happiness,* Ingrid Fetell Lee explains how the objects and spaces we interact with every day can actually have surprisingly powerful effects on our mood. Here are a few research-based examples she shares:

Choosing to wear something colorful, if it's a color you enjoy, can increase your happiness for an entire day. For me, this might mean wearing purple. How about you?

Spending time in sunlight reduces blood pressure, improves mood, productivity and alertness. For me, this might mean taking a walk at lunchtime. How about you?

Doing something unexpected can kick-start feelings of joy. For me, this might mean wearing a pair of rainbow socks with a conservative outfit; buying a fragrant bouquet of flowers at the end of the day; purchasing a small Lego set and basking in childhood memories; or stopping by a junk shop and snapping up the most outrageous tea cup they have. What about you?

The key, of course, is to do as Ingrid Fetell Lee urges and listen to our own hearts.

Today I am experimenting with ordinary activities I think will jolt my joy meter up a notch. I hope you'll do the same.

Thich Nhat Hanh (1926–2022), Vietnamese Buddhist monk, peace activist, author and teacher

JANUARY 10
Relationships First

*A love for learning has a lot to do with
learning that we are loved.*

—Fred Rogers

I used to consider Fred Rogers, the Mister Rogers of my children's childhood, as almost a friend. Sometimes I think I needed him more than my children. His reassurances were cold compresses on my feverish days with two busy little ones. The message that came through loud and clear was always, "You are loved."

Theodore Roosevelt said, "No one cares how much you know until they know how much you care." I think that's right. My children listened to Mr. Rogers' ideas because first and foremost they felt genuinely cared for by him.

When I was teaching, I always worked on forming a loving relationship with each child before doing much else. Come to think of it, I also tried to do the same with colleagues in any work situation. We humans don't like to feel preached at or "instructed." We do, however, enjoy learning together with people who openly care about us.

So today I am remembering that relationships come before all else. I am looking for ways to be more of a loving presence and less of a "know-it-all."

Fred Rogers (1928–2003), American television host and author

JANUARY 11

Feedback Versus Self-Assessment

Don't overestimate yourself because of compliments and don't underestimate yourself because of criticism.

—Amit Kalantri

A friend once told me about the first day she realized she was no longer relying on others' opinions of her in order to feel worthy. Here's her story: She arrived at work to be met with an irate colleague who criticized her harshly for a recent decision. My friend said she paused, took stock, then decided she still believed she had made the right decision. She thanked the colleague for the feedback, then moved on with her day. As she was leaving work that evening, another colleague stopped to shower her with profuse thanks for the enlightened decision she had made, and to pronounce her a brilliant leader. The great thing about both of those incidents, my friend said, was that neither one had much effect on her. She could hear both sharp criticism and copious praise, while staying centered, realizing it was the way she felt about herself that ultimately mattered. Getting to that place of internal calm is quite an accomplishment.

Today I choose to carefully consider feedback from others, while also realizing that my own character assessment is ultimately the most important one.

JANUARY 12

Take Positive Action to Repel Fear

There is nothing that wastes the body like worry.
—Mahatma Gandhi

An older relative once told me that most of the things he worried about in his lifetime never came true. "I wasted a lot of time on needless worry," he said. "I wish I could have those hours back to spend on something better."

I've tried to remember that. When I'm feeling fear, I ask myself if I'm just engaging in "negative future fantasies," or if there's something I can actually do about the fearful situation. Most of the time I realize my fears are pretty irrational. It's highly unlikely, for example, that the plane I'm about to board will fall out of the sky. But in that situation, I can take an action step. I can remind myself that air travel is safer than any other form, and I can focus on bringing along snacks or books for comfort on my journey. If my fears are based on something more substantial, like a concerning medical diagnosis, for example, I can still focus on at least one helpful step to take to support myself. I might ask my doctor to recommend reading material so I can become better informed about options.

Today I am facing any fear I feel head-on. I am being honest with myself about ways I can deal with that fear, and taking at least one action step forward.

Mahatma Gandhi (1869–1948), Indian lawyer, political ethicist and leader of the non-violent campaign for India's independence from British rule

JANUARY 13
Cultivate Joy

The past is gone, the future is not here, now I am free of both. Right now, I choose joy.

—Deepak Chopra

New York Times bestselling author, Mary Pipher, in an article published in *Exchange* magazine, wrote this about cultivating joy in life, "It is never too late to become a happy person. We can set our mind to it and work to acquire the necessary skills. They are gratitude, slowing down, being awake to the wonder all around us, being outside and enjoying the primal activities we humans have enjoyed since the beginning of time. These skills can become healthy habits, just like brushing our teeth or exercising."

It's interesting to think of choosing joy as a healthy habit, but I know this to be true. Each day is a new beginning and another chance to do things that lead to joy. For me it's especially helpful to focus on gratitude and to spend meaningful time in nature.

Today I am claiming my right to be a happy person. Feeling joy is a choice I make today.

Deepak Chopra, Indian-American author

JANUARY 14
Keep Moving

Reflect on what you've lived through - and look, you're still here. Look back at the road you've traveled to get to this place, and know you've built the strength to travel the next stretch - and the next one, and the next one. KEEP MOVING.

—Maggie Smith,
*Keep Moving: Notes on Loss,
Creativity and Change*

Maggie Smith's book, *Keep Moving*, was a gift to me from a treasured colleague. It's an easy read in many ways, but a challenging one in others. It reminds me that all things change, no matter how much I sometimes wish they wouldn't. Things need to keep moving. That's her message, along with her encouragement that I'll always survive the change.

When I think about some of the biggest changes in my life, I realize I often resisted them at first — even fought against them. Now in hindsight I see that there were gifts in even the hardest upheavals.

So today I relax and let change happen around me. I take a breath and stop fighting so much. This is a strange little boat ride we're all on in this life. I think I'll grab a beverage out of the cooler and try to enjoy the twists and turns.

Maggie Smith, American poet and author

JANUARY 15

Learn From Martin Luther King Jr.

If you can't fly then run, if you can't run then walk, if you can't walk then crawl, but whatever you do, you have to keep moving forward.

—Martin Luther King, Jr.

Today, on Martin Luther King Jr.'s birthday, I'm taking his words to heart and focusing on what I am able to do NOW. I'm letting go of where I think I "should" be and celebrating where I actually am at this moment. I am looking down the metaphorical mountain at how far I've already climbed instead of worrying about how far I have left to go.

In the past I would often put off something until I thought I had the time to do it "perfectly." That usually meant I procrastinated for a very long stretch. Over the years I began to teach myself to enjoy doing things imperfectly. Don't have the time to clean out my closet? Just clean one shelf. Don't have the stamina to walk for an hour like I wish? Start with 20 minutes. It's amazing how effective it became to focus on taking small steps. Doing so helped me conquer tasks that had previously seemed too daunting.

So here's to a day of celebrating crawling before walking, and moving forward in whatever way we can.

Martin Luther King, Jr. (1929–1968), American minister and civil rights activist

JANUARY 16
Take My Cue From Nature

*Nature does not hurry, but everything
is accomplished.*

—Lao Tzu

A report published online in 2021 by the United Kingdom's Mental Health Foundation (*mentalhealth.org.uk*), is titled, "How connecting with nature benefits our mental health." For years my daily work focused on the multiple ways meaningful time in nature supports young children's well-being. The reality is, though, that all human beings are better when we spend enough time in the natural world. The UK report describes research showing that "spending time outdoors has been one of the key factors enabling people to cope with the stress of the Covid-19 pandemic." And in what will be a surprise to no one, the report also details how enjoying nature-based activities that engage most of our senses or trigger emotional responses increase "happiness…calmness, joy, creativity, and facilitate concentration."

I've long been intrigued with the Lao Tzu quote above. I've asked myself often if my sometimes frantic need to "get things done" actually works against me. Today I am practicing taking my cue from nature, slowing down and not hurrying. I suspect it might be quite a productive day.

Lao Tzu (believed to have lived in the 6th century, BC), Chinese philosopher

JANUARY 17
Be Kind

*No act of kindness, no matter how small,
is ever wasted.*

—Aesop

Don Miguel Ruiz, in his book, *Mastery of Love*, writes this about our relationships with others:

"You cannot change other people. You love them the way they are or you don't...They are what they are; you are what you are. You dance or you don't. You must be completely honest with yourself — to say what you want, and see if you are willing to dance or not."

Ruiz uses the phrase "wanting to dance" as a metaphor for whether or not we will choose to have close relationships with people. He urges us to stop fooling ourselves that we have the power to change anyone else's behavior. We must decide if we are willing to have a deep relationship with someone exactly as they are. Sometimes the answer will be yes, but many times it will be no.

Even if we choose not to become very close with someone, it is still possible to be kind. This holds true for co-workers, extended family members, or really, any kind of acquaintance. It is quite possible to extend kindness to everyone we encounter, while also holding our strong boundaries.

Today I am remembering what the Dalai Lama said: "Be kind whenever possible. It is always possible."

JANUARY 18
People Have to Earn the Right to Know Me Well

You share with people who've earned the right to hear your story.

—Brené Brown

Brené Brown's TED Talks and writings on shame and vulnerability took the world by storm. Many people related to her message that to experience deep connection we must risk vulnerability. Her message also contained a counterpoint: People need to earn the right to share in our vulnerability.

I have learned over the years to choose carefully who I open myself up to fully. I don't mean that I will be phony with everyone else. I still want to be my authentic self, but that doesn't mean I must reveal every tender part of me. I only share my deepest feelings with those who have, as Brown says, "earned the right" to hear them.

Today I am thinking about the people in my life who have earned the right to share in my vulnerability. And I am asking myself if I have been a safe enough friend to others to earn the right to hear their stories.

Brené Brown, American professor and author

JANUARY 19
Sometimes Allow Problems to Just Be

There is no reason to constantly attempt to figure everything out.

—Michael Singer,
*The Untethered Soul:
The Journey Beyond Yourself*

Here's Michael Singer again, urging us to stop ruminating so much. He describes how the "voice in our heads," will comment on everything, if we let it, and start to drive us to distraction. One thing I've realized over the years is how often something I thought was a "problem," actually worked itself out if I gave it a little space. I don't always have to jump in and try to fix everything. It's a good skill to learn to discern when a situation really does need our immediate action and when it's fine to take a pause. I've been surprised how often the "wait and see" approach turned out pretty well.

Today I am reminding the voice in my head that I don't have to be constantly focused on problems. Today I am relaxing, learning to identify issues where giving them a little space really is the best way to go.

Michael Singer, American author, motivational speaker, former software developer

JANUARY 20
Extraordinary in the Ordinary

*Do not ask your children
to strive for extraordinary lives.
Such striving may seem admirable,
but it is the way of foolishness.
Help them instead to find the wonder
and the marvel of an ordinary life.*

—William Martin,
*The Parent's Tao Te Ching:
Ancient Advice for Modern Parents*

What if the "ordinary" is really the most important part of life? What if I overlook the incredible gifts hidden in what I dismiss as "unimportant?" I love William Martin's writing above. It inspires me to help the children in my life deeply learn what it means to marvel at life's day-to-day goodness. I know that means modeling it myself for them.

It can become a cliché to talk about finding wonder everywhere. To keep myself from throwing around meaningless words, I'm going to see if right now I can find wonder in my "ordinary" surroundings as I write this. Here goes:

I'm watching the flickering of a lemon verbena candle and holding it close to me to enjoy its fragrance.

I'm noticing a small pile of greeting cards from friends and family – a reminder of love sent for my birthday.

I'm looking at a new book I just got from the library, reminding myself what extraordinarily ordinary things libraries are.

Ok. That's a good start. And, you know what? I am indeed experiencing wonder already. I guess it actually is available anywhere if I just remember to look for it.

William Martin, American scientist, minister, therapist and writer

JANUARY 21
Walk Whenever I Can

Now shall I walk or shall I ride?
'Ride,' Pleasure said;
'Walk,' Joy replied.

—W.H. Davies

Living through a global pandemic, especially at the very beginning, brought its share of real challenges, but it also taught me some life lessons I will always remember. One of them is the importance of walking outdoors, preferably in a natural setting. I'd always known at some level that walking was important, but during those first unnerving days of trying to understand what Covid-19 was all about, I calmed myself each evening by taking a walk.

Now walking has become a pleasurable habit that I try to indulge in each day. Sometimes I stick close to my neighborhood, but other times I venture further to a nearby lake. Sometimes I walk alone and sometimes with others. What I've learned is that I don't need to wait until I have the time to go somewhere amazing. Anywhere I walk can bring me solace and inspiration. Just finding the ubiquitous weed pushing its way through a sidewalk crack can remind me of perseverance and that life always finds a way.

As I write this, I think of a friend who takes herself places in her motorized wheelchair. A "walk" for her looks different than it does for me, but in our own ways we enjoy being outdoors, getting from place to place. It really doesn't matter the time we spend or the way we move; the important thing is allowing ourselves to deeply connect with the world around us.

So today, I am making time to enjoy moving from place-to-place outdoors, looking for serendipity along the way, and intending to find it.

W.H. Davies (1871–1940), Welsh poet and writer

JANUARY 22
Choose My View

It's never the things that happen to you that upset you; it's your view of them.

—Epictetus

First, let me acknowledge that choosing my attitude is not always possible. In a crisis, the biological response of "fight or flight" can flood my body with chemicals that may, at first, make a calm reaction nearly impossible. So, depending on the situation, I may need to give myself plenty of time to feel whatever feelings are coming forward. After a while, however, the feelings will begin to flow through me and dissipate. Then I can begin to make some decisions about what attitude I will choose and from what perspective I'll view events.

In any situation, I can eventually select what my ultimate reaction is going to be. I can decide if I will give others the power to hurt me or not. I can decide if I will reside in fear or hope. I can decide to stay immobilized or take action steps. It really is up to me.

So today I am choosing my attitude whenever possible, looking for all the ways my feelings can be mine to determine.

Epictetus (50–135), Greek philosopher

JANUARY 23
Flexibility Feels Good

*The measure of intelligence is
the ability to change.*

—Albert Einstein

I've always been a planner. Sometimes that trait has served me well, but not always. There are times in life when flexibility is the name of the game, and hanging on to the best-intentioned plans is a recipe for heartache (if not disaster). This is true for both the minor and major issues we all face.

As I've gotten older, I've started to develop much more appreciation for flexibility. Now, when I plan a trip with my children and grandchildren, I understand that what we've designed together is merely a suggestion. Inevitably, unexpected twists and turns will pop up that make adjustments necessary. In the past I'd experience these changes with resentment. Today, I make a conscious effort to find the humor and the opportunity in the situation. Being flexible means staying curious. If I ask, "I wonder what's going to happen now?" instead of griping that something went "wrong," I have a much better time and am often pleasantly surprised.

Today I am focusing on the fun in flexibility. Going with the flow sometimes takes me to a much better place.

Albert Einstein (1879–1955), German-born theoretical physicist

JANUARY 24
Humor Helps

Humor is one of the best ingredients of survival.

—Aung San Suu Kyi

According to the Mayo Clinic, research confirms that laughter is good for our health. In an online article called "Stress Relief From Laughter? It's No Joke," the Mayo Clinic staff report that, in the short-term, laughter will:

- "Stimulate many organs (including heart, lungs and muscles).
- Activate and relieve your stress response.
- Soothe tension.

And in the long-term, laughter will:

- Improve your immune system.
- Relieve pain.
- Increase personal satisfaction.
- Improve your mood."

Today I am doing my health a favor and choosing to find humor whenever I can. I am laughing more and stressing less, knowing my immune system is going to thank me.

Aung San Suu Kyi, Burmese politician, author,
1991 Nobel Peace Prize laureate

JANUARY 25
Self-Forgiveness Soothes My Soul

Forgiveness is the answer to the child's dream of a miracle by which what is broken is made whole again, what is soiled is again made clean.

—Dag Hammarskjöld

After having a nationally televised panic attack, news anchor Dan Harris set out to improve his life. The result is documented in his book, *10% Happier: How I Tamed the Voice in My Head, Reduced Stress Without Losing My Edge, and Found Self-Help That Actually Works – A True Story*. He shares a series of short "lessons" that have helped him live a calmer, happier life. One of these is "Go Easy with the Internal Cattle Prod." He writes:

"I had long assumed the only route to success was harsh self-criticism. However, research shows that 'firm but kind' is the smarter play. People trained in self-compassion meditation are more likely to quit smoking and stick to a diet. They are better able to bounce back from missteps."

Harris explains that a person's resilience is much greater when mistakes are accepted as a part of life and seen as an opportunity for growth and learning. Self-forgiveness instead of self-criticism, he says, is a key to living a more contented life.

So today I am listening to how I speak to myself. I choose to replace the internal "cattle prod" with understanding and self-compassion.

Dag Hammarskjöld (1905–1961), Swedish economist, Former Secretary General of the United Nations, Nobel Peace Prize laureate

JANUARY 26

Harness Intention

Our intention creates our reality.

—Wayne Dyer

In his book, *The Power of Intention*, Wayne Dyer includes this quote by globally renowned author, Carlos Castaneda: "In the universe there is an immeasurable, indescribable force which shamans call intent, and absolutely everything that exists in the entire universe is attached to intent by a connecting link." Dyer explains that even though he had been studying the research on intention-setting for years, Castaneda's words caused his thinking to evolve. "Imagine," Dyer writes, "that intention is not something you *do*, but a force that exists in the universe as an invisible field of energy." Connecting to that energy is something everyone can experience.

Dyer clarifies that it's not healthy to set intentions in an ego-driven way ("I want this object because my possessions define me, or I want to have this success because my achievements define me, or I want others to admire me because my reputation defines me"). Rather, healthy intention-setting is a process of identifying with our authentic self and letting go of the lies ego tells us.

For me, healthy intention-setting is very much related to focusing on qualities. I might set an intention for myself to go into a meeting with an open mind and an appreciation for others' ideas. This is very different from the ego's way of setting intentions: "My intention is that everyone will think my ideas are the best."

Today my intentions are focused on my authentic self's way of being, and I am asking my ego to support that process instead of running the show.

Wayne Dyer (1940–2015), American author and motivational speaker

JANUARY 27

Play More

Those who play rarely become brittle in the face of stress or lose the healing capacity for humor.

—Stuart Brown

There's a treasure trove of research on the need for young children to learn through play. As one example, a *Scientific American Mind* online article by Melinda Wenner, "The Serious Need for Play," declares that, "Free, imaginative play is crucial for normal social, emotional and cognitive development. It makes us better adjusted, smarter and less stressed."

And while the quote above was written about children, there is growing evidence that in order to stay healthy, adults also need to play. An *NPR* online article by Sami Yenigun, "Play Doesn't End With Childhood: Why Adults Need Recess Too," has this to say about the benefits of play:

"It helps us maintain our social well-being. And it's not just board games that do this, but soccer leagues, or playing paintball in the woods. And not just after-work recreation, but team-building exercises in corporate offices. Playing is how we connect."

Today I am thinking about what play means for me. I'm not sure I'd like paintball in the woods, but I might pull out my watercolor set and mess around with it – no pressure to make something others might deem as "good." I will share my explorations with people I know won't judge, but will instead rejoice with me in the fun of creation.

Today I am on the lookout for more play in my life. I wonder what play means to you.

Stuart Brown, American medical doctor, psychiatrist, researcher, and founder of the National Institute of Play

JANUARY 28
Educate My Heart

Educating the mind without educating the heart is no education at all.

—Aristotle

ERIC (Education Resources Information Center) is an online library of education research, sponsored by the US Department of Education. On their website, there is a synopsis of a research article by Kimberly Schonert-Reichl and Shelley Hymel, called "Educating the Heart as Well as the Mind: Social and Emotional Learning for School and Life Success."

"The research shows that people cannot – and should not – separate how they feel (about themselves, their relationships, their environments) from teaching or learning...Students do not learn alone, but rather in collaboration with their teachers, in the company of their peers, and with the support of their families."

This need for educating both the heart and mind is not only true for children, but also in the adult world of work. On the *Harvard Business Review* website, an article by Naomi Eisenberger and George Kohlrieser, "Lead With Your Heart, Not Just Your Head," explains, "In the workplace, leaders who show concern and interest in their employees' lives and a predictable set of rules, create a healthy attachment that empowers others to embrace the risk of pursuing success." It is simply not true that schools or workplaces must be impersonal and ruled only by the head. It is also not true in our personal lives. In fact, understanding how our emotions and intellect work together is key to a more contented life.

Today I pay attention to both my emotions as well as my thoughts, valuing each as vital to my well-being.

Aristotle (384–322 BC), Greek philosopher and polymath

JANUARY 29

Weird Can Be Wonderful

In nature, nothing is perfect and everything is perfect. Trees can be contorted, bent in weird ways, and they're still beautiful.

—Alice Walker

The best welcome mat I've ever seen is one that read, "Weirdos Welcome." I'd like to think that all of us have an inner weirdo. That's the part of us that maybe only we truly understand; that sees the world from a different perspective than anyone else we know. Whether we choose to embrace or shun that wild and wonderful weirdness can make all the difference in how we feel about ourselves.

Here's the thing: my weirdness is a unique and precious part of me and it doesn't deserve derision or criticism. James McCrae, in an online *Huffpost* article, "9 Reasons Why It's Okay to Be Weird," writes, "The Ego says that differences are flaws that should be hidden. The truth is that what makes you different is really your superpower. You just haven't learned how to harness it yet. Instead of hiding your weirdness, learn how to use it. Your shyness, for example might make you a better listener…Our quirks, when we master them, contain great power…The world needs more authenticity."

Today I embrace — celebrate, even — my inner weirdness. I hope you do the same.

JANUARY 30
Creativity Calms

Creativity takes courage.

—Henri Matisse

"Expressing yourself through artistic and creative activities is like a prescription for your mental health. Turning to creativity has been proven in extensive research to relieve both stress and anxiety. Creativity also helps lessen the shame, anger, and depression felt by those who have experienced trauma." So write Barbara Field and David Sussman, PhD, in a *VeryWellMind* online article, "How Creativity Positively Impacts Your Health."

Unfortunately, our society tends to want to professionalize creative expression. "I'm not an artist," we say, and no longer allow ourselves to enjoy our doodles. Or we compare ourselves to professional singers, so no longer enjoy singing just for pleasure.

Today I am breaking out of the self-imposed prison of "not good enough" and allowing more creativity into my life. As Matisse says, it does take courage to be creative…the courage to not care about anyone else's judgment…the courage to just enjoy the process.

Henri Matisse (1869–1954), French visual artist

JANUARY 31

Assume Good Intentions

I don't believe that people wake up in the morning, saying, "Who can I treat poorly today?" Always assume positive intent.

—Mary-Frances Winters

One of the most valuable lessons I've learned about life is that each of us is doing the best we can with the tools we possess in this moment. So, does that mean I want to have close relationships with everyone I meet? No, not at all. When people do not yet have the tools to be non-judgmental or accepting, I choose to protect myself by creating boundaries between us. But I do not take anything they do personally. I recognize they are doing their best with what they understand (or misunderstand) about the world.

Learning to not take things personally is a liberating gift. When I remember that we are all "bozos on this bus of life," as a friend of mind says, then I can feel compassion for everyone, even those I disagree with, or choose to keep my distance from.

Today I focus on accepting others while also protecting myself.

February

In the coldest February, as in every other month in every other year, the best thing to hold on to in this world is each other.

—Linda Ellerbee

Linda Ellerbee, American journalist

FEBRUARY 1
February Inspiration

*Never be limited by other people's
limited imaginations.*

—Mae Jemison

In the United States, February has been designated as Black History Month. Below is a sampling of what people have written about its history and significance, and the opportunity for all of us to find inspiration. Today I am pondering these words:

"February is the birth month of two figures who loom large in the black past: US President Abraham Lincoln (born February 12), who issued the Emancipation Proclamation, and African American abolitionist, author, and orator Frederick Douglass (born February 14)."
—Jeff Wallenfeldt, American writer

"Persons from the African diaspora, enslaved and free, provided labor that built the White House, the United States Capitol, numerous government buildings, and the basic infrastructure of American institutions…African Americans have not only picked cotton on plantations and nurtured Euro-American families but we must also be acknowledged for the intellectual, highly skilled creative and artistic acumen that founded colleges and universities; the invention of products consumed daily without thought; insight and contribution to the fields of science, medicine, law, the military, business, theology, finance, and architecture, etc."
—Barbara Peacock, author of *Soul Care in African American Practice*

Mae Jemison, American engineer, physician, and first African-American female astronaut

FEBRUARY 2
Good Enough

The perfect is the enemy of the good.

—Voltaire

Today I am reminding myself to step away from the self-imposed prison of perfectionism. I'm not sure why so many of us think we must be perfect to be worthy, but it's definitely a misunderstanding shared by many humans. Perhaps it comes from a faulty sense of ourselves, a huge misconception that any flaw is an indication that we are somehow damaged.

Today I am remembering that when Navajo peoples braid rugs, they intentionally weave in a flaw to remind themselves — and others — that no human being is perfect. Actually, they believe that flaws can be seen as part of the rug's beauty.

Could it be that my flaws are part of my beauty? I'm working on believing that today.

And I'm telling myself that good is good enough.

Voltaire (1694–1778), French writer and philosopher

FEBRUARY 3
Notice What I Have

*The secret of happiness is to count your blessings
while others are adding up their troubles.*

—William Penn

I know in the past I've been guilty of counting my struggles far more than my blessings. It's easy to get caught up in a recitation of what challenges us, and to a certain extent, sharing our struggles with others is healthy. But I can tell when the balance tips and I'm deep into the rabbit hole of too much self-pity. It's at those times that a healthy session of counting my blessings can restore some equanimity in my life.

So today I'm paying attention to those taken-for-granted blessings all around me. Right now I'm looking out my window at a gorgeous yet imperfect tree that is always there for me to enjoy, but usually overlooked. What if I started every day by taking a moment to bask in the tree's gnarly beauty? I just might find myself smiling a bit more and complaining a bit less.

William Penn (1644–1718), English writer, and influential Quaker who founded the Province of Pennsylvania

FEBRUARY 4
Get a Higher Perspective

*If you're wondering what I mean by 'miracle,'
it's simple: a miracle is a shift in
perspective from fear to love.*

—Gabrielle Bernstein

When I told my college-professor son that I was writing this book, he asked what some of the topics would be. "Well," I said breezily, "One will be about the importance of choosing love over fear." He looked at me for a minute, grabbed his laptop, then said, "Watch this," pulling up a clip from the movie, *Donnie Darko*. In the scene, an insufferable teacher leads her class through an exercise where students must place hypothetical situations on a "life line" divided into fear or love. When the character, Donnie Darko, is asked to do this, he argues that life is not neatly divided into categories and the exercise is inane.

Indeed it was. And I took my son's point. Trying to reduce anything in life to platitudes or certainties is problematic at best. And yet, I believe Gabrielle Bernstein's quote above has something to teach. I have often found myself in situations where by asking, "What's the most loving response I can have here?," I've felt myself shift out of the crippling grip of fear. It's helpful to me to think of the perspective of love as an antidote for fear.

So today I am choosing to pay attention to the choice between riding the energy of fear or love. No, it's not as cut and dried as I'm making it sound, and sometimes I experience both at the same time. All I know is my own experience: I'm better off when I call forward my loving and look for a higher perspective.

Gabrielle Bernstein, American author and motivational speaker

FEBRUARY 5
Thank People

*We must find time to stop and thank the
people who make a difference in our lives.*

−John F. Kennedy

I love to write thank you notes to people, but often the pressures of life get in the way and I don't find time to do what I intended. Today, though, I'm reminding myself that there are so many ways to thank people, not just through written notes or emails (even though I'm going to redouble my efforts to send those).

Honestly, smiling more at the person who checks me out at the grocery store would be a nice way to convey my thanks. I could let my neighbor know how much it means to me that he brings my garbage cans back from the curb after trash pick-up day. I could also thank a colleague for a small kindness that could be easy to take for granted.

Today I'm trying an experiment to see if I can thank ten people before the day is over. I'll start by thanking myself for remembering the importance of expressing gratitude. I have a feeling it's going to make the day a lot more fun.

John F. Kennedy (1917–1963), 35th president of the United States

FEBRUARY 6
Patience, Patience, Patience

> *Even a happy life cannot be without a measure of darkness, and the word happy would lose its meaning if it were not balanced by sadness. It is far better to take things as they come, along with patience and equanimity.*
>
> —Carl Jung

One valuable insight I gained from living through the first intense days of a global pandemic was learning to deal with just the events of the day and not project too far into the future. I remember telling our team, "Let's just deal with what we know today, and we'll tackle whatever comes tomorrow, confident that we will find a way to handle it then."

Actually, I started to find this way of operating very comforting. Even after the most challenging days of the pandemic were over, I continued to try to live this "enough for today" way of being. Carl Jung's urging to "take things as they come" is wise, especially if it's coupled with patience and equanimity.

So today I am reminding myself to not overreact, to practice some patience, and then some more. And for good measure to practice just a bit more.

Carl Jung (1875–1961), Swiss psychiatrist and writer

FEBRUARY 7

Find the Fun

*I am going to keep having fun every day
I have left, because there is no other way of life.
You just have to decide whether you
are a Tigger or an Eeyore.*

—Randy Pausch

Randy Pausch wrote his book, *The Last Lecture*, when he knew he was dying of pancreatic cancer. What has struck me most about the book is Pausch's sense of humor and focus on fun, even while coming to terms with a looming, untimely death. His intention to "keep having fun every day I have left," reminds me that none of us knows how many days that might be.

Today I'm going to think about what having fun means for me. I get to create my own definition. I can remember friends encouraging me to go out with them late at night so we could "have fun" at some pursuit that just wasn't my thing. I sometimes still go, but now I'm more apt to politely decline. I've come to terms with the fact that I like going to bed early, and morning strolls in nature with coffee in hand are more my idea of fun. I also love cozy brunches with a few close friends or family members. I very much appreciate my friends' enjoyment of big crowds, loud music and gatherings way into the night. It's wonderful for them, just not for me.

That's the great thing about fun. We each get to define it for ourselves. At any rate, I am finding some today, my own way.

Randy Pausch (1960–2008), American professor and writer

FEBRUARY 8

Just Breathe

The wisest one-word sentence? Breathe.

—Terri Guillemets

The *Harvard Business Review* published an online piece by Emma Seppala, Christine Bradley, and Michael R. Goldstein titled, "Research: Why Breathing Is So Effective at Reducing Stress."

The authors present compelling research evidence showing that certain breathing techniques can be amazingly effective at reducing people's stress levels. Here's one they describe: Breathe in for a count of four and out for a count of eight. Doing this for "just a few minutes can start to calm your nervous system."

Today, I am remembering to stop and breathe consciously whenever I want to calm myself. Mindful breathing is a tool I have at my disposal anytime, anywhere.

Terri Guillemets, American quotation anthologist

FEBRUARY 9

Gratitude for ALL Things?

Cultivate the habit of being grateful for every good thing that comes to you, and to give thanks continuously. And because all things have contributed to your advancement, you should include all things in your gratitude.

—Ralph Waldo Emerson

Is it really possible to be grateful for all things that come into my life? I'm not sure, but I do know that many things I initially judged as "bad," often ended up teaching me something valuable. Sometimes they led me in a direction that proved better than where I might have ended up otherwise. So, while I may not feel gratitude during a difficult moment as it's happening, I can at least refrain from judging it as "unredeemable" or "disastrous."

Don't get me wrong. Some events in life are, without a doubt, traumatic and need to be recognized as such. We may need skilled support to help us work through them. I don't believe the old adage that "what doesn't kill us makes us stronger." Unless we directly address trauma, it very well may make us weaker. But, when we face our difficult times with honesty, support and self-compassion, then it's possible to come through them with increased strength.

Over the years I've learned that when I face a challenge, it's helpful to be open to the great possibility that something valuable might eventually come from it. That doesn't keep me from feeling sad or frustrated in the moment, but it does help me stay open to unexpected gifts I may have otherwise missed. Today I am giving thanks for so many positives in my life. And if a negative comes along, I am keeping an open mind that perhaps everything that happens to me really does in some way "contribute to my advancement."

Ralph Waldo Emerson (1803–1882), American essayist and philosopher

FEBRUARY 10
Encourage Others

Try to be a rainbow in somebody else's cloud.

—Maya Angelou

One of the best ways to feel better, I've found, is to take the focus off myself and look for opportunities to brighten someone else's day. This works especially well on a Monday when sometimes it's hard to get going, but it's helpful any day. Focusing on surprising a co-worker with a tea or coffee treat, or beginning the day by writing an unexpected thank you email to someone can always do a lot to boost my mood.

So today I am lifting my own spirits by lifting up others. I can't wait to get going.

Maya Angelou (1928–2014), American writer, poet and civil rights activist

FEBRUARY 11
Value My Sense of Humor

People with a sense of humor tend to be less egocentric and more realistic in their view of the world and more humble in moments of success and less defeated in times of travail.

—Bob Newhart

There's a lot of wisdom in the Bob Newhart quote. I also appreciate what English dancer Margot Fonteyn (1919 – 1991) said: "Take your work seriously but never yourself." So today I'm going to lighten up and look for the humor in life.

Especially for any of us who work with children, learning how to laugh whenever possible, especially at ourselves, is a gift. Multiple websites report that children laugh more frequently than adults, although what the actual frequency is seems to be up for debate. Nevertheless, it does seem indisputable that human beings tend to laugh less as they age. Perhaps with a little more awareness, it doesn't have to be this way.

Today I intend to see if I can turn this around.

Bob Newhart, American actor and comedian

FEBRUARY 12

Take a Lesson from Abraham Lincoln

*I am not bound to win, but I am bound to be true.
I am not bound to succeed, but I am bound
to live up to what light I have.*

—Abraham Lincoln

Today, Abraham Lincoln's birthday, I am thinking about what it means to "live up to what light I have." Interestingly, *The Book of Joy*, written by the Dalai Lama, Desmond Tutu and Douglas Abrams, argues that the best way we can share our light with the world is to cultivate our own happiness. They explain, "[S]ome might wonder what our own joy has to do with countering injustice and inequality. What does our happiness have to do with addressing the suffering of the world? In short, the more we heal our own pain, the more we can turn to the pain of others...It is a virtuous cycle. The more we turn toward others, the more joy we experience, and the more joy we experience the more we can bring joy to others."

The authors explain that turning to others' pain does NOT mean taking it on as our own. Instead it means being in a space of loving with them, which we can do best if we have first healed our own pain. "We cannot bring peace if we do not have inner peace," they write. In other words, a focus on our own joy and well-being is anything but selfish. It is the most positive thing we can do for the world.

Abraham Lincoln also said, "Be sure you put your feet in the right place, then stand firm." I think that means cultivating the solid ground inside me, then using that as a base of strength from which to reach out to others. So today I am doing whatever I can to make my own healing and joy a priority.

Abraham Lincoln (1809–1865), 16th president of the United States

FEBRUARY 13

Ask Forgiveness

> *Most especially, in our own families, let us become aware of how we may be wounding our children through harsh or unfeeling words, thoughtless actions, or mindless dismissals of their enormous awareness and sensitivity. To ask forgiveness of one's children is a courageous act, one that can change the entire quality of your relationship.*
>
> —Jean Houston,
> *A Mythic Life*

Parents, as well as teachers, undoubtedly will find opportunities to ask children for forgiveness. I don't think it's possible to spend frequent time with children and not have moments when we lose our tempers or inadvertently "wound" them through "thoughtless action." I believe that when we ask children to forgive us, we model a great life skill. We teach them it's important to know how to admit when we are wrong and to share our intentions of wanting to make things right.

This holds true for one more child – the younger self still residing inside us. Whenever I berate myself with a critical inner voice, I try to visualize young Nancy feeling wounded. I can then take a breath, ask for my own forgiveness, and focus on a kinder way of speaking to myself. The insidious thing about our harsh inner voices is that we often aren't consciously aware of them. They can wreak havoc unchecked if we aren't paying attention.

Today I am making a point to listen to my inner dialogue. If I hear criticism or judgment, I am asking for forgiveness and changing to a more supportive way of being.

Jean Houston, American author, professor and co-founder of the Foundation for Mind Research

FEBRUARY 14

Make It My Own Valentine's Day

The best and most beautiful things in the world cannot be seen or even touched. They must be felt with the heart.

–Helen Keller

I've spent some Valentine's Days alone and others with someone special. Here's what I've learned: I can enjoy them either way. More and more I'm realizing that my happiness is mostly dependent on how I treat myself.

So today, I'm going to take myself on a Valentine's Day adventure by figuring out some small treats my authentic self would really enjoy. These don't have to cost money — although it's ok if they do. I'm thinking of taking a walk in a favorite park, buying myself a cup of "extravagant" coffee and browsing in the library until I find a book that makes my heart sing. And then I'm going to send messages of love to the special people in my life, because sharing my loving with others is one of my favorite things to do.

I'm wondering what your Valentine's Day adventure might be. Here's to a good one.

Helen Keller (1880–1968), American author and disability rights advocate

FEBRUARY 15

Music Keeps Me Young at Heart

Music is the language of the spirit. It opens the secret of life, bringing peace, abolishing strife.

— Kahlil Gibran

"Keep Your Brain Young With Music," an article on the Johns Hopkins website (*hopkinsmedicine.org*), explains that, "There are few things that stimulate the brain the way music does. If you want to keep your brain engaged throughout the aging process, listening to or playing music is a great tool. It provides a total brain workout.

Research has shown that listening to music can reduce anxiety, blood pressure, and pain as well as improve sleep quality, mood, mental alertness, and memory...Music is structural, mathematical and architectural. It's based on relationships between one note and the next. You may not be aware of it, but your brain has to do a lot of computing to make sense of it."

I know how much music helps boost my mood, so it's really good to know it's also helping my brain. Today I am finding many ways to surround myself with music. I think I'll start by singing in the shower.

Kahlil Gibran (1883–1931), Lebanese-American poet

FEBRUARY 16

Avoid Toxic Positivity

When we honestly ask ourselves which person in our lives means the most to us, we often find that it is those who, instead of giving advice, solutions, or cures, have chosen rather to share our pain and touch our wounds with a warm and tender hand.

— Henri Nouwen

"Toxic positivity is the belief that no matter how dire or difficult a situation is, people should maintain a positive mindset. It's a 'good vibes only' approach to life. And while there are benefits to being an optimist and engaging in positive thinking, toxic positivity instead rejects difficult emotions in favor of a cheerful, often falsely positive, facade." So begins an article, "What is Toxic Positivity?" by Kendra Cherry on the *VeryWellMind* website. Cherry continues, "Toxic positivity takes positive thinking to an overgeneralized extreme. This attitude doesn't just stress the importance of optimism, it minimizes and denies any trace of human emotions that aren't strictly happy or positive."

I couldn't agree with this article more. An optimistic outlook is a good thing, but pretending all is well when it isn't is just plain unhealthy. A good rule of thumb is, "First, feel your feelings." We humans have a range of emotions for a reason. Tuning into our feelings provides information about the support we may be needing. Acknowledging our discomfort allows our emotions to be fully present so they can be processed and eventually flow through us. Blocking them keeps us stuck. Dealing with them allows us to take action steps, learn new lessons and grow emotionally.

So today, and every day, I am avoiding toxic positivity. I am keeping an optimistic outlook while honestly acknowledging all my emotions and asking for help if I need it.

Henri Nouwen (1932–1996) Dutch priest, professor, writer

FEBRUARY 17

Get Clear on My Values

*Open your arms to change but
don't let go of your values.*

—Dalai Lama

"Values" can be a loaded word. Sometimes it's used in the political arena so one group can claim superiority over another. That's not my intention in using the word. For me, clarifying values means focusing on what gives my life the most meaning. Do I care a lot about creature comforts or do I value experiences more? In what ways do I want my life to matter? How does being of service to others enrich my life?

Today I am taking a moment to reflect on what matters most to me. It's good to remind myself of my deepest values every once in a while. That way, when change inevitably comes, I can make decisions based on what I hold true as most important.

Poet Mary Oliver asked, "What is it you plan to do with your one wild and precious life?" Answering that question is a great way to get clear on my values.

Dalai Lama, Tenzin Gyatso, spiritual leader
of Tibetan Buddhism and 14th Dalai Lama

FEBRUARY 18

Increase My Emotional Quotient

When you assume negative intent, you're angry. If you take away that anger and assume positive intent, you will be amazed. Your emotional quotient goes up because you are no longer almost random in your response.

—Indra Nooyi

Today I practice assuming good intentions. I remind myself that no one woke up this morning with the intention of making sure I had a bad day. I practice not reacting in haste, but instead taking a breath before I respond. If I feel prickly toward anyone, I check inside and see what tender spot the person may have activated inside me. I do my own work to comfort myself so I do not give others power over my emotions.

Today I celebrate that I am sharing the world with people who all want to love and be loved, as I do. I am reminding myself that just as I am imperfect, so are others. I am holding my boundaries, saying no if I need to, walking away from toxic situations, while also sending good wishes to every one of us who is doing our best with what we understand about this crazy world at the moment.

Indra Nooyi, Indian-American business executive

FEBRUARY 19

Maybe Good Nutrition Really Does Matter

Our food should be our medicine and our medicine should be our food.

—Hippocrates

Just about everything I read about good nutrition mentions certain foods as being especially healthy. You probably know the ones: blueberries, watermelon, broccoli, nuts and seeds...Only recently have I really focused on eating healthy foods in earnest, and wow, I'm convinced! I feel so much better.

In *Brain Food: The Surprising Science of Eating for Cognitive Power*, author Lisa Mosconi, who worked at the Alzheimer's Prevention Clinic at Weill Cornell Medical College during the time she wrote her book, explained:

"There is mounting evidence that adopting a brain-healthy diet is key to maintaining optimal cognitive capacities well into old age...At the same time, eating well and leading a healthy lifestyle have the added benefits of reducing the risk and severity of other medical illnesses that affect the brain, such as heart disease, diabetes and various metabolic disorders...

In the end, science is teaching us that our brain health is dependent on the food choices we make." So today, I am making sure that a lot of my choices are healthy ones.

Hippocrates (460–370 BC), Greek physician

FEBRUARY 20

Say No without Apology

No is a complete sentence.

—Anne Lamott

It's taken me a long time to learn how to say "no" gracefully. I've finally realized that I don't have to offer long explanations or apologies. I can simply decline with kindness. Here's an example:

Friend or family member: Can you come to the dinner next month?

Me: Thank you, I appreciate the invitation and I am not able to. I hope you all have a great time.

That's it. That's all I need to say, no matter the circumstances. Offering long explanations always left me feeling like I'd done something wrong and had to justify my decision. There are so many conflicting ways we could be spending our lives that it's simply not possible to do everything without running ourselves ragged. The sooner we become comfortable with saying no to some things, the more we'll be able to enjoy ourselves when "yes" is the response that works best.

So, today I am practicing saying no without apology whenever I need to, and I'm looking forward to savoring my "yeses."

Anne Lamott, American author

FEBRUARY 21

Joy Is an Antidote

Find a place inside where there's joy, and the joy will burn out the pain.

—Joseph Campbell

In the past, I've held on to a very faulty idea that everything must be "going well" before I can experience joy. Whew. What a way to keep myself imprisoned by perfectionism again. Here's what I've learned over the many years of my life: There's no such thing as a perfect day, and most every day can bring moments of joy if I'm open to them.

My hope is that those of us who have children and/or work with children in any way can help them learn this truth. Joy can be found inside us at any time, and, as Joseph Campbell writes, joy truly can help burn away our pain.

So today I am on the lookout for moments of joy, no matter how small, or no matter how entangled they are with challenges. If I believe they are there, I know I'll find them.

Joseph Campbell (1904–1987), American writer and professor

FEBRUARY 22
George Washington's Wisdom

It is better to be alone than in bad company.

—George Washington

On this anniversary of George Washington's birth, I appreciate his quote above. Choosing who to spend time with is an important part of living a fulfilling life. It's true that we cannot always choose our company, but we still do have a great deal of say about how we spend our discretionary time. Finding people who uplift us rather than deplete our energy, is vital.

Using a quote from George Washington reminds me that even people who have been celebrated as "heroes" are not perfect. No human being is. George Washington owned slaves and struggled with that terrible reality, finally making the decision in his will in 1799 to free the enslaved people on his estate. It's an AND kind of reality. He did admirable things AND regrettable things. As do we all.

The key for me in choosing "good company" is not trying to find perfect people (since there are none), but being clear with myself about how I truly feel. Who do I trust to not use my vulnerability against me? Who makes me laugh? Who appreciates the same qualities in me that I appreciate in myself? Being honest about those questions has been an important way to make choices about the company I keep.

Today I am being kind to everyone around me, while choosing to spend personal time with people who make my heart sing.

George Washington (1732–1799), first president of the United States

FEBRUARY 23
Hope from W.E.B. DuBois

Believe in life! Always human beings will live and progress to greater, broader, and fuller life.

—W. E. B. DuBois

On William Edward Burghardt DuBois's birthday, I've been pondering his quote above. What does it mean to believe in life? Right now, our collective lives often feel fraught with hate, division and misunderstanding. Will we humans really continue to "progress to greater, broader, and fuller life?" I guess the question I'm most wrestling with is, "What can I personally contribute to help make it so?" It's a daunting question.

What occurs to me is an answer that is true for so many things: Begin with myself. Release hatred toward anyone. Look for what I have in common with others instead of focusing on differences. Resolve to stay in my loving more than my judgment. It's ironic that often our way of working for "a better world" is to vilify people we disagree with. I'm certain that the energy of disapproval cannot lead to anything positive.

So today I am focusing on connection and caring. If I find myself judging others, at least for today I am leaving that behind.

W. E. B. DuBois (1868–1963), American author, sociologist, historian and civil rights activist

FEBRUARY 24
My Own Happiness Project

When I discover who I am, I'll be free.

—Ralph Ellison,
Invisible Man

Gretchen Rubin wrote a book called *The Happiness Project: Or, Why I Spent a Year Trying to Sing in the Morning, Clean My Closets, Fight Right, Read Aristotle and Generally Have More Fun.* You can probably tell from the title that her yearlong project was all about finding what would bring more happiness into her life. She tried many things, rejecting some, embracing others and learning a lot about herself in the process. In urging her readers to embark on their own explorations, she writes, "Everyone's happiness project is unique. I enjoyed posting my blog six days a week – a task that some people wouldn't dream of undertaking – but sit in silence for fifteen minutes each day, as my friend urged? I couldn't bring myself to do that."

This book is a bit like my own happiness project, but one I'm sharing with all of you. Some days will give me (and perhaps you) just what's needed. Others may miss the mark. That's ok, though, because through the process I'll be learning more and more about myself and what I really need. So, if I suggest something, feel free to adjust it to something better suited for you. I suspect that when I read through this book again in a year, some of my tastes will have changed and I'll want to make some changes, too. I think that's called life.

So today I am paying attention to my own happiness, embracing what's right for me and letting things go that don't feel like mine.

Ralph Ellison (1913–1994), American writer and scholar

FEBRUARY 25

Support My Curiosity

The beautiful thing about learning is that nobody can take it away from you.

—B.B. King

It's a great goal to try to keep finding new ways of doing things, but sometimes that feels like a lot of pressure. In their book, *A Curious Mind: The Secret to a Bigger Life*, Brian Grazer and Charles Fishman write about how often people are told to be creative or innovative, but aren't supported in learning how to do so. The authors explain that "as indispensable as they are, 'creativity' and 'innovation' are hard to measure and almost impossible to teach…Unlike creativity and innovation, though, curiosity is by its nature more accessible, more democratic, easier to see, and also easier to do… Here's the secret that we don't seem to understand, the wonderful connection we're not making: Curiosity is the tool that sparks creativity. Curiosity is the technique that gets to innovation."

Grazer and Fishman say curiosity is easy. We just need to wonder about the world. Ponder good questions. Channel our inner two-year-old and ask "why?" a lot. And have fun doing it.

Today I am ramping up my curiosity. I am excited about this enjoyable way of interacting with the world.

B.B. King (1925–2015), American singer-songwriter

FEBRUARY 26

Combat Perfectionism

*Progress, not perfection, is what we
should be asking of ourselves.*

—Julia Cameron

Here's my old nemesis perfectionism again. It's not that easy to get out from under its oppressive weight, so today I'll remind myself that perfection is impossible. I love the encouragement to focus on progress. It's important for me to remember, though, that sometimes just being exactly as I am is ok. Self-improvement does not have to be a goal at all times. Perhaps self-acceptance is an equally important goal.

So today I am enjoying being exactly who I am right now. I don't need to "fix" anything to feel good about myself. If I want to learn something new or exercise a bit more, I sure can, but only if it seems fun. I will not beat myself up to attain some arbitrary standard.

I am declaring this day a time of exuberant self-acceptance.

Julia Cameron, American teacher, author and artist

FEBRUARY 27
Prize Myself in Writing

Each person has got a voice inside them.
Communicate with it and take hold of it.
Do not let it push and shove you
around — you are its master!

—Stephen Richards,
Boost Your Self Esteem

For many years now I've been aware how my "voice inside" can either support me or beat me up. One way I've learned to master that voice is to practice writing down positive statements about myself. I call it "prizing myself in writing." The more I've practiced, the more this uplifting voice becomes the one I hear most often. Here's the key, though: the statements have to be ones I believe. I can't write fluff or drivel. My authentic self will automatically reject that. And I can't write something I don't believe and expect it to be effective. So, for example, instead of writing, "You're a fabulous cook" (which by any objective standard I'm not), I write, "You are learning more about cooking all the time, and finding great enjoyment in experimenting." That's the truth, so it feels good.

Today I am finding time to prize myself in writing, teaching the voice in my head to be one of positivity and encouragement.

Stephen Richards, British author, founder of Mirage Publishing in 1998

FEBRUARY 28
Learning Orientation to Life

*We do not learn from experience... we learn
from reflecting on experience.*

–John Dewey

Today I choose a learning orientation to life. I am open to what there is to learn from significant experiences I've had, both enjoyable and challenging. It's usually pretty easy to see the value in enjoyable experiences, but much harder to find the learning in pain. In my younger years I tended to want to bury hurtful experiences, hoping if I banished them from my consciousness I could be free of them. That never worked, though. They were always popping up in very inconvenient ways until I finally realized they were not going away until I'd dealt with them.

Learning from pain doesn't mean dwelling on the past and getting stuck there. Here's a six-part process I find helpful in dealing with hurtful memories: 1. Describe to myself what happened. 2. Name the feelings associated with that experience. 3. Acknowledge the feelings and consciously offer loving to my younger self (at whatever age I was when I had the experience). 4. If I realize I'm blaming or criticizing myself in any way, remind myself I was doing the best I could with the tools I had at the time. Then offer myself caring self-forgiveness for judging myself as wrong. Remind myself that no matter what happened, I am not bad. 5. Ask myself if there is any support I might still need to help heal from the experience. If there is, make a plan. (Do I need to journal about it, talk to a friend, talk to a professional?) 6. Ask myself what gift (e.g. insight, new strength, connection with others) I might have received from having that experience. This last part really only works once sufficient healing has taken place. It really is an "AND" kind of step. I acknowledge the pain I experienced AND I acknowledge any value I've received.

Today I am supporting myself on my ongoing journey of healing and learning.

John Dewey (1859–1952), American philosopher, psychologist, and educational reformer

FEBRUARY 29

Only Once Every Four Years

Today is an ephemeral ghost....A strange amazing day that comes only once every four years. For the rest of the time it does not "exist."...Use this day to do something daring, extraordinary and unlike yourself. Take a chance and shape a different pattern in your personal cloud of probability!

—Vera Nazarian,
The Perpetual Calendar of Inspiration

Whenever a leap year comes along, I will listen to Vera Nazarian's urging to do something unlike myself. I'm thinking about what would feel new and interesting and a bit daring. I think instead of planning what that might be, I will stay open to possibilities and let adventure find me.

So, here's to a leap into the unknown, with trust and excitement!

Vera Nazarian, Armenian-Russian American author and artist

March

Our life is March weather,
savage and serene in one hour.

—Ralph Waldo Emerson

Ralph Waldo Emerson (1803–1882), American essayist and philosopher

MARCH 1
Look for Comfort

*Although the world is full of suffering,
it is also full of the overcoming of it.*

−Helen Keller

Helen Keller's quote is a reminder to roll with life's ups and downs. Some days are more challenging than others, but if I don't fight the rhythm of life, I begin to experience a flow of highs and lows that is actually rather comforting. No matter what is happening, I can be assured that "this, too, shall pass," as Abraham Lincoln was fond of saying.

In Maggie Smith's small but profound book, *Keep Moving: Notes on Loss, Creativity and Change*, she writes, "Let change – even traumatic upheaval – remind you that anything is possible. When the dark cloud of chaos hangs over you, let possibility be the silver lining. Keep moving."

I have a friend who tells me that during times of challenge his go-to word is "curiosity." He asks himself, "I wonder what's next?" and it helps him feel better. Of course, when we know we're in an unhealthy situation, we can't just wait around to be surprised by the future. We have to take action toward our own well-being.

For those days that lean more toward suffering than overcoming, I have a few comfort remedies that help me make it through until I feel better again. Each person's idea of comfort will be different, but for me I like hot baths with cool drinks or driving by myself with my favorite music playing.

Today I am going to find one new "comfort remedy." I'm curious about what I'll come up with. And I'm wondering what you might choose.

Helen Keller (1880−1968), American author and disability rights advocate

MARCH 2
Remember My Why

Very few people or companies can clearly articulate WHY they do WHAT they do. By WHY I mean your purpose, cause or belief...WHY do you get out of bed every morning?

—Simon Sinek,
Start with Why: How Great Leaders
Inspire Everyone to Take Action

I've heard people complain about meaningless meetings at their work places where everyone was made to articulate their "why," but nobody really believed what they were saying. That's not what I'm talking about. It's not helpful to make up a "why" to please someone else. What I want to do is get very clear about my own heartfelt purpose...just for me. Why DO I get out of bed in the morning? What do I contribute to this world? I'm not going to make the mistake of letting my ego convince me I have to find something "grand" that will be noticed by others. That will probably not be purpose; it will most likely be an insecure need to have someone else confirm that I'm worthy.

So today I am reminding myself that I came into this world worthy of love and belonging, just because I'm here. I don't have to try to earn worthiness or do something flashy so others will notice me. My purpose may be as simple as adding a bit more loving to our world. Come to think of it, that's actually a pretty grand purpose.

Simon Sinek, British-born American author and inspirational speaker

MARCH 3
Rejoice in Nature Today

*All my life through, the new sights of
nature made me rejoice like a child.*

—Marie Curie

Today I promise myself to spend time outdoors in the most natural setting I can find. If the best I can do is simply walk down an urban street, I am still determined to marvel at the clouds and let the street trees inspire me by their tenacity to survive in tough conditions.

Time in the natural world always reminds me of the connections we humans share. We bask in the warmth of the same sun. We hurtle through space on the same planet, more linked than we let ourselves realize most of the time. When I was teaching, I always talked to young children about ways the natural world is shared by all humans. The birds in one neighborhood fly long distances to spend time in another part of the globe. The night sky is filled with stars that are seen by our fellow travelers the world over.

I am rejoicing today in this global connection. I promise to hear nature's persistent reminder that we must work together to care for this beautiful planet we all call home.

Marie Curie (1867–1934), Polish-French physicist

MARCH 4
Find My Calm

You are the sky. Everything else - it's just the weather.

—Pema Chödrön

Pema Chödrön's writings urge each of us to cultivate a strong, centered calmness within; a place that can't be disturbed by outside events (the "weather," as she calls it). Obviously this is easier said than done.

Brené Brown, in her book, *I Thought it Was Just Me (But It Isn't): Making the Journey from 'What Will People Think?' to I Am Enough*, writes, "The constant struggle to feel accepted and worthy is unrelenting. We put so much of our time and energy into making sure that we meet everyone's expectations and into caring about what other people think of us, that we are often left feeling angry, resentful and fearful." Or, as Pema Chödrön might say, we decide that the weather around us is more real than the sky.

Often I stir up my own weather and create angst where it isn't necessary. Just yesterday I sent out electronic invitations for a family party and realized, belatedly, that I'd made a typo. No big deal, right? Sure, except all day I kept feeling the "weather" of self-criticism swirling around me. I finally had to stop and ask myself, "If someone would find me unworthy because I made a small mistake, would I really want to have a relationship with them, anyway?" The reality was, as I actually knew deep down, that no one was judging me except ME.

Today, I am the sky. I am calm. I am not letting the weather around me disturb my peace.

Pema Chödrön, American Tibetan Buddhist nun, author

MARCH 5

Service

I slept and dreamt that life was joy.
I awoke and saw that life was service.
I acted and behold, service was joy.

—Rabindranath Tagore

Today I will give some thought to what it means to be of service. One thing I know it does not mean is to make myself a martyr. If, as Tagore writes above, service is joy, how can I experience the kind of service that will fill me up instead of depleting me?

Martin Seligman, Ph.D., in his book, *Authentic Happiness: Using the New Positive Psychology to Realize Your Potential for Lasting Fulfillment*, writes about what research tells us related to service. Seligman explains that "the good life consists in deriving happiness by using your signature strengths every day in the main realms of living." By this he means choosing to use your talents to support **knowledge** (educating children, engaging in journalism, becoming a writer, etc...), **power** (working in technology, engineering, health care...), or **goodness** (the law, policing, firefighting, religion, politics...).

But then he explains, "The **meaningful** life adds one more component: using these same strengths to **forward** knowledge, power or goodness."

According to Seligman, when we discover how to make anything we do better, we are being of service and adding to the joy of life for ourselves and others. Of course it's wonderful when we can contribute in significant ways, but small ways count, too.

Today I am finding a way to be of service by doing one small thing a bit better. Perhaps I will be a little more patient with a child, or I'll offer a more sincere thank you to a colleague. I am remembering that opportunities for service are everywhere.

Rabindranath Tagore (1861–1941), Bengali poet and polymath

MARCH 6
Choose Social Media Carefully

> *The internet is a dangerous place. If you are not careful it will consume you and rob you of your happiness. It can make you angry, jealous, hostile, bitter and lead to the eventual loss of enthusiasm for living your best life. Be wary and avoid overconsumption.*
>
> —Germany Kent

Social media really can be a time black hole and a cause for depression. Here's some more caution from Germany Kent:

"Too often too much social media and the latest internet trends drain us and erode us of creativity, drive, peace of mind and sense of purpose…One should be careful not to buy into the notion that someone else's life is somehow more complete or fulfilling than yours based solely on what you see online."

Today I'm going to be careful I don't confuse what I see on social media with real life. And I'm going to find more fulfilling ways to spend my time than endlessly scrolling through a little screen. I know technology has many positives, and can help us keep in touch with far away loved ones, but I also know it can hurt me. Today I choose to find a healthy balance.

Germany Kent, American print and broadcast journalist

MARCH 7
Don't Wait Until It's Gone

Find ecstasy in life; the mere sense of living is joy enough.

—Emily Dickinson

"Oh earth, you're too wonderful for anybody to realize you," Thornton Wilder's tragic heroine says in his iconic play, *Our Town*. I remember reading it for the first time in middle school and being troubled enough to ask for help, something I usually never did. "I don't get it," I whispered to my teacher, shyly approaching his desk. "She died. Why did we read something so sad?" I still think of his reply as an example of how a teacher can open a mind: "Yes, she died. But you didn't. All the things she misses about life are still there for you."

It's become cliché to talk about an "Our Town" moment, but that one moment with my teacher honestly has enriched the way I look at life. A mundane task like making my bed in the morning is a meditation in gratitude when I think about how much I'd miss smoothing out my quirky striped quilt if I were no longer here on this earth. On my best days I remember that right now many people would give anything just for the chance to sleep in their own beds. A powerful attitude reset happens when I think about what it would be like to lose the things that mean the most to me. When I imagine how sad I'd be without them, it's such a relief to remind myself they're still here. I suspect everyone's "most important" list is remarkably similar: family, friends, health. Knowing I could lose them in an instant is a good gratitude wake up call.

And while my "most important" list keeps me grounded, my "small joys" list makes life more fun. So, today I'm relishing my morning coffee more, drinking it in my favorite cup, a gift from a cherished long-distance friend. Then I'm continuing to pay attention so I don't take for granted the bounty in my life, to be cherished now, in this moment, on this precious day.

Emily Dickinson (1830–1886), American poet

MARCH 8
I Am Certainly Not the First to Face Challenges

You gain strength, courage, and confidence by every experience in which you really stop to look fear in the face.

—Eleanor Roosevelt

As the global pandemic swooped into all our lives in Spring of 2020, I found comfort in reading Eleanor Roosevelt's book, *You Learn by Living: Eleven Keys for a More Fulfilling Life*. It was helpful to immerse myself in her experiences during the influenza pandemic of 1918–1920. She wrote, "Courage is more exhilarating than fear and in the long run it is easier. We do not have to become heroes overnight. Just a step at a time, meeting each thing that comes up...discovering we have the strength to stare it down."

It's natural to put famous people on a pedestal, believing they were born with supernatural powers the rest of us don't have, but the reality is that all human beings are a combination of desirable and unwanted traits: courage and cowardice; altruism and selfishness; hope and gloom.

Reading of Eleanor Roosevelt's many life challenges reminded me that every human being throughout history has faced obstacles, and most have figured out ways to overcome them, even if imperfectly. It helped to realize that my challenges are simply part of the human condition, and I'm not alone in either my moments of despair or triumph.

Today I remind myself that whatever obstacles come along, I can tackle them one at a time, finding new strength with each forward step I take.

Eleanor Roosevelt (1884–1962) former First Lady of the United States, author and activist

MARCH 9

Listen to My Self-Talk

We all have moments of self-deprecation and very often we are too hard on ourselves. Today, start to be caring and supportive of yourself. Observe that little voice in your head and say something positive to yourself instead.

–Elaine Seiler,
Getting Rid of Negative Energy

One of the important things I've learned as I've grown older is that it's crucial to become quite aware of the "voice in my head" as Elaine Seiler calls it (as does my favorite, Michael Singer in *The Untethered Soul*). It's worth reminding myself — often — that I am not that voice, and that my true self is never harsh or critical or unloving. Any disparaging thoughts I hear are simply vestiges of the negative energy we human beings pick up during our time in this "earth school."

Today I am listening to my self-talk and making course corrections as needed. I am being gentle with myself.

Elaine Seiler, American author, global coach and consultant

MARCH 10
Boundaries

Compassionate people ask for what they need. They say no when they need to, and when they say yes, they mean it. They're compassionate because their boundaries keep them out of resentment.

—Brené Brown,
Rising Strong

Indian heart surgeon and author, Mani S. Sivasubramanian, wrote this about our busy lives, "Information overload (on all levels) is exactly WHY you need an 'ignore list'. It has never been more important to be able to say 'No.'" It feels very liberating to realize that it's ok to simply ignore some of the information that constantly bombards us. For me, at least, it's so important to sort out what is necessary to respond to, and what is optional.

The ability to say no is part of having the healthy boundaries Brené Brown references. One of my husband's favorite sayings is, "Having boundaries doesn't make me a jerk; having boundaries keeps me from becoming a jerk." I think that's what Brown means about our boundaries keeping us out of resentment. If we say yes to optional things we don't really want to do, then we won't be showing up with a loving spirit, and others will feel our lack of enthusiasm.

So today I am focusing on what can come OFF my list. It feels good.

Brené Brown, American professor and author

MARCH 11

Let It Go

To live in this world, you must be able to do three things: to love what is mortal; to hold it against your bones knowing your own life depends on it; and when the time comes to let it go, let it go.

—Mary Oliver

One of the hardest life lessons for me has been accepting the value of non-attachment. I have come to understand it to mean that my well-being is not dependent on any object or person. And, paradoxically, my happiness is rooted in deeply loving the people and objects I am with right now. Mary Oliver's urging to let things go when the time comes is both wise and wrenching. Everything within me screams, "No, hold on." And yet, I now realize that acceptance of loss actually opens the door to deeper love. It's not logical, but it is my experience.

In Maggie Smith's book, *Keep Moving: Notes on Loss, Creativity, and Change*, she writes:

"Consider that your ideas about happiness – what you think it should look like, feel like, entail, provide – might be hindering your experience of it. Set aside your expectations. Watch, listen, learn, feel. Keep moving." Perhaps my old expectation that everything I love should remain forever, kept me from experiencing the fullness of life's cycles: the bittersweet letting go mingling with the sweetness of new beginnings.

Today I am accepting the transitory nature of life while at the same time celebrating each delightful gift I can experience right now, this minute.

Mary Oliver (1935–2019), American poet

MARCH 12
I Get to Make Myself Happy

Any happiness you get you've got to make yourself.

–Alice Walker

In the children's book, *The House at Pooh Corner* by A.A. Milne, the main character, Christopher Robin, asks his bear friend, Pooh, a question: "'What do you like doing best in the world, Pooh?' 'Well,' said Pooh, 'what I like best—' and then he had to stop and think. Because although Eating Honey was a very good thing to do, there was a moment just before you began to eat it which was better than when you were, but he didn't know what it was called."

The things we each like most in the world are often hard to explain to others, and are sometimes even elusive to ourselves. What I know for sure is that we are responsible for our own happiness. It's not up to anyone else in my life to "make me happy," so I'd better tune into what my authentic self finds fulfilling and fun.

That doesn't mean I can't find happiness with other people; it simply means that happiness comes from within, not from the circumstances of my life. If outer trappings made us happy, then people with the most money and the fanciest "toys" would be the happiest ones on earth. We all know that is not true. And if we're honest, we understand we can't really have a happy relationship with someone else until the relationship with ourselves is on solid ground.

I love Pooh's description of anticipatory happiness. For me, that moment might come right before I'm about to sip my first cup of coffee in the morning, or when I crack open a book I think I'm going to love. It's also there right before my granddaughters arrive from out of town. Today I'm paying attention to what my authentic self loves. And I'm savoring all the "can't wait" moments I'm able to give myself in this lifetime.

Alice Walker, American writer, poet, and social activist

MARCH 13
Break the Cycle

> *Be the person who breaks the cycle. If you were judged, choose understanding. If you were rejected, choose acceptance. If you were shamed, choose compassion. Be the person you needed when you were hurting, not the person who hurt you. Vow to be better than what broke you - to heal instead of becoming bitter so you can act from your heart, not your pain.*
>
> —Lori Deschene

No one gets out of this life without experiencing pain. All of us have painful experiences from our pasts that we want to transcend. Some of this pain undoubtedly happened in our original family. I have told my own children that everyone learns some things from their parents that they want to keep and other things they want to change. It's ok to acknowledge that some of our old family stories no longer work for us. Some of us have many hurts and misunderstandings that came from our families and others have only a few, but all of us have them.

Today I am becoming more honest about old family patterns that no longer work for me. And I'm finding the courage I need so I can change them. This isn't being disloyal to my family; it's being loyal to myself.

Today I am taking at least one courageous step to break the cycle.

Lori Deschene, American writer

MARCH 14

Deal with Anger

*Letting go gives us freedom, and freedom is
the only condition for happiness. If, in our heart,
we still cling to anything - anger, anxiety,
or possessions - we cannot be free.*

—Thich Nhat Hanh,
*The Heart of the Buddha's Teaching:
Transforming Suffering into
Peace, Joy, and Liberation*

My mother was the daughter of a minister, and she grew up in an era where there were many expectations of a minister's family. "Our family doesn't get angry," she told me when I was a child, certainly a leftover misunderstanding from her own childhood. The reality is, everyone gets angry. Denying anger does not make it go away. It simply becomes buried deep within us, where it continues to burn unless we deal with it.

I still find myself resisting angry feelings, at some level believing I shouldn't have them. The healthy part of me understands how important it is to acknowledge what I'm really feeling. I can remind myself I'm only human and allowed to have the full range of human emotions. Then I can decide what action steps I'll take to deal with my feelings. Mark Twain said, "Anger is an acid that can do more harm to the vessel in which it is stored than to anything on which it is poured," so I know I certainly don't want to hang onto it.

If it feels productive to do so, I can talk about my anger in a calm and non-accusatory way. Or, if talking to someone else doesn't seem right, I can journal about my feelings and deal with the issues inside me that are being poked. I might also choose to take a long walk and think through what's causing my anger and how I can release it.

So today I am practicing accepting any angry feelings that might come up, and I'm finding safe ways to help my emotions flow through me.

Thich Nhat Hanh (1926–2022), Vietnamese Buddhist monk, peace activist, author and teacher

MARCH 15
Be Kind

Be kind. Everyone you meet is carrying a heavy burden.

—Ian Maclaren

Years ago, as a young early care and education director, I was astounded to learn how many staff were coming to work carrying the "heavy burdens" Ian Maclaren references. People would stop by my office to tell me that one of their parents had received a cancer diagnosis; a spouse had just lost a job; or a beloved pet was terminally ill and would be euthanized soon. What I learned from those conversations was that I had no idea how many people in all aspects of my life were facing something challenging I knew nothing about. So while I would like to think that I've always tried to be a kind person, I began being more intentional in my interactions with everyone, including strangers.

A long time ago, as a newly single mother raising two small children on my own with limited financial resources, it was New Year's Eve and I was feeling especially sorry for myself. To try to cheer up, I took my little ones to a restaurant for slices of pie. To my horror, when the check came, I realized I'd underestimated what the bill would be and I was a little short. I sheepishly told my children I would have to ask our server if we could pay the rest later… My daughter, only three at the time, said, "Don't worry mom, an angel will help us." I was taken aback by her words because I didn't remember ever speaking with her about angels. Chalking up her comment to child-like innocence, I steeled myself for the difficult conversation I was about to have. I could hardly believe it when our server breezed over, announcing, "Someone has paid your bill for you. Happy New Year's Eve!" With tears in my eyes, I told my daughter, "Someone has certainly been an angel to us." That experience will always be part of who I am, and it continues to motivate me to find ways to ease others' burdens, especially if I do so anonymously.

Ian Maclaren (1850—1907), pen name of John Watson, Scottish author and minister

MARCH 16
No Praise for Overwork

We think, mistakenly, that success is the result of the amount of time we put in at work, instead of the quality of time we put in.

—Arianna Huffington,
*Thrive: The Third Metric to
Redefining Success and Creating a Life
of Well-Being, Wisdom, and Wonder*

Sometimes life can feel like a competition to prove who works the hardest. I'm not sure where that way of thinking comes from, but I'm ready to let it go. Becoming exhausted is not admirable. Overworking is not a badge of honor.

The people I admire most seem to have figured out how to flow with the rhythm of life – sometimes exerting intense effort, then taking a breath, walking away for a bit and coming back into balance. Arianna Huffington, in her book referenced above, urges all of us to "give up the delusion that burnout is the inevitable cost of success." And while I'm making the decision to walk away from burnout, I'm also reminding myself that I can define success any way I want. I know my definition will not include exhaustion.

Today, I am working and playing at a comfortable pace.

Arianna Huffington, Greek-American author,
co-founder of *The Huffington Post*

MARCH 17

St. Patrick's Day Luck

Luck is believing you're lucky.

—Tennessee Williams

On this St. Patrick's Day, I am claiming some of the "luck of the Irish" for myself. I do believe in Abraham Lincoln's famous quote, "Most folks are about as happy as they make up their minds to be," and I think this holds true for how lucky we feel. Perhaps what people call luck is really just being aware of the abundance in our world that is there for all of us despite our circumstances. During the Great Depression, Judy Garland sang the song, "Life is Just a Bowl of Cherries," that urged people to "live and laugh at it all."

I do realize that laughing in every situation isn't appropriate. It's important not to deny the full range of our emotions. And yet, often we overlook how "lucky" we really are because we focus so much on what we don't have instead of the many glorious gifts we do have.

So today I am remembering my "luck," and giving thanks for the many, many wonderful aspects of my life.

Tennessee Williams (1911–1983), pen name of Thomas Lanier Williams III, American playwright and screenwriter

MARCH 18

Only Me

*Compete against yourself, not others,
for that is truly your best competition.*

–Peggy Fleming

Today I'm giving up any delusion that I have to compete with other people — in any way. The only person I choose to compete with is myself, but even that competition could be dangerous if I'm not careful. If I'm good-heartedly looking to improve some skills or learn something new, then it's a healthy competition. If I'm buying into the misunderstanding that somehow I'm faulty and have to be "fixed," then it's a harmful competition.

Recently, during my evening walk, I've been trying to add a minute or two each day until I'm up to an hour. I'm being careful to think of this "friendly competition" with myself as something fun and not a forced march. If there are days it doesn't work, I'm gentle with myself.

So, today I'm looking for opportunities to grow in healthy ways, while also reminding myself once again that I'm just fine exactly as I am right now.

Peggy Fleming, American figure skating gold medalist,
1968 Winter Olympics

MARCH 19
A Day with No Complaining

When you complain, you make yourself a victim. Leave the situation, change the situation, or accept it. All else is madness.

—Eckhart Tolle

Today I am trying an experiment: Can I get through one day without ever complaining? When I started to pay attention to how often I complained, I was truly shocked. "It's too humid today." "This sandwich is soggy." "There's too much traffic." "I'm annoyed by this politician."

How would my daily experience change if I simply decided not to express any complaints for 24 hours? I'm going to try it. And, just for today, in place of complaints I'm going to try statements of gratitude: "This humidity will be so good for the plants." "I'm so grateful to have food available whenever I want it." "I'm grateful to have such a well-functioning car." "Some politicians are working hard for causes that mean a lot to me."

It's an experiment. I'll be interested to see if I can make it through the whole day. I wonder if you'd like to try it.

Eckhart Tolle, German-born author and teacher

MARCH 20

United Nations International Day of Happiness

Only the development of compassion and understanding for others can bring us the tranquility and happiness we all seek.

—Dalai Lama

From the United Nations website, here's a description of the UN International Day of Happiness, March 20, "Since 2013, the United Nations has celebrated the International Day of Happiness as a way to recognise the importance of happiness in the lives of people around the world. In 2015, the UN launched the 17 Sustainable Development Goals, which seek to end poverty, reduce inequality, and protect our planet – three key aspects that lead to well-being and happiness.

The United Nations invites each person of any age, plus every classroom, business and government to join in celebration of the International Day of Happiness."

Today I am informing myself more about the United Nation's 17 Sustainable Development Goals. I am thinking about how my happiness is deeply connected to the happiness of others. I choose to celebrate today by learning more about the reality of people's lives in places and circumstances very different from my own.

Dalai Lama, Tenzin Gyatso, spiritual leader of Tibetan Buddhism and 14th Dalai Lama

MARCH 21
Unplug

Almost everything will work again if you unplug it for a few minutes, including you.

—Anne Lamott

Today I am thinking about what it would mean for me to "unplug." I know I often spend more time than I intend to on social media. When I'm tired, I sometimes scroll mindlessly through my phone until I realize I've wasted an hour or more. So, I am making a choice to unplug from the world of screens and do something "low tech." I might take a walk, enjoy a bubble bath or read a book. Or maybe I'll try something I've never done before.

Today I am savoring the possibilities open to me when I consciously unplug from technology's grip and look for fresh new ways to relax.

MARCH 22
Rushing People Can Be the Opposite of Love

In our rushing, bulls in china shops, we break our own lives.

—Ann Voskamp,
One Thousand Gifts: A Dare to Live Fully Right Where You Are

One morning, years ago, I was rushing my two small children out the door, ignoring their pleas to look at the puzzles they had proudly put together that morning, so I could make it on time to a workshop I was giving called (I kid you not), "Helping Children Feel Seen and Valued." Hmmm. What's wrong with that picture?

I realize there are times we all need to hurry, but if we aren't careful, rushing can become our default way of being. I think back with chagrin to a time I gave short shrift to a colleague who needed my listening ear because I wanted to get back to writing an article on "Heart-Centered Listening." In situations like those, the irony (and hypocrisy) started to become too great, and I made myself rethink my day-to-day way of being. I made a commitment that I would not value efficiency over loving interactions.

It's still a bit hard for me to stop and lend someone a hand when doing so will mean I'm going to be late for something, but I'm getting more comfortable prioritizing people's significant needs over perfect punctuality.

Today I am paying attention to how often rushing can get in the way of loving. I promise myself I will slow down when it's really important.

Ann Voskamp, Canadian author, blogger

MARCH 23
Be Gentle with Myself

Growth is an erratic forward movement:
two steps forward, one step back. Remember
that and be very gentle with yourself.

—Julia Cameron

One aspect of being gentle with myself is becoming ok with asking for help. In her book, *Composing a Further Life*, Mary Catherine Bateson writes about how reluctant we humans often are to admit we might need someone else's assistance. "This notion of standing on one's own two feet and needing nothing from others resonates with… the mythology of pioneers, frontier scouts and cowboys, but it is by no means limited to males…It is a style that works against mutuality and that risks encouraging taking rather than sharing, exploitation rather than cooperation."

I know in the past I've mistakenly thought that admitting I needed help meant admitting I'd failed. Now I know that, as Julia Cameron says, we all take steps forward and steps backwards. Sometimes we're in a position to offer help to others and sometimes we're the ones needing help.

Today I recognize the ups and downs of life and allow myself to be grateful for the dance of give and take we can all embrace. Admitting I can't do it all isn't a sign of failure; it's a sign of wisdom.

Julia Cameron, American teacher, author and artist

MARCH 24
Tackle Tough Decisions

*May your choices reflect your hopes,
not your fears.*

—Nelson Mandela

One thing I learned over the course of my career was that there would be times I needed to make decisions that not everyone would agree with. I would often listen to team members make the case for two opposite approaches, knowing that no matter what I chose, someone would not be happy. No matter what work we do, or what situations we deal with, all of us at one time or another will encounter those sorts of "no win" decisions.

My solution to those times was to ask myself what the most loving approach would be, and which decision would lead to the greatest chance for learning or healing or forward movement (depending on the situation). When I became clear within myself that I had made the most loving decision I could, then I felt a sense of peace and was ready to face whatever criticism came my way.

Often in life, we are called to choose between two equally difficult options. No matter which way we choose, there will be pain at first. At times like those I like to remember the "splinter analogy." When faced with a painful splinter, we can leave it alone and pretend nothing is wrong (and thereby risk infection and continuing pain), or we can go through the momentary discomfort of removing it, which will then lead to healing and eventually the elimination of pain. When I am tempted to put my head in the sand during times of challenge, I remind myself to look for the splinter, bite the bullet, remove it and get on with the healing.

Today I am making decisions based on what is most loving and, ultimately what is for the highest good of all.

Nelson Mandela (1918–1999), South African anti-apartheid activist and first president of South Africa

MARCH 25
Insist Upon It

*I respect myself and insist upon it
from everybody. And because I do it,
I then respect everybody, too.*

—Maya Angelou

We teach people how to treat us, whether we know it or not. Once I began to believe that every human being was worthy of love and respect, simply because they are on this earth, then I began to act in new ways. I did not allow myself to be treated poorly, and I refused to treat anyone else with less than respect, no matter how vehemently I disagreed with their political positions or felt they had acted badly. I have decided that no matter what anyone else does, I will not add to the negativity that can so easily grow out of control in our world.

So today I intend to act with respect for all, and I'll expect it back for myself. And if things start to feel negative, I'll simply remove myself from the situation, or at the very least, refuse to engage. I will look for the best in each person today, believing that I'm almost certain to find it.

Maya Angelou (1928–2014), American writer, poet and civil rights activist

MARCH 26

Take Pleasure in Eating Seasonally

People who love to eat are always the best people.

—Julia Child

Jane Goodall, in her book, *Harvest for Hope: A Guide to Mindful Eating*, writes about the pleasures of enjoying food that celebrates the seasons. She explains, "We have trained ourselves to plan meals around any food from anywhere in the world at any time of the year. Eating locally means that we need also be reconnected with the season, to think about meals in the way our ancestors did, organizing them around the fresh market vegetables, around seasonal delicacies. An easy way to get started is to eat one local seasonal meal a week."

I realize that eating fresh, local food is a luxury not afforded to all. It can be expensive, and not readily available everywhere. One apartment dweller I know decided to grow fresh basil and chocolate mint in pots sitting on his kitchen windowsill. He finds ways to use these in recipes frequently, savoring the way they can lift his enjoyment of eating.

Today, in whatever way I can, I am savoring fresh seasonal food, and taking pleasure in eating mindfully and gratefully.

Julia Child (1912–2004), American cooking teacher, author, and television personality

MARCH 27
Celebrate What I Have

Acknowledging the good that you already have in your life is the foundation for all abundance.

—Eckhart Tolle

A few years ago I was in a workshop focused on setting intentions. Everyone was paired up with a classmate they didn't know well and asked to talk together about the intentions we wanted to set for our lives. As I began describing how I'd like to make my marriage even stronger, add some new ideas to my job, and make a few improvements around my house, I noticed my partner looking at me with surprise. I stopped and asked what he was thinking. "Oh," he replied. "I'm sorry. It's just that my intentions are to find a relationship, a job and be able to afford a home. It just seems to me that you already have everything I've ever wanted."

His comment changed me. I realized how often I had been focusing on trying to make things better while failing to see how good they already were. So today I remind myself that perfect is the enemy of the good. I give thanks for what I already have, imperfect though it may be. That will be my cue to the universe to continue sending the abundance.

Eckhart Tolle, German-born author and teacher

MARCH 28
Get Some Sleep

*By helping us keep the world in perspective,
sleep gives us a chance to refocus on the essence
of who we are. And in that place of connection,
it is easier for the fears and concerns
of the world to drop away.*

—Arianna Huffington,
The Sleep Revolution

Here's Arianna Huffington again, reminding us to push ourselves less and sleep more. Why is it so hard sometimes to get a good night's sleep? Maybe sleep would come more easily if I thought of it as something pleasant and renewing, instead of something I "needed."

Today I am not scolding myself about sleep. No more saying, "You'd better hurry up and get to bed or you'll be too tired tomorrow," or "I'm just going to finish one more thing tonight, even though I'm really tired." Instead I say: "I'm looking forward to 'refocusing the essence' of who I am. I'm ready to let the fears and concerns of the world drop away."

I look forward to getting cozy tonight and drifting off to a really cool place.

Arianna Huffington, Greek-American author, co-founder of
The Huffington Post

MARCH 29
Choose My Attitude

> *The last of the human freedoms: to choose one's attitude in any given set of circumstances, to choose one's own way. And there were always choices to make. Every day, every hour, offered the opportunity to make a decision, a decision which determined whether you would or would not submit to those powers which threatened to rob you of your very self, your inner freedom.*
>
> —Viktor Frankl,
> *Man's Search for Meaning*

Viktor Frankl was an Austrian neurologist, psychiatrist, philosopher, writer and Holocaust survivor. He is best known for his book, quoted above, that describes his experiences in a Holocaust concentration camp and what those experiences taught him about individual human choice. Frankl describes fellow prisoners, all living under the same horrific conditions, yet not all reacting equally. He explains that he observed a small number of men walking from person to person, offering comfort, sharing their own meager rations with others. It was then Frankl realized that circumstances do not solely control human behavior. Each person has the power to "choose one's attitude."

So what does Frankl's story mean for me? I think it would be a mistake to believe that no matter what is happening, I should be able to keep a positive attitude. That smacks of toxic positivity (see February 16). On the other hand, it does remind me that I do not have to define myself as a "victim" of circumstance. I can choose how I react. I can process my feelings. I can take actions that feel right for me.

Today, in whatever situation I find myself, I am remembering that I have choices in how to react. I am considering all my choices and taking my best next step.

Viktor Frankl (1905–1997), Austrian psychiatrist, writer

MARCH 30

Read

*That's the thing about books. They let
you travel without moving your feet.*

—Jhumpa Lahiri

"What exactly do human beings get from reading books?" asks an article on the *Healthline* website. "Is it just a matter of pleasure, or are there benefits beyond enjoyment? The scientific answer is a resounding 'yes.'"

In "Benefits of Reading Books: How It Can Positively Affect Your Life," Heidi Moawad, M.D. and Rebecca Joy Stanborough write, "Reading books benefits both your physical and mental health, and those benefits can last a lifetime. They begin in early childhood and continue through the senior years...A growing body of research indicates that reading literally changes your mind.

Using MRI scans, researchers have confirmed that reading involves a complex network of circuits and signals in the brain. As your reading ability matures, those networks also get stronger and more sophisticated."

Today I am grateful to learn that in addition to the new places I visit through books and the interesting "people" I meet, my physical and mental health is also benefitting. How cool is that?

Jhumpa Lahiri, London-born American author

MARCH 31
What Will I Find Inside Me?

Happiness is a habit. Cultivate it.

—Elbert Hubbard

There is an iconic legend (author unknown) about two dogs. Both dogs, at separate times, walk into the same room. One dog comes out wagging his tail while the other comes out growling.

A woman watching this goes into the room to see what could possibly make one dog so happy and the other dog so mad. To her surprise, she finds a room full of mirrors. The happy dog found a thousand happy dogs looking back at him. The angry dog saw only angry growling dogs looking back at him.

Meaning: What I see in the world around me is a reflection of my own attitude. Today I cultivate happiness. This doesn't mean adopting a falsely positive outlook. It means finding small ways to feel happy whenever I can.

Elbert Hubbard (1856–1915), American writer, publisher, artist and philosopher.

April

Spring is made of solid, fourteen-karat gratitude, the reward for the long wait. Every religious tradition from the northern hemisphere honors some form of April hallelujah, for this is the season of exquisite redemption, a slam-bang return to joy after a season of cold second thoughts.

—Barbara Kingsolver,
Animal, Vegetable, Miracle

Barbara Kingsolver, American Pulitzer Prize-winning novelist, poet

APRIL 1

April Fool's Day Spirit

Even the gods love jokes.

—Plato

In the spirit of April Fool's Day, I am looking for ways to be light-hearted today.

Kaki Okumura, in her article on the *Forge* website, "The Very Serious Benefits of Being Silly," writes, "There's been little research on playfulness in adults. But recent studies led by René Proyer, a psychologist at the University of Zurich, found that playful people — those who are spontaneous, creative, outgoing, fun-loving, and lighthearted — appear to be better at coping with stress and finding novel solutions to problems."

I think I'll start my quest for light-heartedness by remembering some of the fun-loving things I most enjoyed doing as a child. One of my favorites was a picnic on a blanket in the living room for dinner. I just might try that tonight. How about you? What feels light-hearted in your life?

APRIL 2
Cut Others Some Slack

Three-fourths of the miseries and misunderstandings in the world will disappear if we step into the shoes of our adversaries and understand their standpoint.

—Mahatma Gandhi

I like to remind myself often about the benefits of assuming best intentions. It simply makes life easier and more fun to live that way. I am a firm believer that everyone is doing the best they can with the tools they currently possess. Poet and author Maya Angelou said, "Do the best you can until you know better. Then when you know better, do better."

Each one of us has areas of life where we don't know enough yet to "do better." I certainly hope people will give me grace when I act out of ignorance. I don't have to agree with every action other people take, but I can try harder to understand their worldview. I can set boundaries for myself with people I find difficult to be around, but I can do so with as little judgment and criticism as possible.

Today I am extending the same grace to others that I want for myself.

Mahatma Gandhi (1869–1948), Indian lawyer, political ethicist and leader of the non-violent campaign for India's independence from British rule

APRIL 3

Remember My Resilience

*When we learn how to become resilient,
we learn how to embrace the beautifully
broad spectrum of the human experience.*

—Jaeda Dewalt

When I wrote the book, *Heart-Centered Teaching Inspired by Nature*, I had no idea that a few years later, many of my thoughts would be intensely tested during a global pandemic.

Here's an example. In one chapter I wrote, "How do we weather 'storms' in our lives, and what might we gain from them? Nature uses storms to promote strength. Trees develop sturdy trunks and branches as they weather high winds, pounding rain and heavy snow. Young saplings that stay tied to stakes too long do not develop strong trunks and may easily break in even moderate winds. It's the struggle during the storm that helps a young tree develop resilience. And so it is with human beings, for we too are a part of nature."

During the challenges of the pandemic I had to ask myself if I still believed those words. It took some soul searching, but I found that I truly did. There were times when I got discouraged, but more often than not I began to experience a stronger, more resilient version of myself. When things seemed especially tough I learned that it helped me move away from fear by consciously asking, "What is something I can do to add more loving energy to the world right now?" Each time I found an answer, the better I felt.

So today I am again pondering that question. It's a great one to keep asking. No matter what the circumstances of the day might be, there is always some small way to add love.

APRIL 4
Gratitude is Always Possible

When it comes to life, the critical thing
is whether you take things for granted
or take them with gratitude.

—G.K. Chesterton

I'm a fan of a little book by Lin-Manuel Miranda and Jonny Sun called *Gmorning, Gnight: Little Pep Talks for You and Me.* Here's an example of some short but sweet encouraging words for the beginning and ending of a day:

"Good morning.
Lead with gratitude.
The air in your lungs, the sky above you.
Proceed from there.

Good night.
Curl up with gratitude.
For the ground beneath you, your beating heart.
Proceed from there."

Those passages remind me that gratitude is always possible. Today I am offering great appreciation for my strong lungs and sturdy heart. I have so often taken them for granted, but not today. Today I am remembering to be grateful.

G.K. Chesterton (1874–1936), English writer, philosopher and lay theologian

APRIL 5
BRAVING It

Be bold, be brave enough to be your true self.

—Queen Latifah

On some days it's hard to stay optimistic and hopeful. When I start to feel down, I can remember an acronym, BRAVING, from writer Brené Brown's book, *Dare to Lead*. It's meant to help us strengthen our muscles of courage and trust. Here is my paraphrase of her work:

B – Boundaries: We can't be all things to all people. We need to be clear about what we are able to do and what we are not willing to do.
R – Reliability: We all need people in our lives we can count on. It's important to know who those people really are.
A – Accountability: It's admirable to create standards for ourselves that we always try to meet, but it's also important to remember that accountability doesn't mean perfection.
V – Vault: We all need one or two people we can share anything with, and who will keep our private thoughts in a 'vault' of confidentiality. Be clear about who those people are for us.
I – Integrity: Being a person of true integrity means sometimes having to choose what's right over what is easy.
N – Non-judgment: We all need to find people we can go to for help, knowing that we won't be judged by them, no matter what.
G – Generosity: A helpful rule of thumb is to always assume good intentions. Assume that no one wakes up with the intention of being unkind so there must be a misunderstanding. We might say "I'm sure you didn't mean to hurt my feelings, so I wanted to check what you really meant."

Today I am BRAVING the world, putting these helpful tools to work for me.

Queen Latifah, American rapper, singer and actress

APRIL 6
The Paradoxes of Healing

*Every day begins with an act of courage
and hope: getting out of bed.*

—Mason Cooley

In her inspiring book, *Happiness is Running Through the Streets to Find You: Translating Trauma's Harsh Legacy into Healing,* Holly Elissa Bruno writes about how she helped herself deal with childhood trauma, and how those lessons might be encouraging to all of us. Especially in a world filled with so many challenges these days, Holly Elissa's words bring comfort and support:

"Paradoxes, when the opposite of what I believe to be true is also true, abound in trauma recovery. I accept that dynamic without understanding it. Paradoxes include...Because I am intimate with sadness, my heart knows joy. The more vulnerable I become, the stronger I am."

Today I accept and celebrate life's paradoxes. It helps to know that facing sadness leads to joy and that vulnerability, once embraced, leads to strength.

Mason Cooley (1927–2002), American professor and aphorist

APRIL 7
Positive Self-Talk

Remember that positive self-talk is an intrinsic part of a healthy mind.

—Asa Don Brown

I know the importance of listening to my inner voice to ensure it stays supportive. A good reminder of how to do this comes from an article in *Psychology Today*.

"One of the ways to recognize, promote and sustain optimism, hope and joy is to intentionally fill our thoughts with positive self-talk," writes Dr. Gregory L. Jantz in "The Power of Positive Self-Talk."

"Try the following exercise," he urges. "Write down some of the negative messages inside your mind...Be specific whenever possible, and include anyone you remember who contributed to that message. Now, take a moment to intentionally counteract those negative messages with positive truths in your life...

When you make a mistake — and you will because we all do — you can choose to overwrite that message with a positive one, such as 'I choose to accept and grow from my mistake' or 'As I learn from my mistakes, I am becoming a better person.'

The practice of positive self-talk is often the process that allows you to discover the obscured optimism, hope, and joy in any given situation."

Today I am making the commitment to speak to myself only with love.

Asa Don Brown, American psychologist and author

APRIL 8
Celebrate Important Work

*Success isn't about how much money you make;
it's about the difference you make in people's lives.*

—Michelle Obama

I remember being in a graduate course when the class discussion turned to how each of us hoped to make a positive difference in the world. Most students talked about their lofty goals for meaningful careers. The person I remember best, though, was a student I'll call Sally. She explained that she was supporting herself through grad school by working as a server in a restaurant, a job she had originally thought was not important, but simply a means of getting to her ultimate goal. But then she described how her initial beliefs began to change and how she now knows her work as a server is equally as important to anything she might do in the future. With shining eyes she talked about her opportunities to impact people's lives every day through small kindnesses, heart-centered listening, and honoring the dignity in each person. Sally's story helped me develop my belief that HOW I do something is equally as important as WHAT I do.

So today I am focusing on all the ways I can positively impact people's lives – through my work, through my way of being, and most importantly, through my loving kindness.

APRIL 9

Be the Source of My Own Joy

Sometimes your joy is the source of your smile, but sometimes your smile can be the source of your joy.

—Thich Nhat Hanh

As the quote from Thich Nhat Hanh implies, instead of waiting for something outside ourselves to bring us happiness, sometimes we must become the source of our own joy. I know I have the power to seek out joy and share it with those around me today.

The Persian poet Rumi wrote, "When you do things from your soul, you feel a river moving in you, a joy." I am pondering what it means to do things from my soul. I'm not completely sure, but I'm very eager to find out.

So, today I am actively on the lookout for feelings of joy. I know I'm more apt to find them if I believe I will.

Thich Nhat Hanh (1926–2022), Vietnamese Buddhist monk, peace activist, author and teacher

APRIL 10
Create a Mandala

Each person's life is like a mandala – a vast, limitless circle. We stand in the center of our own circle, and everything we see, hear and think forms the mandala of our life.

—Pema Chödrön

Today I commit to doing some internet research so I can learn more about drawing my own mandalas. I know directions are readily available in many places. "Mandalas are an artistic kind of free expression," explains one article, "5 Benefits of Mandalas," on the *ExploringYourMind* website. "In other words, you can draw them however you like. Of course if you don't want to make the shapes themselves, you can buy books and journals and focus on coloring them in."

The article lists these benefits of mandala-making:

- "They help with balance.
- They bring peace and tranquility.
- Looking at them will give you a feeling of calmness.
- They help with concentration.
- They make it easier to be mindful.
- They push aside thoughts and let your creativity flow."

Although a number of religious traditions incorporate mandalas into their spiritual practice, many people choose to make them for non-religious reasons, simply to enjoy the benefits outlined above.

So today I am looking forward to creating some mandalas as a creative way to relax.

Pema Chödrön, American Tibetan Buddhist nun, author

APRIL 11

Is My Surge Capacity Depleted?

*Just because your light flickers does
not mean it's about to go out.*

—Yohancé Salimu

A few months after the global pandemic began in 2020, Tara Haelle wrote an article published on the *Elemental* website called "Your Surge Capacity is Depleted — It's Why You Feel Awful." In her piece she discusses the science of why most of us could deal pretty well with the first phase of the pandemic, but then began to grow overly weary as it dragged on. "In those early months, I, along with most of the rest of the country, was using 'surge capacity' to operate, as Ann Masten, PhD, a psychologist and professor of child development at the University of Minnesota, calls it. Surge capacity is a collection of adaptive systems — mental and physical — that humans draw on for short-term survival in acutely stressful situations, such as natural disasters. But natural disasters occur over a short period, even if recovery is long. Pandemics are different — the disaster itself stretches out indefinitely.

'The pandemic has demonstrated both what we can do with surge capacity and the limits of surge capacity,' says Masten. When it's depleted, it has to be renewed. But what happens when you struggle to renew it because the emergency phase has now become chronic?" To answer her own question, Haelle discusses the work of Michael Maddaus, M.D., a professor of thoracic surgery at the University of Minnesota, who believes in what he calls a "resilience bank account," which means "gradually building into your life regular practices that promote resilience and provide a fallback when life gets tough. The areas he specifically advocates focusing on are sleep, nutrition, exercise, meditation, self-compassion, gratitude, connection, and saying no."

Today I re-commit to regular practices that help me make nice big deposits into my account.

Yohancé Salimu, American author, Founder
and CEO of Normalize Greatness Global

APRIL 12
Rituals

> *This is what rituals are for. We do spiritual ceremonies as human beings in order to create a safe resting place for our most complicated feelings of joy or trauma, so that we don't have to haul those feelings around with us forever, weighing us down. We all need such places of ritual safekeeping. And I do believe that if your culture or tradition doesn't have the specific ritual you are craving, then you are absolutely permitted to make up a ceremony of your own devising, fixing your own broken-down emotional systems with all the do-it-yourself resourcefulness of a generous plumber/poet.*
>
> —Elizabeth Gilbert,
> Eat, Pray, Love:
> One Woman's Search for Everything
> Across Italy, India and Indonesia

I love Elizabeth Gilbert's encouragement to create my own rituals. I am thinking about what kinds of things I might enjoy. I can imagine having a "pick-me-up" ritual for the end of a long week when I'm feeling depleted and needing to metaphorically recharge my batteries. I can see myself creating a "charging station" area in my house that holds a box full of fun. Perhaps it has some dark chocolates, bubble bath or shower gel, a few interesting magazines and a bottle of my favorite bubbly. My ritual might be to visit my recharging area once a week and dig into the contents of that box.

Today I commit to creating a "just for me" ritual and actually trying it out this week. I can't wait.

Elizabeth Gilbert, American journalist, author

APRIL 13
Plan a Surprise for Someone

The pleasure we derive from doing favors is partly in the feeling it gives us that we are not altogether worthless. It is a pleasant surprise to ourselves.

–Eric Hoffer

Today I am taking pleasure in planning a surprise for someone. It might be a co-worker, a partner or a child. It doesn't have to be elaborate or expensive. I might bring them a favorite beverage, a bouquet of flowers or (in the case of a child), a new set of scented markers. My surprise could also be something just from my heart, like a hand-written note of appreciation.

One of the best ways to cheer myself up is to bring a smile to someone else. Today I look forward to thinking of ways to brighten someone's day.

Eric Hoffer, American social philosopher, author, and recipient of the Presidential Medal of Freedom

APRIL 14

Believe

In the midst of hate, I found there was, within me, an invincible love. In the midst of tears, I found there was, within me, an invincible smile. In the midst of chaos, I found there was, within me, an invincible calm.

—Albert Camus

The second part of the Albert Camus quote above declares, "In the midst of winter, I found there was, within me, an invincible summer. And that makes me happy. For it says that no matter how hard the world pushes against me, within me, there's something stronger — something better, pushing right back."

Today I am finding my "invincible summer."

I believe in my ability to "push back" against challenges. And I believe in this quote from writer John Mark Green, "You are not the darkness you endured. You are the light that refused to surrender."

Albert Camus (1913–1960), French philosopher, author, Nobel Prize winner

APRIL 15

Offer Unconditional Positive Regard

When a person realizes he has been deeply heard, his eyes moisten. I think in some real sense he is weeping for joy. It is as though he were saying, "Thank God, somebody heard me. Someone knows what it's like to be me."

—Carl R. Rogers

Today I am remembering that sometimes the best gift I can give another is a chance to be deeply heard. I can listen to whatever someone would like to tell me without feeling the need to "fix" anything or offer advice. I can listen from my heart without judgment. Carl Rogers termed this way of being with another person "unconditional positive regard." Listening with non-judgment does not mean I have to agree with everything the other person does or says. It is simply a way of letting the other person know that "you do not have to be perfect to be cared for and accepted by me."

While I am at it, today I am giving that same kind of unconditional positive regard to myself.

Carl R. Rogers, (1902–1987), American psychologist and author

APRIL 16

Look for Opportunities in "Failure"

There are opportunities even in the most difficult moments.

—Wangari Maathai,
Unbowed

In my husband John Rosenow's book, *Living Long and Living Well: Inspiring Stories of Creating and Contributing During the Wisdom Years*, he outlines the amazing life history of ingenious Kenyan environmental advocate, tree planter and Nobel Prize winner, Wangari Maathai. He writes:

"As with so many people, it was a combination of Maathai's experiences, each adding to the other, that made it possible for her to be a creative contributor increasingly year by year...Ingenious solutions seldom present themselves whole. Often enough it is the failures that lead to the successes, the lessons learned from trying, falling short, and trying again. Maathai's story dramatically highlights this truth. The things that she tried that didn't work – as well as her persistence – were central to her ultimate success."

Today I am redefining the word "failure." I am realizing that when I try something that doesn't work, I can see it as simply one more opportunity to learn and grow.

APRIL 17

Make Sure to Focus on My Own Needs

Don't give others more than I give myself.
Real change will come when you focus on yourself.

—Ritu Ghatourey

Today I am remembering to treat myself with as much loving kindness as I do others. Because we are caring people, it's easy to deplete ourselves in the service of other people. While that might seem noble, it is actually quite unhealthy. If each one of us, first and foremost, took care of our own emotional needs, I am certain our world would be a much healthier place.

I am considering how often I give more to others than I do myself. I am making a commitment today to restore the balance by putting my needs first sometimes. I am as worthy of my own love and support as anyone else in my life.

APRIL 18
Get to – Instead of Have to

*One way to stop complaining is to practice
gratitude by saying, "I get" to do something,
instead of "I have" to do something. By changing
one word, you will immediately start
to see the glass half full!*

—Alison Doyle

Today I am changing my thinking, as Alison Doyle recommends. What is it I "get to" do instead of "have to" do? If I change from "I have to clean my house," to "I get to clean my house," I remember how fortunate I am to have a safe and comfortable place to live. Many in our world do not. They would love the chance to have a home of their own to clean. It's amazing how one small shift in perspective changes my attitude dramatically.

So today I am on the lookout for ways to change my "have to" thinking to "get to" gratitude. I suspect the day ahead is going to be a lot more fun.

Alison Doyle, American writer

APRIL 19
Indoor Nature: The Power of Plants

Trees and plants always look like
the people they live with, somehow.

—Zora Neale Hurston

One strategy that consistently brings me a lift is to add some indoor nature to my life. Buying a new plant or some fresh flowers is always a day-brightener for me. My favorite experience with this idea happened one day when I was taking a walk along a dirt road and came upon a large swath of sunflowers mixed in among tall grasses. I picked a few to take home, and once I got them into a mason jar, I was delighted at how they lifted my spirits.

So today I am giving myself the gift of beauty by adding a new bit of nature to my indoor spaces.

Zora Neale Hurston (1891–1960), American author, anthropologist and filmmaker

APRIL 20

Stop Worrying So Much

*Worry never robs tomorrow of its sorrow,
it only saps today of its joy.*

–Leo F. Buscaglia

Seth J. Gillihan, in a *Psychology Today* article, outlines the top reasons people worry: "1. If I worry, I'll never have a bad surprise; 2. It's safer if I worry; 3. I show I care by worrying; 4. Worrying motivates me; 5. Worrying helps me solve problems."

Calling these ideas faulty "superstitions," Gillihan explains, "We come to recognize that worry isn't worth what it can cost—tension, poor sleep, irritability, fatigue...general unhappiness." It's not easy to stop worrying, but Gillihan offers five ways to leave the worry habit behind:

"1. Calm the nervous system,,,[with] guided muscle relaxation, meditation, and exercise.
2. Notice when you're worrying...Awareness of the process gives us more choice in how we respond.
3. Embrace uncertainty...as an inherent part of living. We spend so much time trying to eliminate uncertainty that it takes considerable practice to begin to embrace it.
4. Live in the present....focus on everyday activities like taking a shower, walking, or talking with a friend, as well as on more formal practices like meditation or yoga.
5. Face your fears...[W]e can practice deliberately accepting that what we're afraid of could happen: *'It's possible I'll miss my flight.'* At first, it will probably feel frightening. With repeated practice... our fears become less gripping and we can confront them with greater equanimity."

Today I learn from Winston Churchill's words: "I remember the story of the old man who said on his deathbed that he had had a lot of trouble in his life, most of which had never happened."

Leo F. Buscaglia (1924–1998) American author, motivational speaker, professor

APRIL 21
Don't Take Others' Judgments to Heart

When they judge you, yawn.
When they misunderstand you, smile.
When they underestimate you, laugh.

—Matshona Dhliwayo

I've come to realize that the happiest people I know are the least judgmental. I think it's true that we can only treat others as well as we treat ourselves. So people who are harsh and judgmental with themselves tend to be that way with others.

It can hurt when someone judges me, especially if it feels unjustified, but I have come to realize it's probably an indication of how much those people are critically judging themselves.

Today, if I feel unfairly judged by someone, I am not taking their thoughts to heart. Instead, I will stop, slowly breathe in and out, and then focus some compassionate thoughts toward a person I suspect is hurting inside.

Matshona Dhliwayo, Canadian philosopher, entrepreneur, author

APRIL 22

Light through the Cracks

*Kindness begins with the understanding
that we all struggle.*

—Charles Glassman

Rachel Naomi Remen, M.D., in her beautiful book, *Kitchen Table Wisdom*, tells the story of one of her patients, an angry young man whose cancer treatments robbed him of a career in sports. After a life-saving surgery where his right leg had to be removed, she asked him to draw a picture of himself. He drew a vase with a huge crack and furiously scribbled a black crayon over and over the crack. For the next few years, Remen worked with the young man, eventually inviting him to meet with other young people who were experiencing life-changing surgeries. Remen says the change in the young man was dramatic, as he turned his focus from himself to helping others. One of her favorite stories is how he visited a teenage girl who was deeply depressed after having a double mastectomy. She refused to talk with him until one day he turned on some music, unstrapped his artificial leg, let it drop loudly to the floor, and began to hop around the room, snapping his fingers to the music. Startled, the girl finally looked at him, then began to laugh. "If you can dance," she said, "maybe I can sing."

During their final visit, Remen pulled out the young man's picture of the cracked vase. She describes what happened next, "He took it in his hands and looked at it for some time. 'You know,' he said, 'it's really not finished.' Surprised, I extended my basket of crayons toward him. Taking a yellow crayon, he began to draw lines radiating from the crack in the vase to the very edge of the paper. Thick yellow lines. I watched, puzzled. He was smiling. Finally he put his finger on the crack, looked at me, and said, softly, 'This is where the light comes through.'"

Today I consider that the places I feel "cracked" may be what help me share my light with others.

Charles Glassman, American author

APRIL 23

No Regrets

*Nothing can be more hurtful to your
heart than betraying yourself.*

—Roy T. Bennet

Bronnie Ware, an Australian author, songwriter and motivational speaker, wrote a book called *The Top Five Regrets of the Dying,* based on what she heard from patients during her time providing palliative care.

She shares these top five regrets, hoping to help people avoid them while they are still able:

1. "I wish I'd had the courage to live a life true to myself, not the life others expected of me."
2. "I wish I hadn't worked so hard."
3. "I wish I had the courage to express my feelings."
4. "I wish I had stayed in touch with my friends."
5. "I wish I had let myself be happier."

Today I am pondering these regrets, asking myself what I can do to avoid them in my own life. One theme I see is being true to myself and not living only to please other people. It's always a good goal and one I am thinking deeply about today.

Roy T. Bennet, American author

APRIL 24

Unclutter

Beauty is a light in the heart.

—Kahlil Gibran

I know I feel better right after I've straightened my house and worse the more clutter builds up, but now there's research to tell me why. An article on the University of Minnesota website called "How Does Nature Impact Our Wellbeing?," explains:

"Research reveals that environments can increase or reduce our stress, which in turn impacts our bodies. What you are seeing, hearing, experiencing at any moment is changing not only your mood, but how your nervous, endocrine, and immune systems are working. The stress of an unpleasant environment can cause you to feel anxious, or sad, or helpless. This in turn elevates your blood pressure, heart rate, and muscle tension and suppresses your immune system. A pleasing environment reverses that."

So, knowing that, today I am making a commitment to myself to pick up a few items of clutter every morning before I leave the house or each evening when I return home. Doing so is a reminder that I'm worthy of pleasant surroundings, and that I value myself enough to make things nice for me.

Kahlil Gibran (1883–1931), Lebanese-American poet

APRIL 25
Stop Comparing Myself to Others

When you are content to be simply yourself
and don't compare or compete,
everyone will respect you.

—Lao Tzu

In the world of social media and television advertising, a lot of money is made by convincing people to buy products that will help them "fix a flaw" so they can compare positively to others. What a slippery slope that is. And what a faulty premise. No good can come from playing that game.

I'm not immune to feelings of jealousy and wishing I had what someone else has, but here's what I've learned: Those feelings keep me from enjoying my own abundance, which might be different from someone else's but is still very real. My house may be small in comparison to someone else's, but if I look through the eyes of gratitude, I find so much to savor, and my enjoyment kicks in again.

At times I can still get caught by the old "I'm not good enough" misunderstanding. When that happens, I remind myself that I am not meant to have every gift someone else has, and that my authentic self is exactly who I am meant to be.

Today I reject the faulty premise of the "comparison trap." Today I bask in appreciation for everything I have and for all that I am.

Lao Tzu (believed to have lived in the 6th century, BC), Chinese philosopher

APRIL 26
Relish the Simple Things

Sometimes, the simple things are more fun and meaningful than all the banquets in the world.

—E.A. Bucchianeri,
Brushstrokes of a Gadfly,
(Gadfly Saga, #1)

R. Y. S. Perez is both a writer and a writing tutor who enjoys helping students fall in love with words and with life's simple pleasures. I really relate to this sentiment, "I have never been drawn to luxury. I love the simple things; coffee shops, books, and people who try to understand." And here's another, "I hope these simple things are what I forever love about life, for then I will be happy no matter where I find myself."

There's so much wisdom in that way of thinking. It's easy to take for granted the many simple, yet delicious (in all senses of the word) objects and experiences that make life better.

Today I am thinking about what I consider a "simple pleasure." I am going to be on the lookout for them, and I'm playing a game with myself to identify at least ten. Maybe you'd like to join me?

E.A. Bucchianeri, American writer

APRIL 27

Care for My Inner Child

*Caring for your inner child has a
powerful and surprisingly quick result:
Do it and the child heals.*

—Martha Beck

Talking about my "inner child" can feel like a cliché, but I've found it very helpful to spend time thinking about my younger self and all the misunderstandings, hurts and griefs she experienced at a tender age. In trying to make sense of the world, young children often develop faulty theories and misunderstandings to explain frightening or confusing things to themselves. One very common misunderstanding is to blame themselves for things that are happening to adults. How many times have we heard about children taking the blame for their parents' divorces?

Because children usually don't have all the information, the explanations they create for themselves are often incorrect. As adults, it is quite possible, and even necessary to connect with ourselves at a younger age and help update those faulty beliefs. We can also remember times when we may have felt hurt and didn't know how to ask for comfort. We can now commiserate about those long-ago feelings and give ourselves all the consoling we need right now.

Today I am checking in with the younger part of me, helping her update any misconceptions and offering loving care in any way it's needed.

Martha Beck, American author

APRIL 28

Acknowledge Myself

I think it's because I'm a pretty good person.

—Sylvie, age 3

As a brand-new three-year-old, my granddaughter, Sylvie, was proud that she could put her winter coat on all by herself. When she demonstrated one day, I asked, "Wow, Sylvie, how did you learn to do that so well?" She stopped and thought, then smiled and said, "I think it's because I'm a pretty good person."

Her genuine appreciation for herself, without an ounce of self-consciousness, brought tears to my eyes. She simply was tuning in to the wonder of her authentic self. When do we lose that way of being, I wondered. When do we stop expressing self-appreciation for fear of seeming conceited? I hope that twelve-year-old Sylvie can still acknowledge herself as readily as she did at three. I will certainly encourage her to do so, and maybe I can also give the same encouragement to myself.

Today I am taking a lesson from young Sylvie and allowing myself to feel genuine happiness about the "pretty good person" I am.

Sylvie Hadley, Nancy Rosenow's oldest granddaughter

APRIL 29
Find the Best in the Situation

It's good to be in the middle. I get to be two things: your second granddaughter and your middle granddaughter.

—Lyla, age 4

When my granddaughter Lyla was four, she learned that her aunt was expecting a baby, which meant she would no longer be my youngest grandchild. At first she was distraught about losing this title. But after a while she came to me and proclaimed, "You know what? It's good to be in the middle. I get to be two things: your second granddaughter and your middle granddaughter."

I loved the way Lyla found a new perspective that changed a sad situation into one of new possibilities.

Today I am taking a lesson from Lyla and looking for the best in seemingly sad circumstances. I wonder how many times I missed positive perspectives simply because I forgot to look for them.

Lyla Hadley, Nancy Rosenows's second (and middle!) granddaughter

APRIL 30

Feel Wonder Every Day

Who paints the sky?

—Lindy, age 2½

One night my husband and I were at a park with our granddaughter Lindy when the pinks and reds and oranges of twilight were especially vivid. Lindy looked up with awe and asked, "Who paints the sky?" Seeing her joyful curiosity reminded me of how much a sense of wonder can make life more fun. I hope Lindy keeps her unbridled curiosity for the rest of her life.

Today I am taking a lesson from Lindy and allowing my own feelings of wonder and curiosity to surface more often. I can't wait to see what I discover.

Linden "Lindy" Hawthorne, Nancy Rosenow's youngest granddaughter

May

May, more than any other month of the year, wants us to feel most alive.

—Nigel "Fennel" Hudson

Nigel "Fennel" Hudson, English writer, broadcaster, publisher, editor

MAY 1
May Day Fun

*It is spring again. The earth is like a
child that knows poems by heart.*

—Rainer Maria Rilke

May Day is celebrated as a public holiday in some parts of the world, with its origins in ancient festivals. Later it was chosen as the date for International Workers' Day. As a child, May Day for me was a time to pick flowers, put them in homemade paper baskets, leave them on neighbors' doorsteps, ring their doorbells and run away.

Right now I am remembering the innocent fun of May Day as a child and looking for ways to bring some of those feelings into my day today. Maybe I'll buy myself a new plant, or visit a public garden. I could share a bouquet of flowers with colleagues at work or with my family. Whatever I choose, I am doing it in the spirit of child-like fun.

Rainer Maria Rilke (1875–1926), Austrian poet and novelist

MAY 2
Avoid Violent Media

I find television very educating. Every time somebody turns on the set, I go into the other room and read a book.

–Groucho Marx

Research suggests that watching violent media takes a toll on us physically and emotionally. "Repeated Exposure to Media Images of Traumatic Events May Be Harmful to Mental and Physical Health" is the name of an article on the *Association for Psychological Science* website. The article reports on a research study's convincing evidence that watching too much media coverage of traumatic events adversely affects people's well-being.

At times I get into a mindless habit of turning on television news as I'm getting ready in the morning, or at the end of the day. If I'm not careful it's easy to leave it on too long and get overloaded with violent or sad images. Even just the constant negativity present in today's political reality can be disheartening. I do want to stay informed about what's going on in the world, but I know I can be more thoughtful about how I do this.

Today I am mindfully limiting the amount of violent images I bring into my home. I am intentionally choosing to support myself with more positive choices, such as turning on some wonderful music in place of too much television news.

Groucho Marx (1890–1977), American comedian

MAY 3

I Can Let Go of Old Mistakes

*Renew, release, let go. Yesterday's gone.
There's nothing you can do to bring it back.
You can't "should've" done something.
You can only DO something. Renew yourself.
Release that attachment. Today is a new day!*

—Steve Maraboli

Once in a while I find myself ruminating over past actions, wishing I could have a "do over." At times like that, the Steve Maraboli quote above is a good one to take to heart. Instead of beating myself up over decisions I wish I'd handled differently, or interactions with people I feel bad about, I can remind myself that no human being is perfect. More than that, each "bad" decision is a learning opportunity for the future.

It really is a matter of releasing my attachment to the past. It can sometimes feel like a sturdy cord is keeping me tied to my mistakes because I refuse to let them be over and done.

Today I am cutting the cord to actions I regret, releasing myself from any attachment. I am reminding myself that with each mistake I learn from, I am becoming wiser and a better version of myself.

Steve Maraboli, American author

MAY 4

Deal with Burnout Before I'm on Fire

I have a theory that burnout is about resentment. And you beat it by knowing what it is you're giving up that makes you resentful.

—Marissa Mayer

People use the term "burnout" for all kinds of reasons. I'm using it today to describe a feeling I start to get when the ratio of what I'm doing for others gets out of balance with my own needs. I try to recognize the first embers of burnout before they fan into full-fledged flames. Right now I'm planning a party for this weekend, and my enthusiasm is waning. When I look back at the past few months, I realize I've hosted more gatherings than my introverted self enjoys. Each one has been wonderful, but when I add them all up, I start to smell that warning smoke of burnout. Note for the future: Think carefully about the whole picture before I schedule individual events.

Knowing this weekend's party IS happening, what can I do to lessen burnout? First, I can promise myself that once the party is over I will take a nice long break from hosting anything for a while. Then I can acknowledge my feelings. Marissa Mayer is right. I've been feeling resentment about not having enough time to recharge my batteries. Really listening to that resentment helps. It won't change my party responsibilities, but it will improve my outlook. And it will help me remember that I truly am grateful for all the blessings in my life.

Today I am being true to myself. Some extroverts might be totally energized by the gatherings I've held recently, but it's ok to admit that as an introvert it's been too much. Being able to accept my feelings is the first step in putting out the beginnings of an emotional fire.

MAY 5
Cinco de Mayo Appreciation

Cinco de Mayo has come to represent a celebration of the contributions that Mexican Americans and all Hispanics have made to America.

—Joe Baca

Cinco de Mayo is a yearly celebration which commemorates the anniversary of Mexico's victory over the Second French Empire at the Battle of Puebla in 1862, led by General Ignacio Zaragoza. The victory of a smaller, poorly equipped Mexican force against the larger and better-armed French army was a morale boost for the Mexicans. Today, Cinco de Mayo is much more popular in the United States than Mexico. It has come to represent a celebration of Mexican-American culture, and usually includes special food and drink.

Today I embrace the way Joe Baca describes Cinco de Mayo as a celebration of the many contributions to America made by Mexican Americans and Hispanics. I am in appreciation.

MAY 6

Inspiration from Clouds

Clouds are on top for a reason. They float so high because they refuse to carry any burden!

—Jasleen Kaur Gumber

As a child, one of my favorite pastimes was to lie on my back, using my imagination to find pictures in the clouds. I suspect many people had that same experience. I've recently realized that I hardly ever look up at the clouds anymore. I also don't look closely in the grass for bugs like I did when younger.

An online article in the *Guardian* by Phoebe Weston has the long title of "Look up, look down: experts urge us to take a closer look at the concrete jungle: Plants, birds, moths and bugs are all waiting to be noticed and appreciated – and photographed." Weston explains that adults tend to mostly keep our gaze fixed to a relatively small area, mostly straight ahead, and we often miss the pleasures of gazing high at birds and clouds or low at plants and bugs.

I love the quote above about clouds being light because they refuse to carry burdens. Today I am going to find time to lie on a blanket outside and look at clouds. When I do so, I commit to releasing anything that feels burdensome to me, at least for the time I'm cloud-gazing.

Jasleen Kaur Gumber, Indian writer, researcher, marketer

MAY 7
Enjoy Art for Health

Any form of art is a form of power; it has impact, it can affect change — it can not only move us, it makes us move.

—Ossie Davis

A *Smithsonian.com* article by Meilan Solly is called "British Doctors May Soon Prescribe Art, Music, Dance, Singing Lessons." It explains that "a British campaign is expected to launch...that will allow doctors to prescribe therapeutic art, dance or singing lessons for the treatment of ailments such as dementia, a strategy the U.K government calls 'social prescribing' to help build more resilience and happiness at the end of life." It's interesting that the arts are now formally being recognized as a way to build resilience and brain health. That is a good reminder that not being a professional singer, dancer or visual artist does not need to stop me from enjoying those pursuits myself. Not only will I have fun, but I'll be healthier.

So today I am focusing on any kind of artistic expression I choose to enjoy. When our granddaughters were very little, we started having "dance parties" in our kitchen. I still smile when I think about the jubilant looks on the girls' faces as they bopped around in stocking feet. Why haven't I done that recently? Perhaps today I'll bring back the tradition.

Ossie Davis (1917–2005), American actor, director, writer, and activist

MAY 8

Avoid Codependency

Codependents are reactionaries. They overreact. They under-react. But rarely do they act. They react to the problems, pains, lives, and behaviors of others."

—Melody Beattie,
Codependent No More

In her book referenced above, Melody Beattie defines codependency as focusing more on the feelings, problems and behaviors of other people than on our own needs. Codependency often begins in childhood when a parent's problematic behavior affects the household enough that all members begin to walk on eggshells to try to "control" the situation and keep chaos away. A person doesn't need to grow up in an extreme situation to learn codependent behavior. Any time we try to control someone else's actions to make things easier on ourselves, we are engaging in faulty, codependent thinking. It might look like this: We believe we can't be happy at a party unless our partner is, so we bend ourselves into pretzels trying to ensure their good mood. That's a recipe for disaster. Not only is it not possible to "control" someone else's mood, it is also not our responsibility. And it is definitely not true that we cannot experience happiness until everyone else around us is happy. But wow, it's taken me a long time to learn that lesson.

In the past I tried very hard to "ensure" the happiness of others. The cut-to-the-chase reality is that I couldn't. Once I learned to take action steps to support my own happiness, a funny thing happened. When I simply focused on enjoying myself, more often than not that grouchy person began to enjoy themselves as well. The key, though, is to remember I didn't "cause" their happiness. And if they never stopped being grouchy, I could still have fun. (One caveat: Occasional grouchiness is not the same as emotional abuse. It is vital to know the difference.) Today I am fully releasing any codependent misunderstandings.

Melody Beattie, American writer

MAY 9

Use Affirmations

*An affirmation is a positive state of belief,
and if we can become one-tenth as good at
positive self-talk as we are at negative self-talk,
we will notice an enormous change.*

—Julia Cameron,
The Artist's Way

Today I am reminding myself of the power of using affirmations. These are short statements of intent that help me focus on positive outcomes. Actually, the statements I add at the end of each day's encouragement are forms of affirmations.

The key to creating affirmations is to state them as if they are happening now. Saying "I am becoming calmer," is more helpful than "I will become calmer." Our brain takes our words very seriously. If it hears "I will," then it believes we want that to happen in the future, not right now. Stating affirmations in present tense is vital.

So, here I go: Today I am remembering the power of affirmations and I am using them for encouragement and focus.

Julia Cameron, American teacher, author and artist

MAY 10

Let Go of Old Hurt Feelings

When we release the fearful past and forgive everyone, we will experience total love and oneness with all.

—Gerald G. Jampolsky, M.D.

Hanging on to old hurt feelings keeps me stuck. I suspect much of the anger in our world is really old unhealed pain. Only recently did I "unstick" myself from an old painful memory. When I was a child, I was asked to perform a piano piece for my grandparents' anniversary celebration. I had never played in front of anyone, and to my dismay, I learned that all the grandchildren were expected to memorize their pieces. When I was called to perform in what felt like a daunting hall, I was so scared that after the first notes, my mind went blank. I felt my stomach drop and fear turn my neck hot. I sat for a few seconds, then announced, with shaking voice, "I am going to start over." Mercifully I got through the whole piece that time. After walking down the hall's long aisle, I slipped in next to my parents and heard my father whisper to my mother, "How could you let her embarrass us like that?"

I never told my parents how much those words had hurt me. I am certain that wasn't my father's intent. And I'm sure I've said thoughtless things that hurt my own children. But here's the thing: My hurt didn't go away until I acknowledged it. And for a long time it kept me from doing things I wanted, like giving speeches in front of big groups for fear I'd "mess up." I had to first heal my old hurt before I could move on. What worked for me was imagining talking to that little girl, telling her how proud I was. "You didn't give up," I'd say. "You were so brave."

I continue to be on the lookout for old lingering hurts so I can heal them and set myself free.

Gerald G. Jampolsky, M.D. (1925–2020),
American psychiatrist and author

MAY 11
Remember My Impact

*Even on your worst day, you are still
some child's best hope.*

—Larry Bell

I remember reading these words from Larry Bell on a day that, if not my worst, was pretty close. They made such an impression on me and turned my thinking around. As a teacher I understood well that some children counted on their time with me for stability and calm in the midst of a turbulent home life. Even on days I felt brittle and discouraged inside, I knew I was still providing loving care to my youngsters.

Bell's words made me realize that our impact on others' lives doesn't only happen when we are at our best. Trying our best counts, too, even if we fall short.

So today I am giving thanks for the fact that, no matter what, I always have a chance to make a positive difference for someone else.

MAY 12
Access My Inner Wisdom

> *Your inner wisdom will always guide you, if you listen and let it in. If you get quiet inside of your head, then your inner thoughts can come from your inner wisdom. When we are feeling judgmental, or self-conscious, or just plain uncomfortable inside, then usually it is just that noise in our head talking loudly. I call this noise your intellectual thinking which results from your opinions and beliefs. True wisdom holds pretty much no opinions or judgments."*
>
> —Jan Christensen,
> *Magnificent Mind:*
> *Uncover Your Psychological Well Being*
> *So You Can Live in Heaven While on Earth*

Canadian author Jan Christensen worked as a nurse with a B.A. in psychology until a workplace head injury led to depression and a long struggle to regain her health. She explains that it was then that she undertook "the study of developing an understanding of the three principles of mind, consciousness, and thought. This understanding has enhanced my life immeasurably...The result of this knowledge has led me to a life of peace, contentment, and love."

I have already mentioned other writers, like Michael Singer (my favorite) who describe the "noise in our head," which is not our inner wisdom. That wisdom, or authentic self, is never judgmental or critical. It is always supportive and helpful. The problem comes when we mistake our ego-based chatter for our inner guidance. We will know the difference because listening to our authentic self always brings a sense of peace.

So today I am getting still, taking time to let all the ego-based chatter quiet down so I can clearly hear the voice of my inner wisdom speak.

MAY 13
Give Myself a Small Treat Today

One of the secrets of a happy life is continuous small treats. Rituals such as sunset watching, morning walks or a regular call with a friend can make each week more pleasurable.

—Mary Pipher,
"Cultivating Joy," *Exchange* magazine

I was the child of older parents who were more comfortable with intellectual pursuits than the frivolities of small children. I do not remember many times I was allowed to buy something I wanted unless it was practical. One day stands out as being very different, however. My mother and I were shopping for school clothes and we passed a bakery. To my shock and delight she asked if I wanted to go inside and pick out a cookie – any kind I'd like.

This was so contrary to my usual experience that I was simply elated. I suspect that my mother had been overhearing conversations with my two friends who lived on either side of me, one a year older and one two years older. Just that morning they had announced that I was a "baby" and too young to play with them anymore. Even though I tried to hide my tears, I'm guessing my mother knew what was going on. Thus, the special cookie.

To this day I still remember taking my time looking over all the beautifully decorated confections, each one enticing me to pick it. I finally settled on a gorgeous thumbprint cookie, a delicious shortbread with luscious strawberry jam in the thumb-sized hole. Even as an adult, when I want to cheer myself up, getting a thumbprint cookie can do the trick.

So today I'm imagining many things that might feel like treats right now. I'm inviting myself to pick something I'd like, and I can't wait to see what that's going to be. I hope you'll do the same.

Mary Pipher, American clinical psychologist and author

MAY 14
Embrace a Growth Mindset

In a growth mindset, people believe that their most basic abilities can be developed through dedication and hard work—brains and talent are just the starting point. This view creates a love of learning and a resilience that is essential for great accomplishment.

—Carol Dweck,
Growth Mindset

In her bestselling book, *Growth Mindset*, psychologist Carol Dweck tells the story of two groups of young children who were given easy-to-put-together puzzles. All the children accomplished the task, but the first group was told, "You put those puzzles together because you are smart." The second group was told, "You put those puzzles together because you tried hard." Then both groups were asked if they'd like to try putting together harder puzzles. Interestingly enough, many children in the "you are smart" group declined. They were afraid to try a harder puzzle, fail, and risk changing the researcher's belief in their intelligence. Everyone in the "you tried hard" group was game to tackle something more difficult.

The learning here is that how we talk to ourselves (and to our children), is important. Dweck says, "Becoming is better than being." If we believe that it is only through innate intelligence that we can accomplish anything in life, then we limit what we will try. If we understand, however, that it is really through struggle and persistence that we learn, then a whole new world of possibilities opens up for us.

Today I am reminding myself that I don't have to be born with "talent" in order to succeed at a task. I can often learn to do things well with enough effort and commitment.

Carol Dweck, American psychologist and writer

MAY 15

Meditation — My Way

*Meditation is choosing not to engage in
the drama of the mind but elevating the
mind to its highest potential.*

—Amit Ray

If I had a dollar for every time I've read about the benefits of meditation, I think I would at least be able to afford a vacation to someplace relaxing. I really am convinced that meditation is important, but I have to admit I used to have a bit of a block about doing it consistently. My old nemesis perfectionism often got in the way of my being able to relax into the practice. Too often I was asking myself, "Am I doing it right?" That is not a helpful way to experience meditation.

I've only recently been able to break through my resistance by giving myself permission to try lots of things. I've listened to online guided meditations, and I've tried meditating with music only. I've tried some of the meditation techniques Dan Harris includes in his book, *10% Happier*. I've also just experimented with sitting quietly for ten minutes without trying to "do" anything. Here's what I've learned: they all work for me if I just let myself relax and enjoy whatever happens. I've actually become a real fan of meditation. I'm noticing myself generally acting calmer and less apt to experience a stress reaction to every challenge.

So today I am meditating — my way. Any amount of time and any technique is fine. The key is just to do something.

Amit Ray, Indian author

MAY 16
Stop Efforting So Much

Holding on to anything is like holding on to your breath. You will suffocate. The only way to get anything in the physical universe is by letting go of it. Let go and it will be yours forever.

—Deepak Chopra

Deepak Chopra believes that we are actually working against ourselves when we push too hard, try too hard and rest too little. He calls it "efforting" when we are on an unrelenting quest to "make" things happen. He urges us, instead, to pause and focus on making ourselves more comfortable. "You can't make positive choices for the rest of your life without an environment that makes those choices easy, natural, and enjoyable," he says.

Today I am focusing less on "trying hard" and more on allowing beautiful moments to flow through my life.

Deepak Chopra, Indian-American author

MAY 17

Pay Attention to What I Feed Myself Today

If it came from a plant, eat it;
If it was made in a plant, don't.

—Michael Pollan

"'Eat food. Not too much. Mostly plants.' That's the advice journalist and author Michael Pollan offers in his book, *In Defense of Food*." So begins an article on the *NPR* website titled, "'In Defense of Food' Author Offers Advice For Health," that recaps an interview between Pollan and reporter Steve Inskeep. The article explains Pollan's belief that a lot of what we are eating today isn't truly "food," quoting him as saying:

"We are eating a lot of edible food-like substances, which is to say highly processed things that might be called yogurt, might be called cereals, whatever, but in fact are very intricate products of food science that are really imitations of foods...Don't eat anything that your great-grandmother wouldn't recognize as food."

I find it hard to follow hard-and-fast food rules for myself, but I have read enough to believe that our bodies are healthier when we give them more fruits and vegetables and less overly processed products. So today I am paying attention to what I feed myself. I am making more healthy choices and feeling good about taking good care of me.

Michael Pollan, American author and journalist

MAY 18
Spend More Time with People Who Bring Out My Best, Not My Stress

The glory of friendship is not the outstretched hand, not the kindly smile, nor the joy of companionship; it is the spiritual inspiration that comes to one when you discover that someone else believes in you and is willing to trust you with a friendship.

—Ralph Waldo Emerson

Today I am considering carefully who the friends, colleagues and family members are who believe in me in a way that I can feel. Those are the people I want to spend the most time around. I understand that other people don't "give me" my inner strength, but it's nice to surround myself with encouragers, not criticizers.

Today I am giving thanks for the cheerleaders in my life. And I'm redoubling my efforts to be sure that I'm cheering for others as well.

Ralph Waldo Emerson (1803–1882), American essayist and philosopher

MAY 19

Manage My Energy

*To maintain a powerful pulse in our lives,
we must learn how to rhythmically
spend and renew energy.*

—Jim Loehr and Tony Schwartz,
*The Power of Full Engagement:
Managing Energy Not Time is the Key
to Performance, Health and Happiness*

Tony Schwartz, together with Catherine McCarthy, in the *Harvard Business Review* book, *On Managing Yourself*, offers a number of tips on maintaining our energy. Here are a few:

- "Physical energy — Take brief but regular breaks...at 90- to -120-minute intervals throughout the day.
- Emotional energy — Look at upsetting situations through a new lens....ask, 'How can I grow and learn from this situation?'
- Mental energy — Every night, identify the most important challenge for the next day. Then make it your first priority... the next morning.
- Spiritual energy — Identify your 'sweet spot' activities — those that give you feelings of effectiveness, effortless absorption, and fulfillment."

Today I am managing my energy. My intention is to move my body at least every two hours; to focus on what I can learn from challenges; to tackle my top priorities for the day as soon as possible; and to be sure I'm spending time on activities that feel most fulfilling.

Jim Loehr, American performance psychologist and author,
and Tony Schwartz, American journalist and author

MAY 20

Let Go of Over-Consumption to Feel Better

The situation the Earth is in today has been created by unmindful production and unmindful consumption. We consume to forget our worries and our anxieties. Tranquilizing ourselves with over-consumption is not the way.

—Thich Nhat Hanh

At the beginning of the global pandemic, Amazon's stock soared as we all comforted ourselves by buying things from them. That may have been an effective short-term strategy, but Thich Nhat Hanh reminds us that this way of "tranquilizing" ourselves does not ultimately lead to happiness.

Marketers love to sell us on the idea that if we just buy a new car, wear the right clothes or smell a certain way, our problems will be over. At one level we know that's not true, but it's easy to get seduced by "shopping therapy." In the long run, unless we learn to find our happiness inside ourselves, it's likely that all our over-consumption will do is push us into debt.

Today I am reminding myself that over-buying won't make me happy. I am remembering the many things in my life that do bring me happiness, most of which do not come from a store.

Thich Nhat Hanh (1926–2022), Vietnamese Buddhist monk, peace activist, author and teacher

MAY 21

It's Safe to Acknowledge Pain

There is no coming to consciousness without pain.

–Carl Jung

I grew up in a family that valued stoicism and even-keeled emotions. "Don't be so sensitive," I was told often. Fairly early on I learned to hide my tears and pretend that the scrape on my knee really didn't hurt very much. I kept the peace with my parents, but as I grew up I learned that denial of pain came with a price.

As an adult, I am teaching myself to believe Carl Jung's words, that to live a fully conscious life I have to acknowledge pain. I still have a tendency to minimize my feelings if I'm not careful. I have to remind myself that it is actually safe to embrace pain and let it flow through me. It's much worse to deny pain because then it actually gets stuck inside me and can't be processed.

Today I am reminding myself that all human beings experience pain, and that when I do, I have the tools to deal with it effectively.

Carl Jung (1875–1961), Swiss psychiatrist and writer

MAY 22

Memorial Day Is the Last Monday of May

Without memory, there is no culture. Without memory, there would be no civilization, no society, no future.

—Elie Wiesel

In the United States, Memorial Day is the last Monday in May. It is a time to remember and honor people who gave their lives in the pursuit of heartfelt ideals in which they believed. Elie Wiesel's words were written about the Holocaust, a horrendous time in human history, but one that must also be remembered. Spanish writer and philosopher George Santayana proclaimed that, "Those who cannot remember the past are condemned to repeat it."

So when Memorial Day comes this month, I am using it as a time to remember all aspects of human history, the admirable and the regrettable. My hope is to add to efforts to ensure we avoid the worst mistakes of the past so we can make choices in support of a more just and peaceful world.

Elie Wiesel (1928–2016), Romanian-born American writer, professor, Nobel prize winner, Holocaust survivor

MAY 23
Which Is the Most Loving Choice?

*Today I choose life...To feel the freedom
that comes from being able to continue to make
mistakes and choices — today I choose to feel life,
not to deny my humanity but embrace it.*

—Kevyn Aucoin

Today I had to make a choice between what felt like two bad options. I was trying to find the least undesirable choice, which was not a fun position to be in. As I felt my unease increasing, I remembered to ask, "What's the most loving choice here?" That really helped. It didn't mean that the choice I ended up with would be an easy one, but it did feel like it could lead to the most loving place in the long run. Sometimes that's all we can ask.

So today, and every day, as difficult choices come my way, I am remembering to base my decisions on what I believe will add to, not detract from, the sum total of love in our world.

Kevyn Aucoin (1962–2002), American makeup artist

MAY 24
I Choose to Be an Uplifter

How beautiful it could be if we woke up every morning with a burning desire to help others.

—Debasish Mridha, M.D.

Many times I have experienced a lift in my own spirits by being an uplifter for someone else. That's different than being a "fixer." I'm not trying to solve all of someone's problems or give them advice. I'm simply looking for ways to add a bit of sunshine to their day.

I might give them a handwritten note of appreciation or send an email. I might compliment them on their smile or let them know I appreciate their sense of humor. Once I told a complete stranger that I admired the way she was talking to her children. Her reaction was gratifying. "I needed to hear that today," she laughed, shaking her head ruefully. "I was two seconds away from yelling. I'll try to keep my cool a little longer."

Today I am on the lookout for ways large and small that I can bring some cheer to someone else's day.

Debasish Mridha, M.D., American physician and author

MAY 25
Name My Strengths

*You never know how strong you are
until being strong is your only choice.*

—Bob Marley

When I'm feeling really down, but then remember a funny line, make myself laugh and start feeling better, that's a strength. When I'm out on a walk and I stop, arms up, to let a shower of yellow leaves rain down on me, that's a strength. When I find a new book on a subject I've never read about before and dig in with glee, that's a strength.

It's a healthy thing to name our strengths out loud. So today I claim my sense of humor, my appreciation of wonder and my curiosity. I urge you to claim some of yours.

Bob Marley (1945–1981), Jamaican singer, songwriter

MAY 26
I Make a Life by What I Give

We make a living by what we get;
we make a life by what we give.

—Winston Churchill

I'm proud to have spent so much of my life as an early childhood educator and administrator. My work was truly a pleasure most days because I was always aware that I was making a positive contribution to the world. I can attest to Winston Churchill's words. There is something much more important than the amount of money I made over the course of my life. I can honestly say that doing something meaningful was worth more than any material possession I can imagine.

Today I am reminding myself that many times it is when I give that I receive the most.

Winston Churchill (1874–1965), Prime Minister of the
United Kingdom, 1940–1945, 1951–1955

MAY 27

Keep Commitments to Myself — Joyfully

I feel keeping a promise to yourself is a direct reflection of the love you have for yourself.

—Steve Maraboli

I used to give myself lofty goals that I never ended up meeting. That left me feeling discouraged and down on myself. When I finally learned to take my commitments to myself seriously, I started making fewer promises so I could mostly always keep them. Today I take great pleasure in creating a list of nurturing activities that I promise myself I will do each week. I keep this list realistic and fun. It's such a joy to cross things off my list. Steve Maraboli is right. It's a tangible way to express my love for myself.

Today I am thinking carefully about the commitments I make to myself and taking them as seriously as any I make to others.

Steve Maraboli, American author

MAY 28

What Can I Eliminate from My Life?

Too much of anything is the beginning of a mess.

–Dorothy Draper

What I learned when I moved out of the house I'd lived in for 30 years was that it's easy to accumulate a lot of useless stuff. That experience motivated me to give much thought to what I actually needed and wanted in my life. It's amazing how good it feels to clear out clutter. Simplicity can be very calming. I've embraced the way of thinking that says to only keep what is useful or meaningful. I also give myself permission to not save every gift that's ever been given to me. I can keep the memory and good intentions without keeping the "thing."

Today I am remembering how good it feels to keep my surroundings ordered and serene. I do not hesitate to clear my living spaces of unneeded items. I commit to donating these, throwing them away if appropriate, or giving them to someone who might want them more than I do.

Dorothy Draper (1889–1969), American interior designer

MAY 29
The Joy of Donating to a Cause

*Charity brings to life again those
who are spiritually dead.*

—Thomas Aquinas

One thing that always brings me a lift is making a contribution to a worthy cause. It really doesn't matter whether I give money or time; either way I end up feeling better for having contributed. There's something about generosity that reminds me of my responsibility to others. I have always loved what American educator, author and researcher Lilian Katz said:

"Each of us must come to care about everyone else's children. We must recognize that the welfare of our children and grandchildren is intimately linked to the welfare of all other people's children." Indeed.

Today I commit to donating to something I believe is important. I hope you might do the same.

MAY 30

Deal with Anxiety

*We must have a pie. Stress cannot exist
in the presence of a pie.*

–David Mamet

The past years of living through a global pandemic were a crash course in learning to deal with anxiety. Even now as I write, Covid diagnoses are not completely a thing of the past, and especially for parents of young children, anxiety can still be very real. So how does a person cope with frequent stress and worry, no matter the cause? Here are a few things I've learned:

1. Put on my own oxygen mask first. As they teach on airlines, we won't be able to help anyone else if we can't breathe ourselves. As a recovering "fixer," I've learned that making myself sick with worry is not going to help anyone, so focusing on my own emotional needs is vital.
2. Recognize that some days will be harder than others and that's ok. I had to give myself permission to admit that "today is just tough."
3. Breathe. I know it sounds simplistic, but anxiety causes us to take shallow breaths that lead to more feelings of stress. Stopping to breathe deeply is important in keeping ourselves calm. (Also, see Meditation – My Way on May 15.)
4. Write out my feelings. Journaling – my way – continues to be very helpful.
5. Visualize what I want to see. It doesn't help anything to focus on worst-case scenarios.
6. Find my sense of humor. When it's hard to locate, I think of David Mamet's declaration that we must have pie.

Even without a global pandemic, life always gives us chances to practice dealing with anxiety. So today I am holding the intention that no matter what happens, I am equipped to handle it.

David Mamet, American playwright, filmmaker and author

MAY 31

Bring Light

*However vast the darkness,
we must supply our own light.*

—Stanley Kubrick

There are days when the world feels pretty dark. Political division, hatred on social media, war and natural disasters seem to be everywhere I turn. When I begin to feel discouraged, I remember that there have always been dark times in human history. Fortunately, there have also been light bearers. The people who did the most to dispel the darkness weren't ones who fought against it. Instead, they shone their light so brightly that the darkness had to retreat. Mahatma Gandhi didn't secure India's independence from British rule by unleashing an army. Instead, his gentle, persistent non-violent methods eventually led to success.

Perhaps most of us won't do anything as public and momentous as Gandhi, but we can be assured that any time we share our love with others, the light in our world increases. Today I am practicing more patience, more non-judgment, more reaching out to others. If you add your light to mine, I know we can make a significant dent in the darkness.

Stanley Kubrick (1928–1999), American film director, screenwriter

June

Green was the silence, wet was the light,
the month of June trembled like a butterfly.

—Pablo Neruda

Pablo Neruda (1904–1973), Chilean poet, winner of a Nobel prize for literature

JUNE 1

Reminder to Self – I Am Enough Right Now

*Talk to yourself like you would
to someone you love.*

—Brené Brown

One problem I have with many "self-help" books is they imply that something in me is broken and needs to be fixed. I don't find that a helpful premise. What works for me is to focus on first loving myself just the way I am right now. That's an easy phrase to write but not such an easy thing to do. Our society is full of messages about what I "should" weigh, how I "should" look and what possessions I "should" own. It's hard not to buy into those unrelenting dictates. But I'm so much happier if I don't.

Today I am remembering that outer trappings don't define my intrinsic worth. I'm good enough just as I am right here, right now. I don't need to do anything to earn the right to be loved and accepted. All human beings are born deserving of that. I can claim it right now as my birthright.

Today I take a break from self-improvement and focus on self-love.

Brené Brown, American professor and author

JUNE 2

Find the Funny

A day without sunshine is like, you know, night.

—Steve Martin

David Brooks, writing in *The Atlantic*, describes lessons learned during the Blitz in England in World War II that might be helpful for all of us today.

"Societies that build resilience do not hide behind a wall of happy talk or try to minimize the danger… Resilience is built when people confront a threat realistically, and discover that they have the resources to cope with it… During the Blitz, the British told a story about themselves that shaped their reaction to the experience and that shapes their self-perception to this day: They are at their best when their backs are to the wall, they are at their best when they are alone as a nation, and their national strength comes from their ability to be funny and phlegmatic during a crisis."

Humor helped Britons feel stronger, and perhaps we can all learn from their example. In October, 2020, the *New York Times* began an online article, "Laughter May Be Effective Medicine for These Trying Times" with these words:

"Doctors, nurses and therapists have a prescription for helping all of us…Try a little laughter."

One of the things I've noticed about the meanness that's all too prevalent on social media right now is that everyone is so serious. A little gentle shared humor might go a long way.

Today I am lightening up, looking for the funny in situations, and "trying a little laughter." A friend of mine says, "If I'm going to laugh about it later, I might as well laugh now."

Steve Martin, American comedian and actor

JUNE 3

Just Do My Best

I am only one, but still I am one. I cannot do everything, but still I can do something; and because I cannot do everything, I will not refuse to do something that I can do.

—Edward Everett Hale

Edward Everett Hale's wise words can apply to so many things in life. From a lofty perspective, they can relate to working for a more just society or advocating for causes I support. Sometimes my support may seem inadequate, but I remind myself that when each of us does a little, a lot can be accomplished.

On a smaller scale, these words encourage me to focus only on what I'm able to do one day at a time. I realize that sometimes what I expect myself to accomplish in a day might be unrealistic. I am going to keep repeating Edward Hale to myself often, "I cannot do everything."

So today I am doing what I can and calling that enough.

Edward Everett Hale (1822–1909), American author, historian, and minister

JUNE 4
Enjoy Uplifting Images

Art should be something that liberates your soul.

—Keith Haring

It's been a while since I've gone to an art museum and that's a shame because I always leave feeling better than when I came. Right now I am making a commitment to visit one soon, even if it can't be today. Art galleries are also fun to browse, and I'm putting that experience on my list of "To Do Soon."

I'm also thinking of the art I surround myself with daily. One great decision I made recently was to pull out works my children made years ago when they took an art class together during middle school. I hung a few of those creations and now I get a jolt of joy every time I see them. I love choosing art for my home that means something. I have an ethereal photo of a mossy path that my husband and I bought from a street photographer during our honeymoon. It reminds me most of the heartwarming conversation we had with the young man who sold us one of his favorites.

I've always been a fan of framing children's artwork, but I think it's important to choose pieces they've worked hard on and feel proud about. I wouldn't frame any slapdash piece made in haste with no emotional connection. That's not respectful to them. The works I display are ones I know they created with thought and love. It's great to display what I call "refrigerator art," or temporary pieces children create quickly and just for the fun of experimenting. But if I actually frame something, I want to consult with that child and make sure, just as we would with an adult artist, that it's something they love.

Today I'm thinking about the visual images around me and wondering if I'd like to add something new and uplifting. I am taking my cue from Keith Haring, and pondering what will "liberate my soul."

Keith Haring, American artist

JUNE 5
Remember to Take a Walk

We ought to take outdoor walks, to refresh and raise our spirits by deep breathing in the open air.

—Lucius Annaeus Seneca the Younger,
usually known as Seneca

Sometimes when I get busy I remember that it's been a few days since I've taken a long walk. Doing so always renews my energy and lifts my mood. Even a short one helps.

Today I am reminding myself that walking, or in my friend's case, going outside in her mechanized wheelchair, brings us into communion with something greater than ourselves as we feel the connections all humans share to sky and sun and outdoor air. Maybe the peoples of the world would get along better if everyone committed to taking a daily walk where we looked at the sky and remembered we're all fellow passengers on this earth ship.

I like to vary the kinds of walks I take. Sometimes it's fun to stroll through old neighborhoods and enjoy different types of architecture. It's always nice to explore a flower-filled park when I can, or find a hiking trail in a wooded area. When time is short, I make a game of walking around my block and seeing if I can discover something I've never noticed before.

Today I commit to a walk, no matter how I choose to do it.

JUNE 6
Practice Courage

Courage is like a muscle. We strengthen it by use.

—Ruth Gordon

Maya Angelou wrote that "courage is the most important of all the virtues because without courage, you can't practice any other virtue consistently." I think that's right, because to do most things well we need the courage to try and fail, to risk others' disapproval, or to fall short of our own expectations. Finding the courage to learn from "failure" is a vital skill in being able to navigate today's world.

Having the courage to risk being authentic comes before much else of value. It allows me to take chances and try new things, even if I miss the mark on what I want to do. Today I am reminding myself that failing at something is not the end of the world; it is how I learn.

I am choosing to exercise my courage muscle today, remembering that as it gets stronger, so will my ability to show up in the world as my true self.

Ruth Gordon (1896–1985), American actress, screenwriter and playwright

JUNE 7
Watch a Movie — Mindfully

It's not what a movie is about, it's how it is about it.

—Roger Ebert

It was no surprise to me that after the worst of the global pandemic was over, Netflix's stock began to fall. When all of us were stuck at home for long periods, watching movie after movie filled the time. Once we were "liberated," we didn't need that daily crutch as much.

It would be a mistake, though, to write off movie watching as a mindless pastime. It actually can have an important place in a fulfilling life. "The Psychological Benefits of Watching Movies," an online article in *The Acronym*, the student newspaper of the Illinois Mathematics and Science Academy, lists a number of research-based benefits. Here's one: "Film watching has a cathartic effect, allowing viewers to experience strong emotions through an activity. This can be very beneficial for those who have trouble expressing emotions, as films may easily prompt them to laugh, cry..."

A study conducted by researchers at University College London and Vue Cinema found that people who watched movies experienced improved mental focus that helped with cognition and memory. This was reported in an article, "Watching Movies Has Psychological Benefits, and Here is All We Know About It," on *thebridgechronicle.com*. So I'm keeping movie-watching on my list of "Feel Good" activities. Knowing my emotional reactions can be intense, I choose to avoid too much violence, and only pick sad stories if I'm in a good place to handle them. Being mindful of what I watch protects my well-being.

So this week I look forward to finding a fun movie. I'm pondering what I'd enjoy most — something light...serious...informative...funny...? Can't wait to see what I find. I wonder what you'd choose?

Roger Ebert (1942–2013), American film critic and author

JUNE 8
My Sad Feelings Will Change If I Don't Block Them

When you feel pain, simply view it as energy. Just start seeing these inner experiences as energy passing through your heart and before the eye of your consciousness. Then relax.

—Michael Singer,
*The Untethered Soul:
The Journey Beyond Yourself*

You've probably figured out by now that I am a fan of Michael Singer's book, *The Untethered Soul*. It has helped me navigate the ups and downs of life with more grace and equanimity. During times when I'm feeling strong emotion I remember this paragraph, "Relax your heart until you are actually face-to-face with the exact place where it hurts...You must be willing to be present right at the place of the tightness and pain, and then relax and go even deeper. This is very deep growth and transformation. But you will not want to do this. You will feel tremendous resistance...and that's what makes it so powerful. As you relax and feel the resistance, the heart will want to pull away...Keep relaxing...Let go and give room for the pain to pass through you...Just see it as energy and let it go."

Singer is right. Leaning into the pain felt like the exact opposite of what I wanted to do the first time I tried this. But I gave it a shot. With some practice, I've gotten pretty good at saying to myself, "This really hurts right now, and I'm going to just let it be here, knowing it won't last forever and soon it will pass through." If pain seems to linger on, that might mean I need to take action to fully process it — by journaling or talking to a friend, a loved one or therapist. Today, if pain comes, I am leaning into it, trusting that letting the energy flow ultimately leads to healing. And I'm getting myself extra help if I need it.

Michael Singer, American author, motivational speaker, former software developer

JUNE 9
Find Some Comfort Food

Sometimes a little comfort food can go a long way.

—Benjamin Bratt

I really do believe that one important part of eating a healthy diet is not making any food "wrong." If I keep moderation in mind, then I am going to allow myself to try anything I want without guilt. Eating something and then feeling bad about it is a recipe for an unhealthy relationship to food.

Today I am thinking about what feels like comfort food to me. I've already talked about my love for thumbprint cookies (see May 13). Beyond those, I'm remembering a very spicy chili my father would make when I was a child. He got the recipe from his father who got it from a friend who lived in Mexico. It's unusual chili, with no tomatoes and quite a combination of spices. Eating it reminds me of rare childhood moments when people were all in a good mood at once.

Then there's what my own children used to call "Ham & Broccoli Extreme" — a fairly schlocky casserole that uses a lot of canned soup, frozen broccoli, cheese, rice and turkey ham. They liked it immensely. No one would confuse it with great cuisine, but again, it brings back memories of happy times. Finally, there's mashed potatoes. Just because. Mashed potatoes with butter— need I say more?

So, today I'm going to give myself some comfort food, knowing I'm feeding both my body and soul. I wonder what feels like comfort food for you.

Benjamin Bratt, American actor

JUNE 10
Revisit the Idea of Weirdness

Embrace your differences and the qualities about you that you think are weird.

—Sebastian Stan

In January I wrote about becoming comfortable with the idea that we are all a little "weird." Lately I've been wondering how I really feel about that word. Sometimes I love it; it feels like a badge of honor. At other times I worry that it's being used as a weapon in middle schools or high schools or places where people are being unkind to those with different skin tones or gender orientations. I truly hope we can keep it as something we feel good about; a way to celebrate uniqueness.

In middle school, I moved from Pennsylvania, right outside of Philadelphia, to Lincoln, Nebraska when my father got a new job at the University there. I began the first day of school not knowing a soul. The change in culture from an urban Eastern school to a Midwestern one was dramatic, to say the least. Many things that were "cool" in Pennsylvania were not in Nebraska, and vice versa. I don't think most of us in middle school had the inner fortitude to celebrate our "weirdness," especially if others used the term as a pejorative. At least I didn't.

It's taken me a long time to become happy about the things that are uniquely me. Maybe it's a healing step to now be able to call those parts of me "weird." I'll have to think about this some more.

For now, for today, I will say this: I celebrate my uniqueness.

Sebastian Stan, Romanian-American actor

JUNE 11
Cultivate Some Breathtaking Moments

*Life is not measured by the number
of breaths we take, but by the moments
that take our breath away.*

—Maya Angelou

What feels like a breathtaking moment to me? I think it depends on what's going on in my life. When I'm feeling really, really busy, taking a moment to sit on my balcony watching a gorgeous sunset with a glass of wine in hand feels pretty breathtaking. When I've had plenty of time to relax, then attending a spectacular play or musical performance might be it.

Travelling to beautiful places with friends or family, if done in the spirit of relaxation and non-perfectionism, can bring what I call "memory moments." As they're happening I tell myself, "Burn this in your memory and never forget it."

Early in my life when I was a single mother facing pretty daunting financial challenges, breathtaking moments had to happen without spending money. I remember one Christmas when my young children's gift to me was a fabulous performance they had created for my enjoyment, with each of them playing various roles. They worked so hard and I could feel their love and care. It still takes my breath away to think of it.

So today I'm pondering how I can cultivate some new breathtaking moments. I wonder what you'd create.

Maya Angelou (1928–2014), American writer, poet and civil rights activist

JUNE 12
Be Me — Introvert or Extrovert?

> *There is no such thing as a pure introvert or extrovert. Such a person would be in the lunatic asylum.*
>
> —Carl Jung

On personality tests I fall in the middle on the introvert/extrovert scale, but in my heart I know I'm a bit more of an introvert. The book, *Introvert Power: Why Your Inner Life is Your Hidden Strength*, by psychologist Laurie Helgoe, explains what it means to be an introvert. "Introverts gain energy through reflection and solitude. Our culture, however, is geared toward the extrovert. The pressure to get out there and get happier can lead people to think that an inward orientation is a problem instead of an opportunity."

On the other hand, people who identify more as extroverts can also face misunderstanding. Sophia Dembling, in her *Psychology Today* article, "Hurtful Misconceptions Across the Introvert-Extrovert Divide," lists faulty ideas introverts sometimes have: "Extroverts are all noise, no substance...are not as creative as introverts...are afraid to spend time alone...don't listen...are needy...want to change introverts." None of these are true. The reality, as Carl Jung says, is that no one is a pure introvert or extrovert, and people are more alike than different in terms of basic needs. Differences between the two types boil down mostly to style. An extrovert will get just as tired as an introvert from attending a party, but it will probably just happen later for the extrovert. Knowing there is no "better type" means we can all feel fine about however we experience life.

Today I embrace my preferences about how I use my energy, realizing there is no way to be wrong. Whatever I feel is something to be celebrated.

Carl Jung (1875–1961), Swiss psychiatrist and writer

JUNE 13

Be Me — Planner or Go with the Flow?

Do not go with the flow. Be the flow.

—Elif Shafak

When I've taken the Meyers-Briggs Personality Indicator, I am again mostly in the middle on the Judging versus Perceiving category scale. To simplify these two types, if a person has a Judging preference, they mostly prefer things to be neat, orderly, established and settled. People with a Perceiving preference usually like things to be flexible and spontaneous. But just like the Introvert and Extrovert types, we all are a combination of both of these inclinations.

I find it helpful to think about personality preferences because it gives me a tool for understanding myself and others better. In some parts of my life I want to be organized and decided. I like lists for certain things. At other times I absolutely want to keep things open and see what surprises might come up. Understanding that my way of approaching tasks is not better or worse than anyone else's helps me feel fine about my style and be open to other inclinations.

When I go on trips with people I love, talking openly about our different preferences makes things easier. If one of us wants everything planned in advance and one of us wants room for serendipity, we might agree to an every-other-day system, where one day is planned and the next is open for surprises. With colleagues, it also helps to understand our different styles so we can develop a planning versus spontaneity agreement that works for everyone.

Today I embrace who I am and how I like to interact with the world. I give others room to be themselves, knowing their way is not better or worse than mine.

Elif Shafak, Turkish-British novelist

JUNE 14
Be Me — Fiction or Nonfiction?

> *Writing nonfiction is more like sculpture, a matter of shaping the research into the finished thing. Novels are like paintings, specifically watercolors. Every stroke you put down you have to go with. Of course you can rewrite, but the original strokes are still there in the texture of the thing.*
>
> —Joan Didion

I am practicing radical self-acceptance. Who I am is who I am and I don't need to be anything else. The way I see the world is as fine as anyone else's. The flip side to that is accepting others' ways as equally fine.

Today I'm thinking about what I like to read. When my husband and I married more than thirty years ago, our personal reading choices were complete opposites: he stuck with nonfiction and I almost exclusively read fiction. Today, that's flipped. I read mostly nonfiction now and he reads a lot more fiction. It's been fun influencing each other. That only works if it's done in a loving, non-pushy way, though.

Reading brings so much pleasure to my life that I can't imagine not having it all the time. But one of my dear friends does not see the world as I do. For her, reading is a bit of a chore. Her way of relaxing is mostly through art and music. I respect that.

Today I celebrate who I am and what brings me pleasure. And I give thanks for the many, many ways others see the world. If we could all relax a bit about differences, that kaleidoscope of perspectives could start to feel pretty fun.

Joan Didion (1934–2021), American writer

JUNE 15
How to Get Out of a Funk

*You don't need a new day to start over,
you only need a new mindset.*

—Hazel Hira Ozbek

What if a day just seems drab and I don't feel much motivation to do anything? Then what? This might seem surprising, but the first thing I do is just give myself permission to feel down. Sometimes not coming at myself like a frantic cheerleader is kindest. Saying "you can feel any way you want today," is often just what that disturbed part of me needs to hear.

The "new mindset" that Hazel Hira Ozbek talks about might actually be a recognition that I don't need to be "on" all the time. Allowing myself to admit that I'm tired or cranky or sad or feeling overworked is the first step toward restoring equanimity. Yes, it's good to eventually use some of my tools like focusing on gratitude or journaling or taking a walk or listening to good music. But not right away. Doing those things too soon sends the message that "you must never have an off day."

Today, or any day, if I'm feeling down, I will first reassure myself that it's allowed. And I'll remind myself that if I stop judging my feelings, they will eventually flow through me and others will begin to appear.

Hazel Hira Özbek, Spanish poet

JUNE 16
Celebrate Lifelong Learning for Increased Understanding

Education is for improving the lives of others and for leaving your community and world better than you found it.

—Marian Wright Edelman

Years ago, I led a lot of workshops for educators. I remember once talking with a young woman before the workshop began. She told me her principal had signed her up, but she didn't actually want to be there because "I don't like learning new things." I was fairly stunned by her words, wondering why anyone would choose to be a teacher if they themselves didn't enjoy learning. I hope what she really meant was that she was tired and on overload that night.

I've devoted my career to learning, so of course I wholeheartedly agree with Marian Wright Edelman. Education not only provides tools for leading a meaningful life, it can also open doors of understanding between people. Unfortunately, too many of us believe that if we're asked to change our minds about something, then we're being attacked. With a renewed emphasis on social justice issues, it's clear many of us have been feeling defensive as new ideas are brought to the forefront. What I'm afraid is really happening is that many of us are feeling like, "I don't like to learn new things." Perhaps it seems frightening when old ways are challenged; it can be uncomfortable to hear a new reality. But what if we all held this belief: "I don't know everything and I certainly don't know your reality. Let's learn from each other." What if we could do that with no defensiveness at all?

"Establishing lasting peace is the work of education; all politics can do is keep us out of war," said Maria Montessori. Truth. Today I am open to learning more peaceful ways.

Marian Wright Edelman, American activist for civil rights and children's rights and founder of the Children's Defense Fund

JUNE 17
Learn From My Wounds

If you want to know where to find your contribution to the world, look at your wounds. When you learn how to heal them, teach others.

—Emily Maroutian

Holly Elissa Bruno, in her well-loved book, *Happiness is Running Through the Streets to Find You: Translating Trauma's Harsh Legacy into Healing*, wrote: "When I chose to reclaim my life, I made a blind faith decision to heal." Her healing involved coming to terms with the childhood trauma she had long buried. As a result of her courageous journey, she is now a sought-after speaker and best-selling author. Each day she does just what Emily Maroutian urges in the quote above.

The great theologian, Henri Nouwen wrote, "Nobody escapes being wounded...The main question is not 'How can we hide our wounds?' so we don't have to be embarrassed, but 'How can we put our woundedness in the service of others?'"

It would be amazing if each of us could just accept as a given that to live a human life means to sometimes get wounded. What if we all got busy figuring out how to heal our individual wounds so we could openly share our learning with others? What a different world we could have.

Today I am accepting the reality that, because I am human, I have in some ways been wounded. I am learning how to heal those wounds, and I commit to finding ways to share my new wisdom with others.

Emily Maroutian, Armenian-American author and poet

JUNE 18
Stand Up for Children

*If we don't stand up for children,
then we don't stand for much.*

—Marian Wright Edelman

Here's another Marian Wright Edelman quote I love. Having worked for and on behalf of children my whole life, of course her words speak to me. But I don't think they are only meant for educators. I believe she is addressing all adults in our human family, because, if our society is to continue in a healthy way, we must each one of us care about the welfare of all the world's children.

Years ago I was speaking at a school board meeting where a number of us were advocating for some increased funding that would benefit children from low-income families. One father stood up and said firmly, "I don't want any of my money used this way. I'm taking care of my own children and I don't care about anyone else's children."

That way of thinking has come back to haunt us all as "other people's children" bring guns to school and take their hurt and anger out on "our children." The reality is that it will be "other people's children" who grow up to become our healthcare providers; who patrol our streets and keep us safe; who teach our grandchildren; who rob us at knifepoint some dark evening. We are inextricably intertwined with "other people's children." We must care.

Today I commit to renewing my efforts on behalf of all the world's children, taking whatever steps I am able, large or small, to ensure their welfare.

Marian Wright Edelman, American activist for civil rights and children's rights and founder of the Children's Defense Fund

JUNE 19
Juneteenth

*I prayed for freedom for twenty years, but
received no answer until I prayed with my legs.*

—Frederick Douglass

Recently I heard a politician promising that if elected, he would abolish the relatively new "official" Juneteenth holiday. Ah, I realized, here is another case of people feeling threatened by something new. We probably all understand that on some level. When things around us change too rapidly, it can be disconcerting and we might feel out of balance. It's again one reason I hope we can embrace lifelong learning as a must for a healthy society (see June 16).

What would happen if we all expected that new information would be coming to us frequently so we could continue to improve our lives and our whole society? What if, instead of seeing change as frightening, we viewed it as helpful?

Today I am committing to learning more and more about the Juneteenth holiday. I look forward to getting new information that will make my life richer and kinder.

Frederick Douglass (1818–1895), American social reformer, author and abolitionist

JUNE 20

Moderation in All Things — Except Love

The secret to living well and longer is:
Eat half,
Walk double,
Laugh triple,
And love without measure.

—Tibetan proverb

I'm not sure about the "eat half" part in the proverb above, but I get its point. Moderating my overeating would certainly serve me, as would exercising more and laughing even more.

Today I am going to take an informal inventory of my life and look for places I might be out of balance. Where could I stand a bit more moderation? I commit to taking at least one action step that would bring an area of my life into a bit better balance.

And, while I'm at it, I'm going to do my best to remember to "love without measure."

JUNE 21
Look to the Open Door

When one door of happiness closes, another opens; but often we look so long at the closed door that we do not see the one which has been opened for us.

–Helen Keller

In a *Psychology Today* article, Stephen Joseph, PhD writes about the value of change and challenge for all human beings: "To lead an authentic life, we need to take on new challenges that stretch us and give us more opportunities to be ourselves. It is not that the authentic person does not feel the same fear; rather, they are simply more willing to face their fear."

I just got off the phone with a dear friend who has spent the last two months recovering from a seriously fractured tibia. She told me she has been practicing being in acceptance. "You know," she said, "When I look back at the last eight weeks, it is just amazing the amount of blessings that have come to me. I am never again going to be afraid of what the future might bring. I know whatever it is, I can handle it and I will find gifts in it." This kind of attitude doesn't just happen. My friend has been practicing this learning orientation to life for many years, and she is good at it. When the accident happened she didn't minimize her situation. She told me she was in a great deal of pain at first, and she allowed herself to ask for help from others. Very soon, she began to experience serendipitous experiences that ended up enriching her life immensely. I know her accident shut some doors, such as cancelling a long-planned trip. But by shifting her focus, she was able to recognize new doors opening all around.

I'm guessing I've missed my share of opening doors while pining after closed ones, but from now on, if a door slams shut in my face, I'll keep an eye out for what serendipity lies ahead.

Helen Keller (1880–1968), American author and disability rights advocate

JUNE 22
Fun Stuff

You have to treat yourself every once in a while, get to the fun stuff!

—Heidi Klum

Ok. Fun stuff. I am excited for a day of treating myself to something that feels fun. My usual "treats" are often favorite restaurants or fun movies, but today I'm looking for something new. I could keep to the restaurant theme, but go somewhere brand new I've never been to before. No matter how much I enjoy the food (or don't), I'll define the fun part as finding out what an entirely new place is like.

I could also look for a brand new place to walk. I know there are wooded walking trails about a twenty-minute drive away from my home, but I've never investigated them. Today might be the day. Part of the fun of "fun stuff" is figuring out what to do.

Today I am choosing one thing that feels like fun – to me. And I get to define fun however I want. I wonder what "fun stuff" is for you.

Heidi Klum, German and American model, television host, producer

JUNE 23
I Am Nature

We often forget that we are Nature. Nature is not something separate from us. So when we say that we have lost our connection to Nature, we have lost our connection to ourselves.

—Andy Goldsworthy

Dara McAnulty, in his beautiful book, *Diary of a Young Naturalist*, explains how, as a person with autism, the many hours he spends in his traditional school setting, separated from the natural world, are so difficult. "The classrooms at school are claustrophobic. Through the stale air I'm bombarded by fidgets, sighs, shifts, rustles as loud as rumbless...I can't see outside. I feel boxed in, a wild caged animal...I like school, I really want to learn. But... the things we're learning are as captivating as a dripping tap, while outside the world is so much easier to condense, to understand. You can focus on one thing: a flower, a bird, a sound, an insect. School is the opposite. I can never think straight."

McAnulty's words move me deeply. I know the sense of being boxed in is true for so many children. It's why I spent my career advocating for, and creating, natural outdoor classrooms in places around the world, especially in urban school districts where connections with natural spaces would have otherwise been inaccessible to students.

I don't believe it's just children who experience this sense of claustrophobia and over-stimulation. Many work places are bombarded by the "rustles as loud as rumbles," that McAnulty describes. As CEO of Dimensions Foundation, I always urged our team to go outside when they could. I wish I could have done more to bring the natural world into our offices.

In my life now I commit to spending time each day in places where I can "focus on one thing: a flower, a bird, a sound or an insect," and remember that I am nature.

Andy Goldsworthy, English sculptor, photographer, and environmentalist

JUNE 24
Value Quality Relationships

Each friend represents a world in us, a world possibly not born until they arrive, and it is only by this meeting that a new world is born.

—Anaïs Nin,
The Diary of Anaïs Nin,
Vol. 1: 1931-1934

"Quality of friends — NOT quantity — is the key to being happy, and large networks on social media are no match for closeness in real life." So begins an article on *dailymail.co.uk*. Quoting research from the University of Leeds, author Sam Blanchard writes, "Having hundreds of friends on Facebook is no substitute for a handful of close friends in real life, a study has found.

Researchers discovered that people with only a few friends were at least as happy as those with far more if many of theirs were online."

The study results encourage people to focus on cultivating a few meaningful relationships instead of engaging in a competition to "rack up friends" on social media platforms.

Today I am giving thanks for the family members and friends I can count on. It doesn't take many. Just a few deep relationships are enough to make our lives meaningful and happy.

Anaïs Nin (1903–1977), French-born American essayist, novelist

JUNE 25
Celebrate Myself

*It takes courage to grow up and
become who you really are.*

—Edward Estlin Cummings,
often written in all lowercase as e e cummings

Today I am celebrating exactly who I am, with no apologies. I am practicing loving myself because I am here, not because I have met some arbitrary standard I set for myself. Have I made mistakes? Certainly. I won't let that change my ability to love myself. Do I have things I want to "improve?" Sure, but I won't let that keep me from rejoicing in the core me who is wonderful right here and right now.

Let's make this a day of complete self-acceptance. Will you join me?

JUNE 26
Focus on What I Have

*If you look at what you have in life,
you'll always have more. If you look at what you
don't have in life, you'll never have enough.*

—Oprah Winfrey

Today I am reminding myself of the wisdom of Oprah Winfrey's words. I am taking an inventory of all that makes my life rich, focusing especially on things I might take for granted. Here are a few:

- People who do the hard work of running restaurants so I can be nourished by their love of good food;
- Public service workers who keep the trees in my neighborhood healthy, and clear the winter snow off the roads (most of the time);
- Authors who write books that give me new perspectives on life;
- Birdsong that greets me every morning;
- Reporters who still take journalism seriously and work hard to get verified facts out to the general public;
- Friends who call just to ask, "How are you really?"

Once I got started I realized I could have gone on and on. Life can feel tough at times, but even on the most challenging days, all of the things I outlined above are going on, and so much more.

Today I choose to focus on the gifts I might be taking for granted, remembering to give thanks for such abundance.

Oprah Winfrey, American television host, producer, author and actress

JUNE 27
Silence

*There are voices which we hear in solitude,
but they grow faint and inaudible as we
enter into the world.*

—Ralph Waldo Emerson

Does it seem to you that the world continues to become noisier? It does to me. Just the other day I realized that a hotel elevator had a television set in it. Do they really think that in the few seconds it takes to ride an elevator we must be watching TV? Sigh.

I know myself and realize that sound bothers me a great deal – perhaps moreso than many. For anyone with sensory integration challenges, children especially, being in loud surroundings can literally be painful. I find myself wanting to avoid restaurants where the decibel levels soar with each passing hour of the evening. Sometimes a loud and joyful atmosphere is fun, but for me that can't be very often.

Emerson's quote reminds me that it is hard to tune in to the wisdom of my authentic self if that interior voice is always being drowned out by the cacophony of the world. Today I am thinking about how much noise is in my life. I am focusing on ways to bring myself more silent times. Sitting outside in a quiet space during lunch, or meditating for five minutes at the end of a long (and noisy) day, might help me restore some much-needed sensory balance.

Today I am focusing on the necessity of planning for silence.

Ralph Waldo Emerson (1803–1882), American essayist and philosopher

JUNE 28
I Get to Choose What's Important for Me

And every day, the world will drag you by the hand, yelling, "This is important! And this is important! And this is important! You need to worry about this! And this! And this!" And each day, it's up to you to yank your hand back, put it on your heart and say, "No. This is what's important."

—Iain S. Thomas

Wow. I love Iain S. Thomas's words. How many times do well-meaning parents try to "guide" their children onto certain paths or into specific careers? I wonder how many times I gave my children "advice" that was really more about my own life than theirs? When I think about it, why would I ever believe I knew what was best for my children? Or for my friends?

The reality is that each one of us comes into this earth school to forge our own path, learn our own lessons and discover our own way. The kindest thing we can do is to cheer from the sidelines, trusting that each of us has the inner wisdom to guide our life journey.

Today I am putting my hand on my heart and declaring, "This is what's important to me." I support you in doing the same.

Iain S. Thomas, South African writer and new media artist

JUNE 29
Acknowledge My Mistakes

There is no poetry where there are no mistakes.

—Joy Harjo

I love the idea that it is our mistakes that add to the poetry of our lives. I remember reading about a well known business leader, the CEO of a multi-million dollar company, who would ask people he was interviewing to tell him about big mistakes they had made. If interviewees replied that they really hadn't made any serious mistakes, the CEO would respond by saying something along these lines: "I'm sorry, but you haven't had enough good experience to work for our company."

I wish I could say that I'm always able to negotiate my mistakes with equanimity. I'm not quite there yet, but I'm getting better. Looking back on my life, I do see how some of my biggest mistakes taught me the most and honestly did make me a better person. To use Joy Harjo's analogy, the poetry in my life deepened because of them.

Today, and every day, I commit to seeing mistakes as a necessary part of life. I learn from them, grow from them, and celebrate the poetry in them.

Joy Harjo, American poet, musician, playwright, author, and 23rd United States Poet Laureate, the first Native American to hold that honor

JUNE 30
Age Gratefully

I've decided that aging gratefully is even more important than aging gracefully.

—Nancy Rosenow

I'm quoting myself today because tomorrow is my birthday and I've been giving a lot of thought to aging. The culture of the United States does us no favors by celebrating youth above all else. A few years back when I decided to let my hair transition to its natural white, I felt a sense of exuberance. I was no longer betraying myself by using dye to pretend to be younger than I was.

Once I decided to be proud of exactly where I was in life, I think other people could feel my comfort with my own skin. I started receiving more compliments about my appearance than I had for years. The funny thing is, I really didn't crave those kinds of accolades anymore. I did always try to interpret people's comments as expressions of kindness and caring, though, and in that respect they meant a lot.

It would have been helpful to me to embrace the concept of grateful aging earlier in my life. Many cultures actually celebrate their older members with respect and reverence. The cult of youth is a relatively new phenomenon. I suppose part of the reason for it might be a denial of death; a wish to turn away from anything that reminds us of our own mortality. I think there's a better way. I choose to see aging as sacred, celebrating every passing year with gratitude. Karen H. Meyers writes in her book, *The Truth about Death and Dying*, that many African-American communities embrace death as part of the "natural rhythm of life...funerals tend to be life-affirming and to have a celebratory air intermingled with the sorrow."

Today I embrace all the expansive experiences aging has brought. No matter how old or young you are, I urge you to do the same.

Nancy Rosenow, author of this book ☺

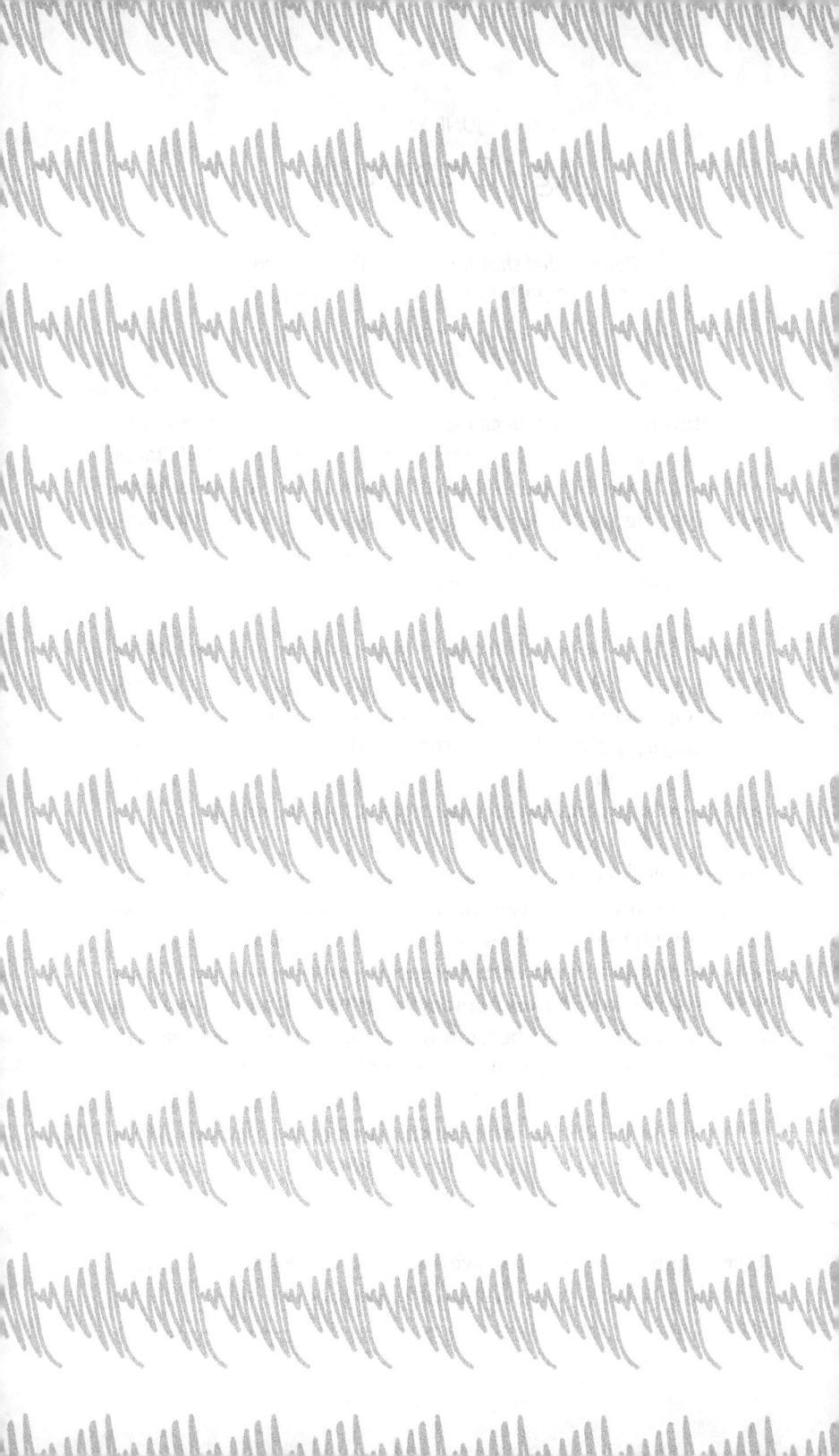

July

The seventh month is strength.

—Lailah Gifty Akita

JULY 1
Live in the Moment

*Life is available only in the present moment.
If you abandon the present moment you cannot
live the moments of your daily life deeply.*

—Thich Nhat Hanh

One of the greatest blessings of my life is that I'm married to my best friend and the person I admire most in the world. My husband John has lived a life of great accomplishment, but more importantly, he continually demonstrates unconditional loving, grace under pressure and service to others. A few years ago, when we least expected it, he was diagnosed with Parkinson's disease. If I admired John before (which I did), watching him negotiate this life detour has exponentially increased my appreciation.

Being told of a life-altering condition tests all our beliefs about life. John and I had often discussed how "everything that happens to us happens for us if we choose to find the gift in it." Well. What about this Parkinson's diagnosis? Was there really a gift in it? It turns out the answer is a resounding, "yes." In fact there have been many gifts. Here are just a few:

- We try to never take any day for granted. It was a goal before the diagnosis, but now we are living our aspiration. Knowing our time is finite focuses gratitude on what we have right now.
- Healthy eating and exercise help manage Parkinson's. We've known for years we "should" be practicing both of those, but now we actually are. I'm benefitting, too.
- One symptom of Parkinson's is memory loss. John keeps detailed notes for his consulting work and compensates well, but at times, memories of our shared past are no longer accessible. That keeps us focusing on the pleasures of the present moment. Philosophers since the beginning of time have urged us to "be here now." Finally, mindfully, we are. Today I invite you to join me in celebrating the present moment so we can, as Thich Nhat Hanh urges, truly live life deeply.

Thich Nhat Hanh (1926–2022), Vietnamese Buddhist monk, peace activist, author and teacher

JULY 2
Vulnerability Opens Doors

> *I do not believe that sheer suffering teaches. If suffering alone taught, all the world would be wise, since everyone suffers. To suffering must be added mourning, understanding, patience, love, openness, and the willingness to remain vulnerable.*
>
> —Anne Morrow Lindbergh,
> Gift from the Sea

The "willingness to remain vulnerable" that Anne Morrow Lindbergh writes about could also be defined as the choice to show up in life as our authentic selves. In their book, *Remembering the Light Within: A Course in Soul-Centered Living*, psychologists Mary and Ron Hulnick explain, "The reality of the Authentic Self is Love; it is altogether different from that of the ego. The Authentic Self has no sense of duality. There's no dividing experiences into right and wrong. At the level of the Authentic Self, you simply see what is."

I was extremely fortunate to be a student in a graduate class taught by the Hulnicks. Early in the course, Mary Hulnick made this statement: "Perfect vulnerability is perfect protection." It took me a while to fully understand what she meant. Over time I came to see that once we become completely comfortable with our authenticity and no longer need the approval of others, we are then free to be vulnerable because others' opinions have lost their power.

Allowing myself to be vulnerable doesn't mean I can't still have boundaries. I don't have to share everything about myself with the whole world. As researcher and author, Brené Brown says, people have to earn the right to hear my deepest story (see January 18). But I also do not have to ever be ashamed of any part of me, either. Today I am remembering that the only opinion about who I am that truly matters is my own.

Anne Morrow Lindbergh (1906–2001), American writer and aviatrix

JULY 3
Have Art in My Life

Simplify, slow down, be kind. And don't forget to have art in your life — music, paintings, theater, dance and sunsets.

–Eric Carle

Today I am thinking about how to have more art in my life. I am again reminding myself that I don't have to be a professional artist, dancer or musician to enjoy experimenting with those means of expression. And I can certainly enjoy nature's amazing artistry with sunsets.

I'm asking myself today what kind of art would bring me the most joy. My husband and I sometimes like going to high school or college theater productions. Not only are they affordable, but the young performers bring a level of enthusiasm that we find so heartwarming. The same is true for college dance productions or musical recitals.

So, what shall I do today? Am I going to create some art myself? Attend a performance? Sit outside this evening and watch the sunset while I drink a cup of tea and enjoy my favorite dessert? Hmmm. Hard choice. Maybe all of the above. What about you?

Eric Carle (1929–2021), American author and illustrator of children's books

JULY 4
Find Independence

America was not built on fear. America was built on courage, on imagination, and an unbeatable determination to do the job at hand.

—Harry S. Truman

Today, on this American holiday, Independence Day, I hope the United States of America can find independence from fear. There seems to be an overabundance of fear lately and an undersupply of love for others (with love being the best antidote for fear I know).

It's easy to write this as if someone else should be doing it. What I really mean to say is that I want to become more loving, less judgmental and less fearful. I want to remember what I have in common with others, even when I may disagree with some of their political opinions.

Today, my vision for a future America is a place where people love themselves enough to be able to love everyone else with generosity, forgiveness and gentle compassion. I know what my part in this is. I am doing the work of learning to fully and unconditionally love myself, right here, right now.

Harry S. Truman (1884–1972), 33rd president of the United States

JULY 5
Learn My Own Lessons

Nothing ever goes away until it has taught us what we need to know.

—Pema Chödrön

I used to notice that friends of mine seemed to have to tackle the same kinds of challenges over and over again. When I looked closer at my own life, I noticed the same was true for me. When I began reading about life as a school, from authors like Pema Chödrön, and Ron and Mary Hulnick (see July 2), it became clear that certain challenges continue to come to us until we've learned the lessons they are meant to teach us.

My family history is full of money challenges, on both my mother's and father's sides. The "family story" I grew up hearing was that a person can never relax about money; it will always be difficult. Not surprisingly, I lived this story as a single mother who struggled to make ends meet. Even after John and I married, other experiences kept coming along to reinforce the belief that "money is always a challenge."

It wasn't until I re-thought the old story and embraced a new way of thinking that suddenly my relationship with money completely changed. Once I came to understand financial stability as a result of trust and service, I began to experience a sense of abundance for the first time in my life. I began to deeply understand the spiritual principle that outer reality is a reflection of our inner reality.

Today, or any day, if I realize that I'm confronting the same kinds of challenges over and over, I am going to ask myself, "What are they here to teach me?" Then I'll get busy learning my lessons.

Pema Chödrön, American Tibetan Buddhist nun, author

JULY 6

Just Relax

No need to hurry. No need to sparkle.
No need to be anybody but oneself.

—Virginia Woolf

Let's make today a time to just relax. I love Virginia Woolf's line, "No need to sparkle." I know just what she means. Today could be a time to "just be."

What might it feel like if I didn't hurry at all today? What if I simply never worried about what anyone else was thinking about me? What if I didn't push myself to improve anything at all about myself? It feels like taking a luxuriously slow, deep breath, doesn't it?

Care to join me?

Virginia Woolf (1882–1941), English writer

JULY 7
Write Thank You Notes

Silent gratitude isn't much use to anyone.

—Gertrude Stein

I have a couple of people I want to thank today, and instead of sending an email (which would be perfectly acceptable), I think I'll create a handwritten note. I actually love the process of finding a beautiful card and using a nice pen to put my thoughts down on paper.

I read once that one of the first things President George H.W. Bush did when he was elected to office was sit down and send handwritten thank-yous to some of the people who had helped him the most. I don't know if this is true, but I hope it is. There's something comforting about that level of graciousness, whether or not you agree with someone's political positions.

I do believe that expressing appreciation does even more good for us than for the people we are thanking. I know I always feel better on days when I remember to thank people in ways small or large.

Today I am enjoying writing something by hand. This is more for my own enjoyment than anything else. If you are someone who'd much rather email your thanks, I fully support that.

Gertrude Stein (1874–1946), American novelist, poet, playwright

JULY 8
Create Some Comforting Phrases

Promise me you'll always remember:
You're braver than you believe, stronger than
you seem, and smarter than you think.

—A.A. Milne

I've noticed something about myself. When I'm in the middle of a painful situation, or I'm experiencing some disappointment, much of what I understand about life goes out of my head. That's why I've created a list for myself of comforting phrases. Here are some of them:

This too shall pass.
Let the pain flow through me.
I wonder what's going to happen next?
I wonder what the gift in this will be?
I have gotten through things just like this before. I can again.
I have the tools to handle this.

When I'm feeling overwhelmed or foggy, reading through these truths calms me.

Today I am remembering that whatever I face, I have the ability to handle it and to comfort myself.

A.A. Milne (1882–1956), English author, popular for his *Winnie-the-Pooh* books

JULY 9
Stop Comparing Myself to Others

Comparison is the thief of joy.

—Theodore Roosevelt

What would life be like if I never again compared myself to anyone else? Much more joyful, I think Theodore Roosevelt would say. Despite my best intentions, I still sometimes measure myself against others. My assessment is often that I'm falling short. "She stays much calmer than you do in a stressful situation." "He is much more informed about current events than you are." "She is so much funnier than you."

Why do I do this? Part of the reason, I suspect, is that we're programmed to do so from a young age. Our school systems are based largely on comparisons — who has the highest scores; who is better, who is worse. We learn early on to assess our worth in relationship to others. What if, instead, children were taught to focus only on their own forward progress, and that what other students were doing was not their concern? My guess is we would have a generation of happier children, and a world where people cooperated more and fought less.

Today I am reminding myself that I am my own unique person. I do not have to have every skill someone else does, just as they won't have all of mine. My value as a human being isn't determined in comparison to others. That's a faulty, ego-based way of thinking. Today I celebrate who I am. What everyone else has or does detracts nothing from my worth.

Theodore Roosevelt (1858–1919), 26th president of the United States

JULY 10
Stay Soft

Be soft. Do not let the world make you hard. Do not let pain make you hate. Do not let the bitterness steal your sweetness. Take pride that even though the rest of the world may disagree, you still believe it to be a beautiful place.

—Kurt Vonnegut, Jr.

Kurt Vonnegut's words bring a tear to my eye. They remind me again that we live in an AND world. Yes, there is darkness and horror AND there is still so much beauty. I want my grandchildren, and indeed all children, to grow up with a sense of the world's sweetness. It is there despite all the challenges.

Here's what I am reminding myself of today: People can be cruel AND most people are basically kind. Environmental problems are very real AND there are many of us working hard to overcome them. Hatred rears its ugly head on social media AND there are many compassionate people who reach out to strangers, offering words of support and offers of service. Pollution chokes rivers AND people plant pollinator gardens as havens for bees and butterflies.

Today I choose to focus on being soft. I am reminding myself and others that our world is indeed beautiful in so many senses of the word.

Kurt Vonnegut, Jr. (1922–2007), American author

JULY 11
Lean Into Acceptance

Accept — then act. Whatever the present moment contains, accept it as if you had chosen it. Always work with it, not against it...This will miraculously transform your whole life.

—Eckhart Tolle

I'm finally understanding what it means to lean into acceptance. I've gotten good at accepting serious situations like my husband's Parkinson's diagnosis. And John and I deal with disturbing issues, such as racism, by accepting that it exists and then taking action steps, remembering that acceptance does not mean agreement. Interestingly, when it came to mundane circumstances, my acceptance was often more like grudging tolerance. A recent experience gave me a chance to practice Tolle's urging to "accept it as if you had chosen it." I'd planned a housewarming party for a family member, excited for out-of-town relatives to see her new place. Since many children were coming, I bought a wading pool and other outdoor games. The weather had been beautiful for days. The forecast predicted more of the same.

On the morning of the party, everything changed. A sudden rainstorm blew in and I grumbled grudgingly, "This is disappointing, but I guess I'll have to accept it." Suddenly the Tolle quote came to mind and I wondered, "What if I had chosen this weather? Maybe the children won't play outside, but what if I put the pool in the garage with wind-up toys like 'swimming' sea turtles?" Soon I came up with a host of new ideas. You can probably guess that the party turned out to be great fun. The children loved the revised activities. By the end of the evening the rain left and everyone mingled outside, enjoying balmy temperatures and an impressive sunset. Most importantly, the new homeowner basked in our love; really the only thing that mattered. Today I exercise my acceptance muscles in situations large and small, remembering that acceptance is the first step toward positive action.

Eckhart Tolle, German-born author and teacher

JULY 12
Clear Some Clutter

Have nothing in your house that you do not know to be useful, or believe to be beautiful.

—William Morris

It's time again to remind myself how good it feels to clear away clutter. My daughter always says there is so much going on in her mind that she needs her surroundings to be clear to help her focus. I agree. Simplicity calms.

I take William Morris's advice to heart. I no longer keep things that "might come in handy someday." If I don't have a known use for something, then it only weighs me down and makes my surroundings feel oppressive. It's a relief to let it go.

A present-day decluttering expert, Marie Kondo, writes this in her bestselling book, *The Life-Changing Magic of Tidying Up*, "The space in which we live should be for the person we are becoming now, not for the person we were in the past." Reading that helps me remember that hanging on to too many "memories from the past" leaves no room for making new ones.

Today I release anything from my physical surroundings that isn't useful or that doesn't bring me joy.

William Morris (1834–1896), English textile designer, architect, poet

JULY 13
How Do I Define Success?

*Success is liking yourself, liking what you do,
and liking how you do it.*

—Maya Angelou

I don't think I could do much better than Maya Angelou's definition of success. Although a friend once told me he'd seen a t-shirt that said, "What matters in life is what we brought – not what we bought." That's good, too. Sometimes t-shirt wisdom is as good as what poets create.

It's hard not to get confused about the value of buying versus bringing. Advertising messages certainly tell us to define our success by the size of our home or make of our car. They usually never ask, "What of value are you adding to our world?" But I can ask myself that. And at the end of the day, I hope my answer will be something that's rooted in love.

Today I am letting go of the misunderstanding that success is measured by a life of consumption. Today I am focusing on living a life of loving.

Maya Angelou (1928–2014), American writer, poet and civil rights activist

JULY 14
Remember the Importance of Sleep

*A good laugh and a long sleep are
the best cures in the doctor's book.*

—Irish Proverb

Today I am again reminding myself of the importance of getting enough sleep. "A good night's sleep is incredibly important for your health. In fact, it's just as important as eating healthy and exercising." So begins an article on *healthline.com*, "10 Reasons to Get More Sleep," by Joe Leech. The article explains that good sleep helps us maintain a healthy weight, strengthen our heart, fight off depression and improve concentration, among many other benefits.

When I'm tempted to push myself too hard and trade sleep for "getting more done," I will remember that I'm doing so at the expense of my health. I can trade the "exhaustion is a badge of honor" misunderstanding for a new mantra: Rested people are rad. (Ok, maybe I need to ask for help in creating good mantras.)

Today I am making sleep a top priority. I am not scolding myself about my sleep patterns. Instead, I am gently supporting myself in getting the sleep I deserve.

JULY 15
Break the People-Pleasing Pattern

I can't tell you the key to success, but the key to failure is trying to please everyone.

—Ed Sheeran

The people-pleasing pattern began for me in childhood when I desperately tried to earn the approval of my parents and teachers – both to gain their praise and avoid their anger. By carrying that habit into adulthood, I caused myself unnecessary hardship in my twenties. I can look back and see myself trying frantically to please absolutely everyone in my life. It seemed terribly important, I thought, that everyone approve of me. Well. Ed Sheeran's right. It is the key to failure. In my case, the person I failed most was myself.

I was pretty good at twisting myself into pretzels trying to keep everyone around me happy. For the most part it worked, but at the end of the day, there was always someone who didn't want to be pleased, because they were simply unhappy with life. That didn't mean I didn't run myself ragged trying to get them to cheer up. After almost a decade of this impossible dance, I came to a sudden realization that life this way wasn't tenable. It was then I began my liberating journey to break that old destructive pattern.

Paulo Coelho, the Brazilian writer most famous for his book, *The Alchemist*, asserts that, "Stress, anxiety and depression are caused when we are living to please others." Today I am pretty good at remembering that. I can care about others, but it is not my job to "live to please them."

Today I am pleasing myself. That is enough.

Ed Sheeran, English singer-songwriter

JULY 16
Lighten Up

Your attitude is like a box of crayons that color your world. Constantly color your picture gray, and your picture will always be bleak. Try adding some bright colors to the picture by including humor, and your picture begins to lighten up.

—Allen Klein

It's good to not take myself so seriously. Life is full of fun if I let myself find it. Yes, there are difficult challenges in our world. Always. But that's all the more reason to laugh often — especially at myself.

The Book of Joy, by the Dalai Lama, Desmond Tutu and Douglas Abrams, has this to say on the subject: "*Humor*, like *humility*, comes from the same root word for *humanity: humus*. The lowly and sustaining earth is the source for all three words. Is it any surprise that we have to have a sense of humility to be able to laugh at ourselves and that to laugh at ourselves reminds us of our shared humanity?"

Today I am lightening up. I plan to add some bright yellow to my life picture today.

Allen Klein (1931–2009), American author and lecturer

JULY 17

Because I Read

I've lived a thousand lives and I've loved a thousand loves. I've walked on distant worlds and seen the end of time. Because I read.

—George R.R. Martin

My life becomes harder when I don't make time to read. Reading transports me, as George R.R. Martin said in the quote above, "to distant worlds." It helps me negotiate this world with more equanimity when I can visit someplace else once in a while.

So today I am reminding myself of the value of reading. If I say I'm "too busy," then I deprive myself of the renewal that helps me tackle tasks again with more ease and grace.

One of my friends told me reading was such an ordeal for him as a child that it's ruined it for him for life. First, I'm so sorry when school children start to see reading as something punitive. I love what children's book author, Mem Fox, says, "When I say to a parent read to a child, I don't want it to sound like medicine. I want it to sound like chocolate."

That's my wish, too, for every child in every classroom and every bedroom in the world. Reading can be such a lifelong pleasure. Let's please don't ruin it. My wish for my friend is that he might someday dip his toe back in the reading water and find that it feels better this time.

Today I am finding time for the joys of reading. It's a gift I give myself gladly.

George R.R. Martin, American novelist, screenwriter, television producer

JULY 18
Mindfulness Really Does Matter

The little things? The little moments?
They aren't little.

—Jon Kabat-Zinn

In his book, *Wherever You Go, There You Are: Mindfulness Meditation in Everyday Life*, Jon Kabat-Zinn writes, "Practice sharing the fullness of your being, your best self, your enthusiasm, your vitality, your spirit, your trust, your openness, above all, your presence. Share it with yourself, with your family, with the world." I love his description of living in the present moment, or practicing mindfulness as it is popularly called. It's more than being aware of my surroundings. It's showing up with all my "enthusiasm, vitality…openness."

But here's the paradox. In order to show up that way, Kabat-Zinn says, "We must be willing to encounter darkness and despair when they come up and face them, over and over again if need be, without running away or numbing ourselves in the thousands of ways we conjure up to avoid the unavoidable." In other words, being fully present means experiencing EVERYTHING in the present moment – darkness and light both. Blocking the pain means I won't feel the joy, either.

Luckily people like Michael Singer (author of *The Untethered Soul*) remind me that if I allow my difficult feelings to be fully present, they will soon flow through me and dissipate. So there's no need to block anything.

Today I am showing up in each moment – fully present.

Jon Kabat-Zinn, American professor and author

JULY 19
Do a Puzzle — Slow Down

The nice thing about doing a crossword puzzle is, you know there is a solution.

—Stephen Sondheim

I understand why many people are enjoying the Wordle puzzles that the *New York Times* publishes. There's a sense of delightful slowing down that happens when I focus on them, even if it's brief. And Stephen Sondheim is right. It's comforting to work on something that I know can be solved. It's a nice respite from so much that I do in my life that's uncertain.

Crossword puzzles take more time than Wordle so I don't do them often, but today I'm going to give one a try. Maybe you'd like to join me.

Stephen Sondheim (1930–2021), American composer-lyricist

JULY 20
Find My Spiritual Center

Believe in your infinite potential. Your only limitations are those you set upon yourself.

—Roy T. Bennett,
The Light in the Heart

It helps to frequently stop and remember the strength I have that comes from the core me. That power is available for every human being. When I remember my spiritual center, problems seem more manageable. I can relax and know all is well.

Jean Houston, in her book, *The Mythic Life*, calls this strong center our Essence. "There is real science within this phenomenon of accessing Essence...When we tap into Essence, we unleash extraordinary abilities — rapid healing, overcoming pain, accelerated response time, and focus and endurance beyond our usual capacity."

Gary Zukov, writing in his book, *The Seat of the Soul*, describes the concept of Essence this way, "When we align our thoughts, emotions, and actions with the highest part of ourselves, we are filled with enthusiasm, purpose, and meaning. Life is rich and full...We are joyously and intimately engaged with our world. This is the experience of authentic power."

Today I tune in to my Essence, my spiritual center and experience the strength and meaning available to me.

Roy T. Bennett, American author

JULY 21
Heal Old Hurts

Healing old hurts can only begin when the children we once were feel safe enough to speak their hearts to the adults we are now.

–L.R. Knost

Today I am going to take a moment and invite the unhealed parts of myself, left over from childhood, to come and speak with adult me. Healing old hurts is like peeling an onion. I do a little, and then a little more, and through the process I will probably cry.

Each time I think I might be done, I find there's still another layer. That's ok. The process will be finished when it is. Period. No need to push or judge, just love myself.

Today I am promising any part of me that still needs healing that I am here to listen. And react with compassion and love.

L.R. Knost, American author

JULY 22

Proclaim it a Day of Fun

*Never, ever underestimate the
importance of having fun.*

—Randy Pausch,
The Last Lecture

Here's some more wisdom from Randy Pausch. You'll remember him as the professor who wrote a wise and touching book as he knew he was dying of pancreatic cancer (see February 7).

Sometimes I have to admit that I can get too serious, and before I know it I've forgotten to add any play to my day...or my week. This isn't healthy or fair to myself.

So today I am proclaiming a Day of Fun. I might try something I haven't done for a while. Go to a baseball game? Maybe. Swimming? Could be. Picking the funniest movie I can find and getting a big tub of popcorn? Hmmm. How about going to my favorite ice cream store and getting some peanut butter chocolate chip ice cream? (Ok, I've done that recently, but I really like it.) If I'm not feeling like spending money right now, how about taking a walk in a brand new place? Could be fun.

I look forward to pondering all my options. Whatever I choose today, the important factor is that it feels like play. Can't wait.

Randy Pausch (1960–2008), American professor and writer

JULY 23
Know the Futility of Worry

*Worry does not empty tomorrow of its sorrow,
it empties today of its strength.*

—Corrie ten Boom,
Clippings from My Notebook

Over five hundred years ago, during the French Renaissance, writer Michel de Montaigne, declared: "My life has been filled with terrible misfortune; most of which never happened." Many famous people have said something similar. That's because it's part of the human condition to worry – unless we decide to intentionally change that destructive habit. In the workplace, one common fear among today's employees is that they "aren't getting enough done" at work. Perhaps that's because so many workplaces reward exhaustion. Expectations cause people to worry they aren't good enough unless they are pushing themselves hard.

In 1948 Dale Carnegie wrote *How to Stop Worrying and Start Living*. Here's some of his advice, just as relevant today as when the book was first written, "Think of your life as an hourglass. You know there are thousands of grains of sand in the top...and they all pass slowly and evenly through the narrow neck in the middle. Nothing you or I could do would make more than one grain of sand pass through this narrow neck without impairing the hourglass. You and I and everyone else are like this hourglass...if we do not take [tasks] one at a time and let them pass...slowly and evenly, then we are bound to break our own...structure." Carnegie's guidance is that working at a relaxed, steady pace accomplishes the most and is best for us in the long run.

Today I will work at a productive pace, but not harder than is healthy for me.

Corrie ten Boom (1892–1983), Dutch watchmaker and writer

JULY 24
Claim My Qualities

There are no greater treasures than the highest human qualities such as compassion, courage and hope. Not even tragic accident or disaster can destroy such treasures of the heart.

—Daisaku Ikeda

Today is a good time to claim some more of my qualities. As a child I was told so often to be careful not to "blow my own horn." What I didn't understand then but do now, is that acknowledging myself is not the same thing as being conceited. When I appreciate myself, I'm not dependent on others in an unhealthy way. I don't need them to confirm that I'm ok. I get to do that for myself.

So today I am appreciating my kindness, my perseverance and my courage. What about you? What qualities are you claiming?

Daisaku Ikeda, Japanese philosopher and writer

JULY 25
Find the Best

*Treat people as if they were what they
ought to be and you help them to become
what they are capable of being.*

—Johann Wolfgang Von Goethe

I very much took Von Goethe's words to heart during the years I served as CEO of Dimensions Foundation. I made a commitment to myself to seek out and celebrate the strengths in each team member. I believed in them, sometimes more than they did themselves at first. Over the years, I got to watch people flourish. They sometimes surprised themselves with what they were able to do and be.

What I believe actually happened with some people was that I simply held a vision of their authentic selves for them until they could come into more awareness of all their gifts. Teachers can do this for students, too, and parents for children.

Today I commit to seeing people for who they truly are, even if they don't quite believe it yet themselves.

Johann Wolfgang Von Goethe (1749–1832), German poet, playwright, novelist, and scientist

JULY 26
Leave It Behind

*Write it on your heart. Finish every day
and be done with it.*

—Ralph Waldo Emerson

As I talk to family and friends, I so often hear, "I couldn't sleep very well last night because I was worried about..." Often their source of unease was something that had happened during the previous day. I understand that. I have also experienced some of those sleepless nights in the past. They sure aren't fun.

One of the best things I've done for myself, though, it to practice "finishing a day and being done with it," as Emerson recommends. That practice takes discipline. I must remind myself, firmly, "Worrying does NO good. It only makes you lose sleep and then you'll be less able to cope with anything tomorrow."

In order to let things go, here's what works for me: 1. Acknowledge what I'm thinking ("I hated how I made that presentation. It wasn't what I wanted.") 2. Feel the feelings fully ("I'm so mad at myself. I'm so disappointed. I'm so embarrassed.") 3. Let the feelings flow through me. (See Michael Singer's advice, June 8.) 4. Practice self-forgiveness. 5. Picture myself firmly closing the book on the day, knowing it's the very best thing for all concerned.

That's it. Over.

Today, and every day, I am writing it on my heart that as soon as a day is done, it is DONE.

Ralph Waldo Emerson (1803–1882), American essayist and philosopher

JULY 27
Eat Colorful Food

*The more colorful the food, the better.
I try to add color to my diet,
which means vegetables and fruits.*

—Misty May-Treanor

An easy way to eat a healthier diet is to simply add more colorful foods. The Rogel Cancer Center at the University of Michigan explains that colorful foods are rich in phytochemicals – or plant chemicals – that are beneficial in many ways, including fighting cancer. According to an article on their website, "Eating Rainbows" by Joan Daniels, R.D., and Nancy Burke, R.D., (*rogelcancercenter.org*), these are some of the best choices:

- Red: tomatoes, watermelon, pink grapefruit, guava, papaya, cranberries,
- Orange: carrots, mangos, cantaloupe, winter squash, sweet potatoes, pumpkins, apricots,
- Brown: beans, chickpeas, lentils,
- Green: broccoli, cabbage, bok choy, brussels sprouts,
- Purple: blueberries, eggplant, blackberries, prunes, plums, pomegranates, beets, purple cabbage.

Today, and every day from now on, I am choosing at least three foods off the "colorful" list. Want to join me?

Misty May-Treanor, American beach volleyball player

JULY 28
Make a Commitment to Myself

*Today the materials and skills from
which a life is composed are no longer clear.
It is no longer possible to follow the
paths of previous generations.*

—Mary Catherine Bateson,
Composing a Life

In her book referenced above, Mary Catherine Bateson (1939–2021), the daughter of Margaret Mead and Gregory Bateson, wrote that creating our own lives is like engaging in an improvisational art form. We can no longer simply repeat the way the last generation lived. Life is moving too fast, throwing too many twists and turns our way. She urges us to view our challenges, unexpected interruptions and conflicts as a source of wisdom. Those twists in life are what help us find the path that is right for us, if (and this is an important if) we make a commitment to ourselves above all else.

Bateson says we must realize that we can only be as good to someone else as we are to ourselves. Rather than viewing that focus on our own well-being as selfish, we can instead realize it to be essential. As they say on an airplane, we must first put on our own oxygen mask before we are able to help anyone else.

Today I am renewing my commitment to my own well-being. My happiness is worthy of my time and attention. If I hope to have anything to give to the world, my first task is to give to myself.

Mary Catherine Bateson (1939–2021), American writer and cultural anthropologist

JULY 29
Grow Hope through Action

Hope is often misunderstood. People tend to think that it is simply passive wishful thinking: I hope something will happen but I'm not going to do anything about it. This is indeed the opposite of real hope, which requires action and engagement.

–Jane Goodall,
The Book of Hope: A Survival Guide for Trying Times

Today, instead of feeling discouraged by the world's problems, I am choosing to do as Jane Goodall urges and focus on real hope, which comes through action and engagement. My first action is to consider HOW I'm showing up in the world, not just what I'm doing. Then my goal is to look for the next positive actions to take.

Mother Teresa said, "I will always attend a peace march but never an anti-war march." The energy of how we act is vital. I have learned that being against something only adds to the negativity in the world. To grow hope, I choose to focus on positive actions. What am I for? What positive qualities am I trying to nurture in the world?

Today I am pondering what my next action is going to be to add hope to the world.

Jane Goodall, English primatologist, anthropologist and writer

JULY 30
No Need to Ration Joy

> *If I had my life to live over...I would have burned the pink candle sculpted like a rose before it melted in storage...I would have eaten less cottage cheese and more ice cream.*
>
> —Erma Bombeck,
> *Eat Less Cottage Cheese and More Ice Cream:
> Thoughts on Life from Erma Bombeck*

Today I'm allowing myself to have all the joy I can muster. I'll not be rationing ice cream or naps or walks in the park. I'll do as much as I want of everything, trusting my body to know what I need. And if what I need is too much candy, well, for one day that's not the end of the world.

I declare today a "No Moderation Day." Once in a while we all need to dive into life with both feet, laughing and shouting and splashing with abandon.

Today is that day for me. I plan to enjoy it. I invite you to join me.

Erma Bombeck (1927–1996), American humorist and newspaper columnist

JULY 31
Quiet My Ego

*Ego is to the true self what a
flashlight is to a spotlight.*

—John Bradshaw

I've heard people say, "If I could only get rid of my ego, I'd be so much better off." Actually, no, without our egos we really couldn't function. According to a *Scientific American* article, "The Pressing Need to Quiet Our Egos," by Scott Barry Kaufman, we don't need to eliminate our egos, but simply learn how to keep them more in balance. He explains:

"In recent years, Heidi Wayment and her colleagues have been developing a 'quiet ego' research program grounded in Buddhist philosophy and humanistic psychology ideals, and backed by empirical research in the field of positive psychology. Paradoxically, it turns out that quieting the ego is so much more effective in cultivating well-being, growth, health, productivity, and a healthy, productive self-esteem, than focusing so loudly on self-enhancement.

To be clear, a quiet ego is not the same thing as a *silent* ego. Squashing the ego so much that it loses its identity entirely does not do yourself or the world any favors. Instead, the quiet ego perspective emphasizes *balance* and *integration*. As Wayment and colleagues put it, 'The volume of the ego is turned down so that it might listen to others as well as the self in an effort to approach life more humanely and compassionately.'"

Today I am helping my ego turn down its volume. I can find the balance between "what about me, me, me, me, ME?" and "It doesn't matter what I want as long as everyone else is happy." Between those two extremes, my quiet ego can still look out for my needs while keeping an awareness of other people's desires as well.

John Bradshaw (1933–2016), American educator, counselor, author

August

*August of another summer, and once again
I am drinking the sun, and the lilies again
are spread across the water.*

—Mary Oliver

Mary Oliver (1935–2019), American poet

AUGUST 1
Keep Myself Centered

In the midst of movement and chaos,
keep stillness inside of you.

—Deepak Chopra

Most mornings, whenever I can, I begin the day with what I think of as my centering time. I settle in on a cushy chair with a cup of coffee or tea and some soft music. I pick my quality cards for the day (see January 3), write in my gratitude journal (see January 4), and do some meditation (see May 15). Those three practices have been remarkably effective in helping me experience more calm and equanimity in my life. Even when I was working 40 plus hours each week, I made sure to get up early enough to have this time.

Earlier in my life, as a single mother with two small children, my mornings were such that I couldn't fit in this kind of practice. What I did instead was wake up a bit earlier than my children and read in bed for fifteen minutes. I chose books that sustained and uplifted. Even then I knew I needed some sort of centering practice in my day.

Today I am remembering how important it is to connect with the stillness inside. That calm center sustains me, no matter what may come my way today.

AUGUST 2
Find My Truth

Cheers to not quite knowing who you are anymore because you've stopped pretending to be what other people want or need you to be and are instead finally getting to know the truth of you.

—Lisa Olivera

I've done a lot of thinking over the years about who I am at my core; about what it means to be my most authentic self. I don't believe I've fully met her yet, and that's ok. Perhaps that is the work of our lifetimes, to eventually awaken to the realization of everything we truly are.

In a graduate class in spiritual psychology that I took, we were taught to journal with our "Inner Counselor," the wise part of ourselves that is always there but not always readily accessed. This journaling takes the form of a written dialogue where I ask questions and the Inner Counselor answers. I have found this practice remarkably helpful. At least once a week now I look forward to this time.

Today I am open to learning more about the truth of who I am. Cheers to no longer pretending to be what I think other people want me to be. Hurray for times that help me discover my truest self.

Lisa Olivera, American writer, therapist

AUGUST 3
It Takes Courage to Have Courage

*My courage and my bravery at a
young age was the thing I was bullied for,
a kind of 'Who do you think you are?'*

–Lady Gaga

I admire people who stand up for what they believe. I admire people who push boundaries in their careers, looking at things in new ways. And I admire people who are afraid to do something but do it anyway. US President Franklin Roosevelt said, "Courage is not the absence of fear but rather the assessment that something else is more important than fear."

There are countless examples of people who are bringing courage to the workplace in every setting imaginable. Here's just one: Early childhood educator, Nick Terrones, in his book, *A Can of Worms: Fearless Conversations with Toddlers*, writes about how he made the brave decision to lean into uncomfortable conversations with young children, instead of shifting back to "safe" subjects. He explains, "I want to stay true to my goals for children and myself, goals which are less about content-driven teaching and learning, or focusing on developmental skills, and more about practicing thinking about complex ideas and about becoming comfortable with uncertainty... This has been (and continues to be) a learning process for me. I've worked to feel comfortable with my own discomfort when complex issues come up in the classroom, and to be as compassionate with myself as I am with the children when I'm unsure how to respond."

Every day, in workplaces all over the globe, people make the decision to do something scary because they think it will bring positive change to our world. It's what keeps humanity moving forward, and it is worthy of huge celebration. Today I celebrate my own courage and the courage of so many who continually make the assessment that something is more important than fear.

Lady Gaga, professional name for Stefani Germanotta, American singer, songwriter, and actress

AUGUST 4
Say 'Yes' to Myself

*When you say 'yes' to others,
make sure you aren't saying
'no' to yourself.*

—Paulo Coelho

When I take stock of how many obligations I have made to others lately, I realize that if I'm not careful, I'll soon be on overload. I truly enjoy doing things for and with friends, family, and colleagues, but I can always feel the introvert part of me start to bristle when my alone time becomes dangerously short.

I love Paulo Coelho's admonition to consider whether saying "yes" to someone else is really saying "no" to myself. Sometimes it isn't. Sometimes I'm able to say yes in a way that works for me quite nicely. But if obligations become too much, I'll remember that when it's time to say no to someone else, that's really saying yes to me.

Today, and every day, I am considering carefully before I make commitments.

Paulo Coelho, Brazilian author and lyricist

AUGUST 5
Seven Types of Rest

Creating the culture of burnout is opposite to creating a culture of sustainable creativity.

—Arianna Huffington

An article by Saundra Dalton-Smith, M.D., on the website, *Ideas.Ted.Com*, is called, "The 7 types of rest that every person needs." Dalton-Smith's ideas hit home for me. Here's how she explains why it's important to understand our need for various kinds of rest:

"Have you ever tried to fix an ongoing lack of energy by getting more sleep — only to do so and *still* feel exhausted? If that's you, here's the secret: Sleep and rest are not the same thing, although many of us incorrectly confuse the two.

We go through life thinking we've rested because we have gotten enough sleep — but in reality we are missing out on the other types of rest we desperately need. The result is a culture of high-achieving, high-producing, chronically tired and chronically burned-out individuals. We're suffering from a rest deficit because we don't understand the true power of rest. Rest should equal restoration in seven key areas of your life."

So, for the next seven days I'm going to be focusing on the seven kinds of rest Dalton-Smith outlines, one per day. I look forward to finding new ways to support myself.

Today I begin the journey of learning to rest well. Of course, if I ever have a time where fatigue persists continually, even after trying all these ideas, I will not hesitate to consult my doctor.

AUGUST 6

Day One – Physical Rest

Passive physical rest includes sleeping and napping, while active physical rest means restorative activities such as yoga, stretching and massage therapy that help improve the body's circulation and flexibility.

—Saundra Dalton-Smith, M.D.,
"The 7 types of rest that every
person needs," *Ideas.Ted.Com*

Today I am considering all the ways I can rest my body physically. It's more than sleeping. As Saundra Dalton-Smith explains, practicing yoga, or simply spending time stretching is also restful for my body's physical health. Recently my husband John and I have learned about Qigong, a system of coordinated meditative movements and breathing. We enjoy watching YouTube videos where online instructors lead us through the actions. John has been told this type of exercise is helpful for his Parkinson's disease, but it's great for me, too. I consistently experience increased energy after a session.

Massages always leave me feeling wonderful, but I don't often remember to schedule them. Massage therapy schools offer very affordable appointments with their students, so that is a great option if budgets are tight. I plan to schedule one soon.

Today I am committing to providing my body with supportive ways to rest physically.

Saundra Dalton-Smith, M.D., American internal medicine physician and writer

AUGUST 7
Day Two — Mental Rest

*There can be no peace without
but through peace within.*

—W.E. Channing

When it feels impossible to turn off our nagging thoughts, then it's very likely we have a mental rest deficit. Having a mind that's constantly on overdrive is exhausting. I can tell this is happening to me when I wake up during the night with my mind racing. Saundra Dalton-Smith (see August 5) recommends, "Schedule short breaks to occur every two hours throughout your workday; these breaks can remind you to slow down. You might also keep a notepad by the bed to jot down any nagging thoughts that would keep you awake."

I have also found that scheduling even five minutes of meditation into my day can give me a mental rest. It also helps to check in with my internal self-talk. When I find myself in a loop of "shoulds," I can intentionally tune that chiding dialogue to a gentler channel.

Today I am paying attention to ways I help support my mental rest.

W.E. Channing (1780–1842), American Unitarian minister

AUGUST 8

Day Three — Sensory Rest

Bright lights, computer screens, background noise and multiple conversations — whether they're in an office or on Zoom calls — can cause our senses to feel overwhelmed.

—Saundra Dalton-Smith, M.D.,
"The 7 types of rest that every person needs," *Ideas.Ted.Com*

Fluorescent lights, loud sounds and blinking computer screens confront us in most workplaces. A blog called "3 Ways Lighting Affects Students in the Classroom (and What to Do About It)," on *alconlighting.com*, reported that, "Unfortunately, fluorescent light flickering is linked to not only lack of concentration among students, but also to mood." Studies in adult workplaces report similar adverse effects. If it's not immediately possible to replace fluorescent lights with LED lighting, which does not have the same issues, then simply turning off the fluorescents for stretches of time can be beneficial. Saundra Dalton-Smith urges that we take sensory breaks throughout the day by simply closing our eyes for a few minutes every once in a while.

Today I am paying attention to how much my senses are being bombarded by light and noise. I am taking sensory breaks by walking outdoors when I can, meditating for a few minutes if possible, or simply closing my eyes every so often.

Saundra Dalton-Smith, M.D., American internal medicine physician and writer

AUGUST 9

Day Four — Creative Rest

*The desire to create is one of the
deepest yearnings of the human soul.*

–Dieter F. Uchtdorf

For anyone who spends a great deal of time brainstorming new ideas, solving problems, or producing creative products, it's imperative to find time for creative rest. Spending time in the beauty of nature is one of the best ways to recharge creative batteries. But there's more.

Saundra Dalton-Smith, M.D. (see August 5) explains that "creative rest isn't simply about appreciating nature; it also includes enjoying the arts. Turn your workspace into a place of inspiration by displaying images of places you love and works of art that speak to you. You can't spend 40 hours a week staring at blank or jumbled surroundings and expect to feel passionate about anything, much less come up with innovative ideas."

Children need to learn in classrooms that are thoughtfully curated to include beauty and order. They can be their best creative selves within these surroundings. The same holds true for adult work spaces.

Today I commit to finding some ways to experience creative rest. I am planning a walk in a beautiful spot, and I'll take a look at my work space. I think some time spent to move it from jumbled to serene will be very helpful.

Dieter F. Uchtdorf, German aviator

AUGUST 10

Day Five — Emotional Rest

Half of the troubles of this life can be traced to saying yes too quickly and not saying no soon enough.

—Josh Billings

If we're the person everyone depends on, or the one people call whenever they need a favor, or the people-pleaser who has a hard time saying no, we are probably in need of emotional rest. To give ourselves a break, we can practice expressing our feelings and needs more honestly. We can respond with an honest "no" rather than a reluctant "yes" so as "not to hurt feelings."

Today I am remembering that I do not need to "earn" love by people-pleasing. That's not real love anyway if I have to get it by betraying myself. My needs matter just as much as anyone else's. And "no" is not a dirty word.

Josh Billings (1818–1885), pen name for Henry Wheeler Shaw, American humor writer and lecturer

AUGUST 11

Day Six — Social Rest

If you're in need of emotional rest, you probably have a social rest deficit too. This occurs when we fail to differentiate between those relationships that revive us from those relationships that exhaust us. To experience more social rest, surround yourself with positive and supportive people.

—Saundra Dalton-Smith, M.D.,
"The 7 types of rest that every
person needs," *Ideas.Ted.Com*

It's important to be able to admit that some people drain my energy while others invigorate me. That doesn't mean I don't like, or even love the people who drain me. What I think it means is that I have very different styles and personality types than some of my friends or relatives, and that's okay.

On the other hand, there are some people who are consistently negative, and choose to always see the glass as half empty. Those are the people I know I have to limit time with because I end up feeling very depleted if I'm around them too much.

Today I am getting very honest with myself about the people in my life who revive me and the ones who exhaust me. I can make choices about how I spend my time accordingly.

Saundra Dalton-Smith, M.D., American internal medicine physician and writer

AUGUST 12
Day Seven — Spiritual Rest

Begin doing what you want to do now.
We are not living in eternity. We have only
this moment, sparkling like a star in our
hand and melting like a snowflake.

—Marie Beynon Ray,
How Never to Be Tired

When I go long periods of time without experiencing a sense of purpose or enjoying a strong feeling of love and belonging, then I know I am in need of spiritual rest. So many of the ideas I am writing about in this book have helped me find spiritual renewal. But I know when I spend too many days not "doing what I want to do now," as Marie Beynon Ray puts it, then I'm in danger of suffering some spiritual fatigue.

Listening to what my spirit is calling me to do and honoring that call is the best way I know to combat spiritual exhaustion. Today I am encouraging myself to spend at least a little time on those pursuits that really make my heart sing. (See tomorrow, August 13, for some ideas of how to connect with spiritual purpose.)

Marie Beynon Ray (1886–1969), American writer

AUGUST 13
What is My Entelechy?

*Everybody is a genius. But if you judge
a fish by its ability to climb a tree, it will
live its whole life believing that it is stupid.*

—Albert Einstein

Scholar, author, philosopher and teacher, Jean Houston, in her book, *A Mythic Life*, describes the concept of *entelechy*, "a Greek word meaning the dynamic purpose that drives us toward realizing our essential self, that gives us our higher destiny and the capacities and skills that our destiny needs for its unfolding. It is the entelechy of an acorn to be an oak tree. It is the entelechy of a popcorn kernel to be a fully popped entity. And it is the entelechy of a human being to be...."

That is the question each of us must answer for ourselves. What is our entelechy? What is unpopped in us that needs to burst forth? The key to finding out what is uniquely ours is to resist comparing ourselves to anyone else. Otherwise we will end up feeling like the fish Einstein describes who feels inadequate for its inability to climb trees.

I believe part of my entelechy is to be an encourager. Writing this book helps me express that drive to support others; to bring some hope into the world. I can feel when I am in the flow of that "dynamic purpose" Jean Houston writes about because the words flow almost without effort. I write without worrying about how my thoughts will be received; what matters is to record what wants to be expressed.

Today I am honoring my entelechy and trusting the process of being true to my own unfolding. I support you in discovering your own entelechy.

Albert Einstein (1879–1955), German-born theoretical physicist

AUGUST 14

Brain and Heart

*Only when our clever brain and our
human heart work together in harmony
can we achieve our true potential.*

—Jane Goodall

Rachel Naomi Remen's book, *Kitchen Table Wisdom*, mostly shares stories about her cancer patients, but one of the most powerful is about herself and how she learned to value both her head and heart. As a young professor she was invited to participate in a research project at the Esalen Institute. Once a month she met with influential thinkers such as Abraham Maslow, Gregory Bateson and Joseph Campbell. With these brilliant scholars she discussed radical new perspectives on the practice of medicine. Remen soon began to suffer panic attacks before each Esalen visit. When she set up a meeting, attempting to resign, the wise project director asked if she wouldn't like to understand what the panic was about, urging Remen to close her eyes and allow any image to emerge. Remen saw a flat, white rectangle, declaring, "It's a business card." "Are you sure?" the director questioned, urging an open mind to other interpretations.

Days later Remen again saw the rectangle, but this time it began to puff up. She began to feel panic, but then an insight emerged. "The white rectangle was not a business card at all. It was a marshmallow that had been subjected to a steady external pressure for many, many years... But now, this pressure had been released. Its shape was changing and it was terrified. But the marshmallow was not dying, it was returning to itself." Remen explains that her very academic family held only contempt for "the non rational." The free thinkers at Esalen were affecting her deeply. "Their willingness to entertain questions that were larger than the available tools of research, had begun to release the pressure that had held me in a shape that was not my own...Although I could be analytical and pragmatic, by nature I was an intuitive, even a mystic."

Jane Goodall, English primatologist, anthropologist and writer

AUGUST 15
My Actions Speak

*What you do speaks so loudly
I cannot hear what you are saying.*

—Ralph Waldo Emerson

I can't help but think that every politician should read these lines and take them to heart. Then again, the same holds true for me. I can talk all I want about noble ideas, but if I don't live them, then my words are pretty hollow.

Today I am thinking about the parts of my life where there's a disconnect between what I do and what I say. The reality, really, is that none of us does anything perfectly all the time, even if we wish we could. I write a lot about positive self-talk, but there are still some days I'm awfully mean to myself. I can imagine the little girl inside me saying, "You're not practicing what you preach." True, but that doesn't mean I won't keep trying.

I am doing my best today to sync up my words and actions, but I'm granting myself grace for those times I can't quite do it.

Ralph Waldo Emerson (1803–1882), American essayist and philosopher

AUGUST 16
Remember Those Who Help Me

We don't accomplish anything in this world alone and whatever happens is the result of the whole tapestry of one's life and all the weavings of individual threads from one to another that create something.

—Sandra Day O'Connor

Today I am thinking of all the people in my life — so many — who helped me when I was younger, in so many situations, and those who help me now. I realize some of the people who gave me the most were ones I thought of as "difficult" at the time. They often pushed me to learn from my mistakes or clarify my values so I didn't take paths that weren't right for me. And of course there have always been delightful mentors and friends who believed in me through it all.

I think it's a good practice to stop every so often and give thanks for the support I've had throughout my life — and continue to have. I love the imagery of a tapestry where each person has contributed a thread that weaves its way through the strong garment that now wraps me.

Today I am grateful for all those who have warmed me along life's journey.

Sandra Day O'Connor, first female United States Supreme Court justice

AUGUST 17

Value Impermanence

> *We need to learn to appreciate the value of impermanence. If we are in good health and are aware of impermanence, we will take good care of ourselves. When we know that the person we love is impermanent, we will cherish our beloved all the more.*
>
> —Thich Nhat Hanh,
> *The Pocket Thich Nhat Hanh*

Thich Nhat Hanh's quote has been true for me when it comes to the people in my life, and also when applied to material objects. A few years back as my husband and I prepared to sell the home we'd lived in for thirty years, where our children grew up and our grandchildren loved to visit, I had to face the challenge of impermanence. I would be "losing" not only my beloved home, but many of the possessions I'd enjoyed for years, including my beloved piano. We were giving it to the new homeowner's children. That felt good, but still I grieved. My first task in learning to truly accept – and ultimately appreciate – impermanence, was the hardest: coming to terms with my own mortality. It feels easier sometimes to pretend we just might be immortal. What helped me get beyond that irrational denial was slowly coming into balance with life's rhythms and finding beauty in them. I could see the rightness in passing our home on to a young couple who would love it as we had, including my piano. I began to think of packing up our home as a meditation in liberation from greed, ego and small-spiritedness.

Slowly I fell in love with the part of me that could say, "I've had my turn and now it's time for someone else." Doing this not as a martyr but as a generous person felt great. That lesson carried over into other parts of my life. When it was time for me to retire from a job I loved, I could hand over the CEO reins to my successor with joy and excitement for her future...and mine. Today I celebrate the many gifts of impermanence.

Thich Nhat Hanh (1926–2022), Vietnamese Buddhist monk, peace activist, author and teacher

AUGUST 18

Cultivate a New Quality

*What we cultivate internally,
we pass that on to the world.*

—Purvi Raniga

While it's supportive to keep acknowledging the positive qualities I claim as mine, I think it's also healthy to sometimes cultivate a new one. In my set of quality cards, I can look at "Kindness," "Generosity" or "Humor" and allow that those are traits I have. But I keep looking at the word "Risking" and passing it by, thinking, "Ick, why is that even considered a good quality? I don't like it." But today I decided to think more about how being a risk-taker could be positive.

To be honest, I actually have taken a number of risks throughout my career, but I like to think they were smart ones, and I only took them because I thought it was the right thing to do. I certainly never LIKED taking risks. At least I don't think I did. I know it was risk-taking that kept the work moving forward and interesting. It's what brought new ideas to fruition and allowed us to support more children, families and educators in better ways. So...

Hmmm. Perhaps "Risking" simply means being open to trying things with uncertain outcomes. Still seems a bit scary, but I would like to be able to do that with less resistance and more trust.

Ok. Deep breath. Today I am choosing "Risking" as one of my qualities. I plan to keep nurturing it until I feel I can really claim it. What quality might you like to begin cultivating today?

Purvi Raniga, author, United Kingdom

AUGUST 19
A Compassionate Definition of Health and Healing

> *If there is a single definition of healing it is to enter with mercy and awareness those pains, mental and physical, from which we have withdrawn in judgment and dismay.*
>
> —Stephen Levine,
> *A Year to Live: How to Live This Year as If It Were Your Last*

One of the issues I have with the positive psychology movement is that sometimes it feels like we are being shamed for having any medical issues. Surely with enough positive thinking we can keep ourselves completely healthy, the "you create your own reality" writers seem to imply.

I certainly believe our thoughts influence us in many ways, but I also believe it is harmful and inaccurate to say that all health challenges are somehow a result of faulty thinking. Stephen Levine, in his book referenced above, invites us to adopt a new way of viewing illness and healing. He encourages making peace with our "pains, mental and physical" so that we might stop judging them (and ourselves). Rather, Levine invites us to consider that there are many forms of health and many ways to heal.

Often there are gifts to be discovered when we are able to stop judging our physical illness so we can come into acceptance and cooperation with whatever action steps we can take. This has certainly been the case for my husband John and me as we deal with his Parkinson's diagnosis (see July 1).

Today I am recognizing how important it is to view "with mercy and awareness" any physical or mental affliction that I may have previously been judging.

Stephen Levine (1937–2016), American poet, author and teacher

AUGUST 20

Find Magic

The greatest secrets are always hidden in the most unlikely places. Those who don't believe in magic will never find it.

—Roald Dahl

Today I'm on the lookout for magic. Not the kind found in *Harry Potter* books, but the magic made by nature, by human connection, by love.

Our world has so much magic in it, but many of us don't much notice it. When children come into the world, they see it. But it's not long before they become as oblivious to it as the rest of us.

I remember one Fall day when my husband and I were with our then two-year-old granddaughter, Sylvie, at a nearby park. A huge gust of wind swept up suddenly, bringing with it a shower of golden leaves that danced around all of us, but especially Sylvie. She stood stock still, arms reaching for the sky, looking up with an expression of sheer delight, her whole body a celebration of enchantment. She stayed that way for many minutes, letting the leaves dance through her hair, alight on her shoulders and rest at her feet. I turned to my husband. "Wow," was all I could think to say. I'm really not sure I would have noticed the magic if I'd been there alone. Sylvie felt it in a visceral way, and because she did, we did also.

Since that time, whenever I walk around the block by my home on an Autumn day, I make a point to stroll by a tree with beautiful golden leaves. Once in a while, if I'm lucky, I'm there on a windy day just when the leaves take flight, and I stand like Sylvie, arms up, letting the magic transport me.

Today I am ready for more magic. I wonder what I'll find. I wonder what you'll find.

Roald Dahl (1916–1990), British novelist

AUGUST 21

Stains and Wrinkles Are a Good Sign

Our wrinkles are our medals of the passage of life.

—Lauren Hutton

I find it very sad when anyone feels the need to pretend to be younger than they are, as if age is a shameful thing. In my seventh decade, I am grateful for all the experiences that have brought me to a place where I feel more peace and contentment than ever. I can honestly say that once I let go of the "need to be young," I've experienced each new decade as more joyful than the one before. The soft wrinkles and white hairs I notice feel like friendly reminders of a meaningful life.

I have gratefully adopted an attitude that celebrates wrinkles and stains. I see them as indications of a life well-lived. I wouldn't want to have immaculate furniture because the subtle stains I notice remind me of exuberant times with my granddaughters. The "good" dishes with cracks bring me joy because they announce that we choose to live our lives exuberantly – with family dinners that value connecting with loved ones more than curating pristine dishware.

Today I am reminding myself that perfection is overrated (and impossible). A life with no stains or wrinkles would be a pretty bleak one.

Lauren Hutton, American model

AUGUST 22
Stop Measuring My Worth

Your worth is determined by you, not the judgmental measuring cups of a fickle world.

—Katie St. Claire

I've noticed lately that there are a lot of numbers in my life that are meant to assess if I'm okay or not — my weight, my age, my blood pressure, my credit score, my bank account...even my Wordle score. Now all of these measures are certainly useful in some way. But it's important to get very clear about the fact that they do not define my worth, in the same way that children's scores on standardized tests don't define theirs

In my book, *Heart-Centered Teaching Inspired by Nature*, I wrote: "I believe one of the most detrimental aspects of our current educational system is the over-emphasis on point-in-time measurements. While these ways of assessing learning have their place, the unintended consequence of over-emphasizing them has been to confuse us into thinking the real goal of education is the score on a test. Of course, the real goal of education is to help students become motivated and capable lifelong learners who will help move humanity forward in positive ways. Imagine how our schools would change if every student arrived each day looking forward to the joy of ongoing learning."

And imagine how our adult lives would change if we put less emphasis on our measurements and more on our imaginations, or our loving, or our service. Don't get me wrong. I want to know my blood pressure and my credit score. I just want to remember that there's a whole lot more to me than that.

Today I am remembering what is most important in life, and those are usually things that can't be given a number.

AUGUST 23

Get the Facts

*Everyone is entitled to their own opinion,
but not their own facts.*

—Daniel Patrick Moynihan

For years my brother was a newspaper reporter for the Kansas City Star. Quite a while ago he began expressing concern for the lack of journalistic integrity on the internet. Anyone could post anything and call it fact, even if it wasn't. He said we'd all be in trouble if no one knew what to believe anymore. I'm afraid that day has come.

My promise to myself is that I am going to get my news from reputable sources that have trained reporters who studied journalistic integrity at reputable journalism schools. My brother taught me about the necessity of having multiple credible sources before a story could run. Once the story was published, people were free to have their own opinions about what was happening, but no one used to question the basic facts of the report.

Today I am considering carefully where I find news. It is my hope that we humans can discover a way to agree on facts, while allowing everyone to have individual opinions about how they feel about those facts.

Daniel Patrick Moynihan (1977–2001), American politician

AUGUST 24
Give a 20-Second Hug

A hug a day keeps the demons at bay.

—German proverb

An article, "Reasons Why You Need at Least 8 Hugs a Day," on the *happify.com* website, lists these benefits of hugging:

- Hugging is Heart Healthy.
- Hugging Reduces Stress Naturally.
- Hugging Babies Helps Them Become Well-Adjusted Adults.
- Hugging is Important for Adults, Too, To Combat Lonely Feelings.
- Hugging Can Regenerate Muscles.
- Hugging Can Make You a More Mindful and Present Person.
- Hugging Can Minimize Fears.
- Hugging for Longer Periods of Time is Better for the Body.

The article quotes a study that provides evidence that when people hug for 20 seconds or more, the hormone oxytocin (the "feel-good" hormone) is released, which then boosts the immune system and reduces stress.

Today I am on the lookout for opportunities to give and receive hugs (with permission, of course). I am eager to try out some 20-second hugs.

AUGUST 25

Hot Showers or Baths Are Good for Me

There is no problem on earth that can't be ameliorated by a hot bath and a cup of tea.

—Jasper Fforde

Could it be that taking a hot bath or shower might be just as beneficial as exercise? "Yes," say researchers at Loughborough University in the UK. Steve Faulkner, research associate at Loughborough, in his article, "A hot bath has benefits similar to exercise," on The Conversation website, *theconversation.com*, reports:

"Water immersion resulted in a greater increase in body temperature compared with exercise, as well as a greater reduction in average arterial blood pressure. This is important, as a reduction in blood pressure is closely associated with a reduced risk of developing heart disease. This study points to the promising effect that may result from passive heating. It also suggests some of the cardiovascular effects of passive heating may be comparable with those of exercise...[and] there is evidence to suggest that there may be beneficial metabolic effects as well – such as better control of blood sugar."

Now we know. Passive heating, which means soaking in a hot tub, or taking a warm bath or shower, is not only relaxing, it's good for our health.

Today seems like a good time for me to relax in a bubble bath.

Jasper Fforde, English novelist

AUGUST 26
Let Emotions Flow Through

Life is your seesaw. You may not stay balanced long, but you can aim for a high after every low.

—Sanita Belgrave, M.D.

When my emotions seem difficult to manage, it helps me to remember the ebb and flow of life. When I'm experiencing a "down" time, I remind myself that right around the corner there will inevitably be an "up" time. Accepting this "seesaw" of feelings keeps me from fighting against it.

"We are fragile creatures, and it is from this weakness, not despite it, that we discover the possibility of pure joy," write the Dalai Lama, Desmond Tutu and Douglas Abrams in their *New York Times* bestseller, *The Book of Joy: Lasting Happiness in a Changing World*. That quote reminds me that without the down times, the up times wouldn't feel half as sweet.

Today I accept the ups and downs of life as inevitable and even beneficial.

AUGUST 27
In Praise of Care

Care is an ethic. Care is a moral code by which we live our lives. Care shines a light on life's path — illuminating our shared dependency as our strength through each step of the way.

—Carol Garboden Murray

Carol Garboden Murray, the author of a beautiful book, *Illuminating Care: The Pedagogy and Practice of Care in Early Childhood Communities*, has written about the concept of care at all phases of life. She explains, "It will take courage to challenge the notion that care is subordinate to education or that care is women's work and a private family matter. It will take courage to lift care from an association with weakness and fragility and align care with strength and power. It will take courage to free care from gender roles, and make care attractive to men and women, to all people, and to position care as a human right and a public good." Her description of the nobility of care is moving to me. The care we provide for children at the beginning of life and for loved ones at the end has often been undervalued. Somehow in our society many of us have picked up the mistaken notion that we should be able to care for children and elderly parents without missing a beat back at the job.

When my own mother died, I was with her, but within three hours I was back at work at an "important" meeting I didn't feel I could cancel. Looking back, I'm sad I didn't allow myself the very human need to grieve uninterrupted. I can't imagine my colleagues being upset with me for missing a meeting because of my mother's passing. What societal messages, I wonder, make us deny our need to take time for caregiving — at any stage of life? It's time for new messages.

Today I am celebrating caregiving in every phase, and encouraging others to do the same.

Carol Garboden Murray, American educator and author

AUGUST 28
Set an Intention of Calm

Everything we do is infused with the energy with which we do it. If we're frantic, life will be frantic. If we're peaceful, life will be peaceful.

—Marianne Williamson

I have found Marianne Williamson's quote to be one that can calm me down when I find myself feeling frantic. She is so right. In scary or challenging situations, the more I am able to take a deep breath and find a feeling of calm inside, the better I am able to deal with anything that comes my way.

In my role as CEO of Dimensions Foundation for years, I was very aware that in moments of challenge, people were taking their cues from me about how to react. When I stayed calm and focused, so did they. If I let myself fall into "pushing, frantic, hectic" energy, then I started to feel that all around me.

Today I am setting an intention to keep a calm center. I can stay in peaceful energy no matter what the world brings to me.

Marianne Williamson, American author, speaker

AUGUST 29

Learn Something New Today

Change is inevitable. Growth is optional.

—John C. Maxwell

Today I am going to remember the fun of learning new things. Change happens whether we like it or not, so embracing growth as a part of change makes life a lot more interesting. Here's an example:

John and I live in a complex of individual townhouses that are cared for by a management company. One of the reasons we picked the place we live was because of the beautiful view of five scotch pine trees. Over the last year, one by one each tree has died because of a fungus that attacks those kinds of trees.

I can't pretend I haven't been sad to lose such beauty, but I have used all my skills to cope. I remind myself of impermanence as a way of life and that helps. I remember to let emotions flow through me so the sadness doesn't get trapped inside. And I think about how this change can be an opportunity to learn and grow.

My husband asked to meet with the management company of our complex to make a plan for replacing our much-loved trees, but first we did some research about some good options for tree replanting. It was helpful to learn something new (like how many kinds of pine trees there actually are) and to be able to take a positive action in the face of a disappointing situation.

Today I am remembering that with every change comes an opportunity to learn and grow – if I choose to look for it.

John C. Maxwell, American author

AUGUST 30

Reach Out to Others

*Never underestimate the lingering effects
of a dash of spontaneous comfort.*

–Gina Greenlee,
*Postcards and Pearls: Life Lessons
from Solo Moments on the Road*

One of the unfortunate effects of living through a global pandemic is that we all learned to view each other with some level of suspicion. "Will that person be the one who infects me? I've got to stay far away." That distancing from each other was necessary, and the worrying was understandable, but I fear it carried over into other areas besides health concerns. Has it made us look at each other with more distrust than we used to? Is it one of the reasons our politics have become so contentious?

It's time I focus on more genuine appreciation for strangers as fellow human beings. Here are my intentions: I am smiling at people in line with me at the grocery store. I am striking up a conversation with the cashier, asking how they are and genuinely wanting to know. I am giving out spontaneous compliments.

Today I am encouraging the best in myself to connect with the best in others. I look forward to moments of mutual "spontaneous comfort." We all could use more of that.

Gina Greenlee, American author, speaker, teacher

AUGUST 31

How is My Vulnerability My Strength?

*To speak up for wounded children,
I claimed my truest voice. My greatest
vulnerability became my greatest strength.*

—Holly Elissa Bruno,
*Happiness is Running Through
the Streets to Find You*

James Hillman is a psychologist who has taught at places such as Yale University and the University of Chicago. He is also the author of a number of books, including one I've just reread called *The Soul's Code: In Search of Character and Calling.* He explains his reason for writing this particular book: "Because the 'traumatic' view of early years so controls psychological theory of personality and its development...the language of our personal storytelling [has] already been infiltrated by the toxins of these theories... We are, this book shall maintain, less damaged by the traumas of childhood than by the traumatic way we remember childhood as a time of unnecessary and externally caused calamities that wrongly shaped us."

Hillman asserts that if we focus too much on our challenges, we lose sight of "what must be recovered: a sense of personal calling...a feeling that there is a reason my unique person is here." He tells stories of people whose difficult early years later turned out to hold unexpected gifts that led to their contributions to the world. As Holly Elissa Bruno explains in the quote above, her greatest strength came from using her childhood hurts to become a strong advocate for vulnerable children.

Today I am pondering whether areas of my life I have written off as "difficult" might also contain seeds of strength I've overlooked. Tonight I intend to journal more about this.

Holly Elissa Bruno, American author and speaker

September

There is a clarity about September. On clear days, the sun seems brighter, the sky more blue, the white clouds take on marvelous shapes; the moon is a wonderful apparition, rising gold, cooling to silver; and the stars are so big.

—Faith Baldwin

Faith Baldwin (1893–1978), American writer

SEPTEMBER 1

What Can Be Learned from Labor Day?

All labor that uplifts humanity has dignity.

—Martin Luther King Jr.

September is the month that contains the US holiday, Labor Day. Wikipedia describes its meaning this way, "Labor Day is a federal holiday in the United States celebrated on the first Monday in September to honor and recognize the American labor movement and the works and contributions of laborers to the development and achievements of the United States."

It seems to me that this holiday can help us remember how each of us is inextricably dependent on others who work at jobs that support the common good, no matter where we live in the world. How often do I remember to thank the people whose lives make mine easier? The sad truth is not at all often enough, but that can be changed.

Here is my list of people I plan to thank soon – either through emails or thank-you cards:
- The nurses who worked over holidays when my husband was in the hospital having surgery;
- The people who deliver groceries to our home when we are unable to make it to the store;
- The librarians who knowledgeably and patiently advise about new books at our local library;
- The skillful early care professionals who provide loving experiences for our granddaughter;
- The servers at restaurants who do their very best, even on days there is a staff shortage.

I could go on and on, but I'll start with these. I'm wondering who might be on your list.

Martin Luther King Jr. (1929–1968), American minister and civil rights activist

SEPTEMBER 2
Pay Attention to My Uplifters

Who do you spend time with? Criticizers or encouragers? Surround yourself with those who believe in you. Your life is too important for anything less.

—Steve Goodier

In earlier parts of my life, I found myself trying very hard to win the favor of people who chose to look at life with a negative bent. Quite frankly, this was exhausting. Now I know that I am happier and healthier when I spend more time with people I call "uplifters."

They are the folks who want to know the real me. Who don't expect me to be perfect. Who are sympathetic to my mistakes and help me think through how I can grow from them. When I get to choose how I'll spend my time, it's always going to be in the company of those uplifters.

Today I am grateful for the people in my life who warm my heart. Who are your uplifters?

Steve Goodier, English writer

SEPTEMBER 3
Enjoy a Simple Pleasure — a Great Beverage

There's not a man, woman or child on the face of the earth who doesn't enjoy a tasty beverage.

–David Letterman

Today I am treating myself to something hot and cozy to drink, or maybe something cold and refreshing. Who knows; I might choose to have both. The key is to remember to savor this simple pleasure.

No matter what else is happening in my life, I always feel nurtured if I take a moment to hold my morning mug of coffee or tea with both hands, feeling the warmth and inhaling the fragrant steam. If I've gone for a long walk on a hot day, nothing beats a glass of ice cold water, except maybe a cold beer.

Once when I was feeling pretty sad, I heated some milk and grated in real chocolate that melted into decadent goodness. I'm not usually much of a chocolate fan, but somehow that creamy hot comfort was just what I needed.

Today I am remembering that simple pleasures are not insignificant, and relishing them makes my life much better.

David Letterman, American television host

SEPTEMBER 4
Do Something to Be of Service

*The best way to find yourself is to lose
yourself in the service of others.*

—Mahatma Gandhi

A few years ago I was on a densely packed bus that was taking sightseers to a high point in Zion National Park. It was standing room only and I was one of the standers. As the bus rounded a curve, I started to lose my balance and a man nearby reached over and held me upright. When I thanked him, he said, "It was my pleasure. Whenever I can do something to be of service for someone else, it's a good day."

I've always remembered his words, but some days I forget to take all the focus off myself and look for ways to be a bright spot in someone else's life. So today I'm remembering how good service feels, and finding opportunities large and small to put it into practice.

Mahatma Gandhi (1869–1948), Indian lawyer, political ethicist, leader of the non-violent campaign for India's independence from British rule

SEPTEMBER 5

Try Some Evening Appreciations

Self appreciation is a sign of maturity.

—Sivaprakash Sidhu

In my book, *Heart-Centered Teaching Inspired by Nature*, I wrote, "I invite you to begin collecting ideas for healthy ways to celebrate life 'just because.' You might want to try out one of your ideas at least once a week." I then provided some suggestions to get people started. Since writing that book awhile ago, I realize that my thinking has undergone a subtle change. Sure, it's still good to celebrate life by choosing something fun to do. In fact, I highly recommend it. But I've learned another way to celebrate that can be done daily. I call it "Evening Appreciations." I'll explain. If you live with someone else and they agree to participate, then find a moment at the end of the day to share appreciation together. When my husband and I do this, we begin with ourselves and then the other person. It might sound like this:

- **Nancy:** "One thing I appreciate about myself is that I spent time enjoying the sunrise this morning. One thing I appreciate about you is that you brought me a cup of coffee this morning."
- **John:** "One thing I appreciate about myself is that I enjoy reading about new subjects. One thing I appreciate about you is that you listen to me tell you what I'm learning."
- **Nancy:** "One thing I appreciate about myself is that I kept my cool when someone cut me off in traffic today. One thing I appreciate about you is that you love taking walks in nature with me."

You get the idea. We've found three rounds to be just right. Honestly, it felt a little hokey at first, but once we got over ourselves, we started to experience a lift every night. During times I'm home alone, I like to say my appreciations out loud to myself. It felt weird at first; now I like it. Today, I am celebrating how focusing on what's working is such a great antidote to negativity.

Sivaprakash Sidhu, Indian actor, author

SEPTEMBER 6

Take a Deep Breath

I've learned that you can tell a lot about a person by the way he/she handles these three things: a rainy day, lost luggage, and tangled Christmas tree lights.

—Maya Angelou

There are many things in life that I understand to be only annoyances, not tragedies. I think of these as "deep breath moments." If someone is unreasonably upset about lost luggage, then I know they are reacting to something much deeper than the situation at hand. I think we are seeing so many more examples of public "bad behavior" these days because we haven't quite figured out how to deal with the ongoing effects of unusual stressors such as...Covid, severe weather, wars, financial challenges, political unrest...choose one or all of the above.

No one has offered a "wise voice" to all of us, explaining that we will probably feel angrier or sadder than usual. And no wise voice has told us we should be proud of ourselves for living through one of the most unsettling times humans have faced in years.

Today if I face a deep breath moment, I will stop and remind myself it is only an annoyance. If I feel my blood pressure skyrocketing, I will talk calmly to myself until I regain my equilibrium. Here is what I might say, "Wow, you have faced so many challenges over the last few years. Now this challenge feels really bad, too, but it actually isn't. It is simply annoying, not dangerous. Take a deep breath and remember that you have the skills to deal with (that luggage, the unexpected rain, or those tangled lights). This will pass soon and you will be ok."

Today I am the "wise voice" for myself that I've been needing for quite some time.

Maya Angelou (1928–2014), American writer, poet and civil rights activist

SEPTEMBER 7

Perfection is Overrated

Perfection is overrated, boring. It's the imperfections — the vulnerabilities, the weaknesses, the human elements — that make us who we are, that make us real, beautiful... necessary.

—Guy Harrison,
Agents of Chaos

I'm a recovering perfectionist. Most of the time I can keep from jumping down the rabbit hole of self-criticism by remembering that perfection is the enemy of excellence. Usually that works. But today I just dove down that hole before I could stop myself. I woke up feeling foggy and not quite myself, with a slight headache. I knew I had a Zoom call to do soon, but didn't double check the time. It was a meeting I was quite looking forward to, with people I admire. The work we do together to bring more equity to children from diverse populations is gratifying. I don't see them often, and was happy for a chance to connect. I decided to get some coffee, curl up in a blanket, hoping a few minutes of calm would clear my head. When I finally checked the time of my meeting, I realized to my horror that it had begun two minutes ago. I jumped up, splashed my face with water and threw on a random sweater over my pajama top. I apologized for being late, looked at my disheveled hair on the Zoom screen and cringed inside. I tried to remain focused, but the internal critical spiral had already begun to spin out of control. I did my best to be present, but was distracted by the shaming going on inside.

After the call, it took me a while to regain my equilibrium. I reminded myself, "No one is perfect; I forgive myself for expecting unattainable perfection." Then I started to laugh about the crazy sweater and spiky hair. Not one of my best looks. Ah well. I suspect my colleagues still like me. The important thing is that I still like my less-than-perfect but very human self. Today I remember that perfectionism is actually quite boring and vastly overrated.

SEPTEMBER 8
Thank Five People Today

*Appreciation can change a day,
even change a life. Your willingness to
put it into words is all that is necessary.*

—Margaret Cousins

One of my favorite ways to get myself going in the morning is to create some kind of "game" to play during the day. Today my game will be a challenge to see if I can find five people to sincerely thank.

What I suspect is that being on the lookout for reasons to thank people will help me notice the positivity all around me. It is true that we often find what we expect to see. I am certain that I often overlook opportunities to express gratitude. I love to think that Margaret Cousins could be right and that some appreciation expressed could even change a life.

I'm excited to see who I can find to thank today. I'm eager to get going. Want to join me?

Margaret Cousins (1878–1954), Irish-Indian author

SEPTEMBER 9

Celebrate Art

Before a child talks, they sing.
Before they write, they draw.
As soon as they stand, they dance.
Art is fundamental to human expression.

—Phylicia Rashad

Young children begin creating art with joyful abandon. In the beginning, no one says, "I can't do it," or, "I'm not good enough." Only when our society's sense of comparison and competition begin to interfere with children's innate delight in creation do those negative feelings start to appear. Wouldn't it be wonderful if we could all go back to our earliest selves who sang, drew and danced with abandon? Maybe we can.

Today I am allowing myself to enjoy some artistic expression in any way I'd like. I am remembering there is absolutely no way I could possibly do it "wrong."

Phylicia Rashad, American actress and dean of the College of Fine Arts at Howard University

SEPTEMBER 10

Just Take a Step

*It's worth remembering that it is often
the small steps, not the giant leaps,
that bring about the most lasting change.*

—Queen Elizabeth II

My daughter asked me a surprising question the other night. We were outside enjoying beautiful summer weather and a nice glass of Chardonnay. I was telling her about how my husband and I were experiencing retirement, he from Arbor Day Foundation; me from Dimensions Foundation. That's when she looked at me quizzically and asked, "How in the world did you each come up with such large visions of how to create foundations that would do so much good in the world?" I was taken aback by the question because her premise was mistaken. The reality is, as I explained, that neither of us began with a grand vision. What got us started were ideas about small steps we could take that might do some good in the world. Those first steps led to more, and then more. Soon other people joined us and offered thoughts on new steps. The only real vision was service. Neither of us began with a full-blown plan. Things evolved organically as we were guided by what seemed possible and might do the most good.

If someone had told me that I'd need a detailed vision of all that was needed to start Dimensions Foundation, I'm sure I wouldn't have begun. The vision needed to grow slowly, in collaboration with many wonderful people. I'm afraid there's often a misconception that it takes something exceptional to be able to make a difference in the world. I don't believe that. I just think it takes a desire to be a positive influence and a willingness to take one step at a time. Today my one step is working on this book. I don't know how it will be received, but that's not the point. I will offer whatever encouragement I'm able and then trust it will find the people it's meant to reach.

Queen Elizabeth II (1926–2022), Queen of the United
Kingdom and Commonwealth realms from 1952–2022

SEPTEMBER 11
Find Calm in Chaos

*When little people are overwhelmed by
big emotions, it's our job to share
our calm, not join in their chaos.*

—L.R. Knost

I understand that L.R. Knost is writing to adults about their reactions to children, and I agree with her. But it also occurs to me that somewhere inside each of us are those old fears and misconceptions we created for ourselves as small children. That part of us very much needs our adult calm.

When I find myself feeling turbulent and chaotic, it's a clue that my younger self has taken control. I know then that it's time for the rational adult part of me to take charge with firmness and as much calm as I can muster. When I'm struggling emotionally, it helps to talk to myself like I would a small child.

Today I am remembering that there's still a part of me that needs comforting. I am enlisting the help of the rational adult me to provide it.

L.R. Knost, American author

SEPTEMBER 12

Take Some Love Actions

Love is an action, never simply a feeling.

—bell hooks

After the tragic shooting at Sandy Hook Elementary School in Newtown, Connecticut in 2012, ABC news interviewed first grade teacher, Kaitlin Roig, who huddled in a bathroom with her class to help keep her students safe during the terrifying time. Here is part of what she said:

"I told them, 'I want you to know I love you all very much.' I don't know if that was ok, you know...but I wanted it to be the last thing they heard." I was so touched by her bravery, but it also struck me that she was questioning whether it was ok that she, a teacher, had said, "I love you," to her children. I can't imagine a more appropriate response at that time. I know why she asked the question, though. A friend of mine who teaches preschool in a public school reports that their staff has been told that saying "I love you," to students is inappropriate. Here's what I find inappropriate: spending hours every day with young children and not being able to express genuine human emotions with them. My four-year-old granddaughter is with her early care teachers for eight hours a day. During that time I sincerely hope she feels loved.

But here's the good news: Love can be communicated through more than what we say. In fact, people often experience our love the most through our actions. Today I am thinking about the kind of love Carl Rogers calls "unconditional positive regard," that can be expressed to anyone. What will my love actions be today? I am on the lookout for authentic ways to express love.

SEPTEMBER 13
Try Some Grounding

*Forget not that the earth delights to
feel your bare feet and the winds
long to play with your hair.*

—Kahlil Gibran

A *USA Today* online article, "Have you heard of 'grounding' or 'earthing'? What it is and why it's getting attention," by Sara M. Moniuszko offers these key points:

- Earthing (or grounding) is the practice of placing your bare feet on the ground for health purposes.
- Being barefoot can help your body absorb Earth's electrons and in theory offers health benefits.
- People who practice earthing say they have found both physical and mental health benefits.

According to the article, the more often we humans have a chance to reconnect to the Earth's electrons, the better we'll feel. The key is finding a place to walk or stand with bare feet on grass or soil. Moniuszko quotes Clint Ober, an earthing expert, as saying, "Anything that is conductive (like a ground rod, metal, a human body, an animal) that touches the earth, the body absorbs electrons from the Earth and equalizes with the Earth...These electrons are thought to be used by the body to help improve function and reduce inflammation, leading to myriad health benefits."

Today I am making a commitment to give grounding a try. When I take a walk this evening, at least some of it will be with bare feet.

Kahlil Gibran (1883–1931), Lebanese-American poet

SEPTEMBER 14
Become Just a Bit Kinder

Kindness can become its own motive.
We are made kind by being kind.

–Eric Hoffer

In his *Mindful* magazine article, "The Power of Kindness," Dacher Keltner discusses research showing that people who are successful leaders share certain traits. The following characteristics can help anyone, leader or not, to simply become kinder human beings.

"Empathy: Ask a great question or two in every interaction...Listen with gusto...When someone comes to you with a problem, signal concern... Avoid rushing to judgment and advice...

Gratitude: Make thoughtful thank-yous a part of how you communicate with others...

Generosity: Give praise generously...Share the limelight."

Today I am becoming just a bit kinder by intentionally practicing empathy, gratitude and generosity.

Eric Hoffer (1902–1983), American philosopher and author

SEPTEMBER 15

Celebrate Things That Give Life Meaning

Work like you don't need money. Love like you've never been hurt. Dance like nobody's watching.

—Satchel Paige

I have very much appreciated rereading *Man's Search for Meaning*, the iconic book by Holocaust survivor, Viktor Frankl. It's good once in a while to remind myself that generations before me faced challenges and overcame them, just as I will...just as we are all doing right now.

Only eleven months after Frankl was liberated from the concentration camps, he gave a series of lectures. Here's an excerpt from one that I found helpful:

"[I]magine that you are sitting in a concert hall...and your favorite bars of the symphony resound in your ears, and you are so moved by the music that it sends shivers down your spine; and now imagine that it would be possible...for someone to ask you in this moment whether your life has meaning. I believe you would agree with me...that in this case you would only be able to give one answer...'It would have been worth it to have lived for this moment.'

Those who experience not the arts, but nature, may have a similar response, and also those who experience another human being. Do we not know the feeling that overtakes...*The fact that this person exists in the world at all, this alone makes this world, and a life in it, meaningful.*"

Music, beauty, nature, relationships. Those were some of the things that helped Frankl find meaning in life, even after his horrendous experiences during the Holocaust. Today I am remembering that those gifts are available to me, also.

Satchel Paige (1906–1982), American professional baseball player

SEPTEMBER 16
Find Some Cultural Recipes

Food history is as important as a baroque church. Governments should recognize cultural heritage and protect traditional foods. A cheese is as worthy of preserving as a sixteenth-century building.

—Carlo Petrini

My son-in-law, Chad, gave me the book, *Salt Fat Acid Heat* by Samin Nosrat. I was touched by the author's description of her childhood love affair with food. She writes, "My parents left Tehran for San Diego...shortly before I was born in 1979. I grew up speaking Farsi, celebrating No-Ruz, the Iranian New Year...but the most delightful aspect of the culture was the food...Rare were the nights when our aunts, uncles, or grandparents didn't join us at the dinner table, which was always filled with plates mounded high...Invariably, I was the one who snagged the ...tahdig, the golden crust that formed at the bottom of every pot of Persian rice Maman made."

Her words made me wonder why I didn't have more family recipes that reflect my cultural heritage. Then I realized what probably happened. My mother, whose family came to the US from Germany, was born right after World War I. The children had been bilingual, but as the war began, everyone stopped speaking German and the traditional German food was replaced by typical American fare. My father's family had English and Irish roots, but he didn't much want to talk about Irish influences since Irish immigrants were often looked down on and did not have an easy time. There were no Irish dishes served in his home - ever.

Because we live in an AND world, I'm sure everyone's family histories have both heartwarming stories AND some difficult ones. We can acknowledge that we humans treat each other badly at times while always working to make our world more loving. Today I'll search out some traditional German or Irish dishes. What recipes might reflect your cultural heritage?

Carlo Petrini, Italian editor, founder of
the International Slow Food Movement

SEPTEMBER 17

Help Myself by Helping Others

*An effort made for the happiness of
others lifts us above ourselves.*

–Lydia Maria Child

"Scientific research provides compelling data to support the anecdotal evidence that giving is a powerful pathway to personal growth and lasting happiness," writes Jenny Santi in her *Time* magazine article, "The Secret to Happiness is Helping Others."

She explains, "Through fMRI technology, we now know that giving activates the same parts of the brain that are stimulated by food and sex. Experiments show evidence that altruism is hardwired in the brain—and it's pleasurable. Helping others may just be the secret to living a life that is not only happier but also healthier, wealthier, more productive, and meaningful."

I am going to be alert in many situations today to ways I might be able to help other people. It could be something as simple as opening a door for a mother whose arms are full carrying children. It's nice to know that one of the best ways to help myself feel good is to do nice things for others. I look forward to seeing how many opportunities I find today.

Lydia Maria Child (1802–1880), American journalist, novelist, abolitionist, women's rights and Native American rights activist

SEPTEMBER 18
Make Time for Good Conversations

*Be brave enough to start a
conversation that matters.*

—Margaret Wheatley

I've learned that I have to make space for them if I want good conversations in my life. They don't usually happen at crowded parties. And they certainly don't happen if I'm not open and available.

Mostly I have to be ready for those moments that begin with a spark that ignites into real connection. Good conversations happen best when I can be fully present and able to listen from my heart, with interest, acceptance and non-judgment. They need enough time so no one feels rushed.

Having a meaningful conversation with people I care for, about things that matter, is one of life's great pleasures for me. Today I am open to brave discussions about important topics. It's one excellent way to share love.

Margaret Wheatley, American author

SEPTEMBER 19

What Have I Been Taking for Granted?

The whole world is a series of miracles...but we're so used to them we call them ordinary things.

—Hans Christian Andersen

I want to see if I can discover things in my life that I've been taking for granted... the miraculous in the ordinary that Hans Christian Andersen speaks of. I've made a pretty good effort to appreciate my abundance, but I wonder what I've overlooked.

After some serious thought, what occurred to me is that two things I think of as ordinary are really momentous. Here's the first: the fact that I can always get healthy food for myself and my family whenever I want. I know this is not true for so many people throughout our world. According to the United Nations, during 2020, the first year of the global pandemic, one in three people did not have access to adequate food. While this number is slowly improving, it still remains shockingly high. Realizing that readily available healthy food is actually not ordinary, but indeed miraculous, helps me experience my good fortune with appropriate gratitude.

Here's another: clean, reliably available water. According to the World Health Organization, one in four people throughout the globe do not have access to a safe drinking water service where they live, available when needed and free from contamination. Knowing that my reality is not true for so many people changes the way I go about my daily round.

Today, each time I turn on the tap or put a bite of food in my mouth, I plan to express silent, heartfelt appreciation for my often taken-for-granted good fortune.

Hans Christian Andersen (1805–1875), Danish author

SEPTEMBER 20

Just a Little Each Day

*Success is the sum of small efforts,
repeated day in and day out.*

—Robert Collier

In her best-selling book, *The Happiness Project*, Gretchen Rubin creates a list for herself of what she calls "Secrets of Adulthood." One of these secrets is this:

"By doing a little bit each day, you can get a lot accomplished."

It's so simple, but so true. I firmly believe it, but often forget. I sometimes hear myself saying, "I don't have enough time to organize that closet. I'll have to wait until I have at least a half day." Good luck with that. It's likely to be quite a while until that happens, which means the closet will keep frustrating me each time I open it.

If I would try Gretchen Rubin's secret right now, organizing just a bit each day, it wouldn't be long before I'd be able to find some gloves without a tangle of scarves and baseball caps falling on my head.

Today I am remembering the power of accomplishing a lot by doing just a little at a time every day.

Robert Collier (1885–1950), American author

SEPTEMBER 21

Make Friends with My Body

As I often tell my students, the two most important phrases in therapy, as in yoga, are "Notice that" and "What happens next?" Once you start approaching your body with curiosity rather than with fear, everything shifts.

—Bessel van der Kolk, M.D.,
The Body Keeps the Score

I know I'm not always a very good friend to my body. Nevertheless, it's served me well, even when I haven't treated it the way it deserved. Today I'm ready to make amends. Using Bessel van der Kolk's question, I'm asking myself "What happens next?" I think an apology is in order.

So, body, I'm sorry for spending so many hours slouching. I promise to pay attention and sit up. Really. And I actually know how important it is to drink water, so I'm sorry I keep forgetting. I'll do better. And I'm sorry I've overworked my eyes. When they start to get tired and achy, I promise I'll take a break. And, listen, despite my best intentions, I'm pretty cruel to you sometimes when I make disparaging comments about weight or lumps or sags. You don't deserve that rudeness. You actually are pretty wonderful. I promise to remember that.

Today I am creating an improved relationship with my body, focusing on how miraculous it actually is.

Bessel van der Kolk, M.D., American psychiatrist, author, researcher

SEPTEMBER 22

Stop Saying I'm Busy

The trouble with being in the rat race is that even if you win, you're still a rat.

—Lily Tomlin

"A study in the Journal of Psychological Science shows that we're much happier when there's a lot going on in our life. But if keeping active and 'busy' is positive for our health, why do we often feel overwhelmed or exhausted by our list of responsibilities?" So begins a Washington Post article, "Six reasons you'd be happier if you stopped saying 'busy,'" by Megan Wycklendt.

Wycklendt answers her question by explaining that when we keep telling ourselves and others that we're "busy," we program in unnecessary feelings of stress. She writes:

"When I complain about how busy I am, it is as if someone put all these things on my plate without my approval. When in fact, I make my life the way it is...The question is: Is it all worth it? If it is, be grateful and proud of everything you do. If it's not, make a change."

Today if I find myself complaining about being "busy," I commit to stopping and taking stock of all I'm doing. Is most everything worthwhile and something I would still choose? Then if so, I'll say "my life is eventful and gratifyingly full." If everything is not worthwhile, I'll begin taking steps to make a change.

Lily Tomlin, American actress, comedian

SEPTEMBER 23
Accept Disappointment as a Part of Life

Disappointment builds character and strength.

—Nafessa Williams

If Nafessa Williams is correct, I was recently given a chance to build my character. After avoiding Covid 19 for years, my husband woke this morning with a sore throat. Sure enough, our home Covid test quickly turned positive. Suddenly plans for dinner with friends needed to be canceled, and we were no longer able to attend a party for out-of-town relatives or take a long-planned birthday trip with delightful in-laws. I know we are not unique. Folks have been making adjustments to their lives for years now. Weddings, graduations and funerals have been missed. So I realize our cancellations are nothing tragic. And I'm grateful my husband is feeling fine. Yet, I'm still disappointed. And it's important that I not deny that feeling. So I'm using this new situation as an opportunity to practice a healthy way of dealing with disappointment.

It helps to remind myself I'm not alone. Beyond humanity's recently shared pandemic experience, disappointment in general is simply part of the human condition. Much has been written over the centuries about what disappointment can teach. Sir Bayle Roche, an Irish politician who died in 1807, declared, "Disappointment is the nurse of wisdom." And Eliza Tabor, a novelist who lived in Victorian England, wrote, "Disappointment to a noble soul is what cold water is to burning metal; it strengthens, tempers, intensifies, but never destroys it." Perhaps disappointment builds character by helping us practice acceptance. I realize I have a choice today: I could continue fretting about how unfair it is that we'll miss all our gatherings. Or I could accept my disappointment, let the feeling flow through, then decide what my positive action step will be. I choose option two. I think maybe I just got a little wiser.

Nafessa Williams, American actress

SEPTEMBER 24
Choose Good Music

Music can lift us out of depression or
move us to tears — it is a remedy,
a tonic, orange juice for the ear.

—Oliver Sacks

I am being intentional about my choice of music today. I'll change things up and enjoy a variety of styles. What I'll listen to when I first get up in the morning will be different from what I tune in to as I'm driving. What I choose this evening will lift me up and bring me some "ear orange juice."

British musician Elton John has said that "music has healing power." I know that's true for me. I sometimes forget how great it is when I find just the right musical "medicine."

Today I am remembering to savor music as "a remedy, a tonic" - always available any time I need it, any time I want it.

Oliver Sacks (1933–2015), American author and neurology professor

SEPTEMBER 25
Be Open to Serendipity

Whatever you are looking for is also looking for you. You see, don't only look. Be available and ready when it shows up.

—Sahndra Fon Dufe

As someone who appreciates the value of planning, I have also come to celebrate the importance of serendipity. Serendipitous surprises happen when something vital comes into my life at an unexpected time or in an unpredictable way.

Looking back, I'm quite certain I sometimes shut the door on serendipitous gifts because they weren't part of my plan. But I hope now I am more eager to welcome them in.

The older I've gotten the more I feel ready to be surprised by life. I've learned to listen to "crazy" ideas, consider unexpected invitations and change plans when a better way comes along.

It's interesting; when I'm ready to be pleasantly surprised, I often am. Today I'm open to serendipity. Come on, life. Amaze me.

Sahndra Fon Dufe, Cameroonian author, actress, CEO of African Pictures International

SEPTEMBER 26

My Best Is Enough

*You must accept that you might fail; then,
if you do your best and still don't win, at least
you can be satisfied that you've tried.*

—Rosalynn Carter

Today I am reminding myself that in any life situation, all I can control is my input, not the outcome. The good news, though, is that if I've done my best, that's all that matters. And by the way, doing my best does NOT mean being perfect.

On some days, when I was a single mom with two small children, doing my best meant serving breakfast before we all left for work and school, even if breakfast was just a bowl of cereal. Recently, sometimes doing my best might mean saying no to one more thing and taking a rest.

Today I am releasing misguided beliefs that I can "make" anything happen. Instead I am celebrating myself for showing up, doing what I'm able, and trusting that whatever outcome occurs will ultimately be for the best.

Rosalynn Carter, former First Lady of the United States

SEPTEMBER 27
Visit a Nourishing Place

Don't forget to pause and nourish yourself a bit along the way. When you're born to help others, sometimes you forget to help yourself.

—Paula Heller Garland

When I first became the director of an early care and education program, I realized right away how self-sacrificing most of the educators were. They did indeed feel a calling to help others. And while this is admirable and important, it can become unhealthy if the sacrifices go too far. Caregivers must be good at caring for themselves, not just everyone else. Otherwise exhaustion will set in, and then resentment, and finally, burnout.

This is true for all of us, no matter what profession or life circumstance we're in. I know I must check in with myself frequently to be sure I'm not "starving" myself to "feed" others. One way I nourish myself is by visiting places that feed my soul. In my own town these include a beautiful arboretum on a university campus, a lovely art museum that is generously free to the public, and a wooded walking trail that shows off nature's artistry. I have other favorite places if I travel, but I need nourishing spaces close to me.

Today I commit to making plans to visit a nourishing place - soon. I'm wondering what places feel nourishing to you.

SEPTEMBER 28
Ask for Help — Unapologetically

*Asking for help is never a sign of weakness.
It's one of the bravest things you can do.
And it can save your life.*

–Lily Collins,
*Unfiltered: No Shame,
No Regrets, Just Me*

When I was younger I believed that asking for help was a sign of failure. That way of thinking came from parents who had lived through the Great Depression as young children. They were taught to keep a stiff upper lip and figure things out for themselves. I was taught that "nice girls" don't get angry or complain. They always, always "look on the bright side."

Well. I'm here to tell you those teachings are based on misunderstandings. And they're impossible. I do get angry. I speak up if something isn't working. I find the bright side by first facing the storm. And I have learned to ask for help. Unapologetically. As Lily Collins says, asking for help is an act of bravery. Let's all agree on that.

Here's how requests for help might sound in a number of hypothetical situations:
- I realize I have more work on my plate than I can complete on time without making myself sick. I'm going to talk with my supervisor about getting me extra help.
- I haven't been sleeping well for weeks, no matter what I've tried. I'm going to ask my doctor for suggestions.
- I don't have a clue what to buy for my 16-year-old nephew's birthday. I'm going to get some advice from a friend who has a teenager.
- I've been feeling extra stress and sadness lately. I think it would help to talk to a professional.

Today I celebrate the fact that asking for help is a sign of strength.

Lily Collins, British and American actress, writer

SEPTEMBER 29
Forget Multitasking

Now, more than ever, I believe that the antidote to our ever-expanding to-do lists, the distractions of modern life, and the fragmentation of our attention is to do one thing at a time.

—Thatcher Wine,
*The Twelve Monotasks:
Do One Thing at a Time
to Do Everything Better*

Dan Harris, in his book, *10% Happier*, writes about working with a woman named Janice Marturano, an attorney who discovered the remarkable benefits of adopting a mindfulness practice and began teaching it to others. "A big part of Marturano's success" in teaching mindfulness, writes Harris, is "that she talks about it not as a 'spiritual' exercise but instead something that…enhanced your 'creativity and innovation.'"

Harris describes how "Marturano recommended something radical: do only one thing at a time. When you're on the phone, be on the phone. When you're in a meeting, try actually paying attention. Set aside an hour to check your email, and then shut off your computer monitor and focus on the task at hand."

While the idea of leaving multitasking behind felt radical to Harris, the same advice was actually being given by people like Dale Carnegie as early as the 1940's (see July 23). But sometimes each generation must "discover" an idea for themselves in order for it to become truly their own.

Today as I focus on one thing at a time, I am looking for opportunities to bring positivity to the world in each individual situation. Not only will I be fully present when I'm on the phone with someone, but I'll remember to hold loving energy for them. Doing things one by one will help me bring my best to all I do.

Thatcher Wine, American author, founder of Juniper Books

SEPTEMBER 30
If I Can't Laugh about It, I Don't Want It

Progress is nothing but the victory of laughter over dogma.

–Benjamin De Casseres

English author and philosopher G. K. Chesterton (1874 - 1936) wrote, "It is the test of a good religion whether you can joke about it." I think it's a pretty good test of most anything. If I can't joke about it, I'm not sure it's for me. I'm not talking about mean-spirited humor. I'm thinking of heart-warming laughter and the "whistling-in-the-dark" banter we humans have always used to get through tough times.

To me there's something quite brave about humor. It's like a declaration of belief in the power of joy.

Today I'm celebrating laughter. Care to join me?

Benjamin De Casseres (1873–1945), American journalist

October

I will cut adrift — I will sit on pavements and drink coffee — I will dream; I will take my mind out of its iron cage and let it swim — this fine October.

—Virginia Woolf

Virginia Woolf (1882–1941), English writer

OCTOBER 1

Eat for Energy

Healthy does NOT mean starving yourself EVER. Healthy means eating the right food in the right amount.

—Karen Salmansohn

At times when I feel my energy lagging, I've learned that eating the right kind of snack can really give me a boost. Instead of reaching for candy (which lifts me quickly but very soon sends me crashing), I feel better when I choose something tasty, healthy and easy that will sustain me. Here's my "Top Ten" list:

1. String cheese and a pear
2. Apple slices with nut butter
3. Cottage cheese and grapefruit wedges
4. A handful of trail mix
5. Roasted edamame
6. Baked pita chips and cheese wedges
7. A smoothie made by blending frozen fruit with Greek yogurt
8. Hard boiled egg, wheat crackers, and cherry tomatoes
9. Carrot and celery sticks with hummus
10. Coconut milk yogurt mixed with banana slices

And because sometimes low energy actually is a result of dehydration, I drink plenty of water while I munch.

Today I'm remembering the great benefits of a healthy snack. It feels good to take care of myself this way.

OCTOBER 2

Practice Self-Forgiveness

*Be courageous enough to forgive yourself;
never forget to be compassionate to yourself.*

—Debasish Mridha, M.D.

Finding the courage to forgive myself is most difficult when the voice inside my head keeps scolding, "You knew better." Those are the mistakes I regret the most. Part of me doesn't believe I deserve my own compassion. The old vestiges of perfectionism tell me it's unforgivable to do something I knew in my heart was not a good choice.

It's precisely at moments like those, though, that I most need my own love and understanding, my unconditional positive regard, my own permission to be human and "mess up." Once again I must gently but firmly remind myself that perfectionism is impossible. Making mistakes does not make me less worthy of love and acceptance.

Here's what works for me after an episode of harsh self-criticism: I put my hand on my heart and say, "I forgive myself for buying into the misunderstanding that I must be perfect. I forgive myself for forgetting that I'm allowed to be human." Then I remind myself that I can learn from my mistake and do better next time.

Today I am taking a deep breath and releasing myself from the prison of self-judgment. I'm finding the courage to love and forgive myself, no matter what.

Debasish Mridha, M.D., American physician and author

OCTOBER 3
Stop Judging Others

*Judging a person does not define
who they are. It defines who you are.*

–Wayne Dyer

When I find myself feeling judgmental of someone else, it's a good indication that I'm probably still holding on to some self-judgment. Because here's the thing: the more I stop judging myself, the less I feel the need to judge others.

Life becomes so much happier and healthier when I can approach other people with acceptance. That doesn't mean I have to agree with everything they do; it simply means I don't have to be their judge and jury. I can offer as much grace for their imperfections as I do for my own.

Today I am approaching those around me with unconditional positive regard. It sure does make life easier and more fun.

Wayne Dyer (1940–2015), American author and motivational speaker

OCTOBER 4

Increase Intentions of Beauty

*When you're connected to intention,
you see beauty everywhere and in everything
because you're radiating the quality of beauty.
Your perceptual world changes dramatically.*

—Wayne Dyer,
The Power of Intention

When I am successful in first releasing judgmental feelings toward myself and then toward others, I am able to move into a new way of experiencing the world around me. It comes from holding an intention to find the best in each person and situation.

I'm quoting Wayne Dyer again, who studied and wrote about intention for years. He explained it this way, in his book referenced above: "At the higher energy of intent, you see beauty in everyone, young or old, rich or poor, dark or light, with no distinctions. Everything is perceived from a perspective of appreciation rather than judgment."

In moments when I'm able to rise to that level of perception, I'm much more likely to feel the connections we humans all share. I remember that each of us is doing the best we can with the tools we have right now. And I remind myself that hateful behavior is usually rooted in fear, so as someone who also struggles with fear, I can be compassionate to those who have been overtaken by fear's tyranny.

That never means that I excuse hateful behavior, but compassion helps me stay out of the energy of judgment. Once an acquaintance of mine made this statement about a political party: "I hate them because they're such haters." I don't think he realized the irony of his words.

Today it is my intention to stay in the energy of appreciation. I look forward to finding beauty all around.

Wayne Dyer (1940–2015), American author and motivational speaker

OCTOBER 5

Another Way to Play

Play keeps us vital and alive. It gives us an enthusiasm for life that is irreplaceable. Without it, life just doesn't taste good.

—Lucia Capacchione

It's time for some more intentional play. Today I'd like to try something I haven't done for a while: draw with my non-dominant hand. According to an article called "Non-dominant hand writing" on the UK-based website, Psychologies (*psychologies.co.uk*):

"Art therapist Lucia Capacchione's longitudinal work confirms that writing with your non-dominant hand helps stress and anxiety. It is also a great way to access the voice of your inner child. You can even use the process to gain insight into relationship dynamics and it can go as far as alleviating some physical pain."

Plus, speaking from past experience, it can be a whole lot of fun.

So today I am going to grab some crayons and paper and see what happens when right-handed me draws with my left hand. I promise not to censor myself in any way, but to just enjoy the process...to just enjoy playing.

Lucia Capacchione, Italian-American psychologist, art therapist and writer

OCTOBER 6

Listen to Constructive Feedback

An acquaintance merely enjoys your company, a fair-weather companion flatters when all is well, a true friend has your best interests at heart and the pluck to tell you what you need to hear.

—E.A. Bucchianeri,
Brushstrokes of a Gadfly

There's a flip side to not letting other people's opinions determine how I feel about myself. That's being open to others' constructive feedback. Here's an example from when I was a relatively new early childhood director: I had just completed a team meeting when one of the teachers asked to talk. She said she didn't want to hurt my feelings but had information that might be helpful. Taken aback, I told her I'd very much like to know. She explained that often when people shared ideas in our meetings I jumped in too quickly to explain why something wouldn't work. "I think if you'd let ideas percolate longer," she said, "more people would be willing to share. And sometimes valuable ideas can flow from impractical ones."

I had to shush the insecure part of me that felt ashamed to have done "something wrong," and call forth the healthy me who could thank the teacher profusely for such valuable feedback. And valuable it was. It changed my leadership style for the better and was the beginning of a wonderfully satisfying collaborative relationship with creative colleagues.

Being able to learn from "course correcting" observations makes life better. Just the other day a friend gave me information that stung a bit, but turned out to be so helpful. I still have to get past my initial "oh no, I've done it wrong" feeling, but I'm getting better at silencing my inner critic. I look back with gratitude to friends, family and colleagues who cared enough to be honest with me. Their generosity has been such a gift. I'm open to more.

OCTOBER 7
Embrace Humility

*If you aren't humble, whatever empathy
you claim is false and probably results from
some arrogance or the desire to control.
But true empathy is rooted in humility and
the understanding that there are many people
with as much to contribute in life as you.*

—Anand Mahindra

In *The Book of Joy*, Douglas Abrams asks his fellow authors, the Dalai Lama and Desmond Tutu, this question: "Can you explain the role that humility plays in cultivating joy?"

"I think that the Archbishop was laughing about the question even before I had finished asking it," Abrams explained. "He did not want to claim to be an expert on humility. Nonetheless he and the Dalai Lama were saying that humility is essential to a life of joy." *The Book of Joy* provides this description: "Humility allows us to celebrate the gifts of others, but it does not mean you have to deny your own gifts or shrink from them."

On days when I'm especially hard on myself and perfectionism shows up insistently, remembering humility can help. After all, perfectionism is a kind of ego trip. It's telling myself I'm superior enough to accomplish something no one else can - live a life with no mistakes. Humility reminds me that mistakes are an inevitable and even necessary part of my ordinary human life. The Dalai Lama says that people with humility can laugh at themselves. He and Desmond Tutu describe "the importance of a proper sense of humor, and especially the ability to laugh at our own foibles, as essential to the cultivation of joy."

Today I embrace humility, learning to laugh at myself and accept who I am, flaws and all.

Anand Mahindra, Indian business executive

OCTOBER 8

Water is My Friend

*If there is magic on this planet,
it is contained in water.*

–Loren Eiseley

"If you don't think of water as being nutritious, think again," writes Lisa Mosconi, PhD, in her book, *Brain Food: The Surprising Science of Eating for Cognitive Power*. "Water is undeniably vital to human life and, as it turns out, also to our intelligence...water is involved in every chemical reaction in the human brain...In fact, brain cells require a delicate balance of water and other elements such as minerals and salts to work efficiently at all."

Mosconi reports that less than twenty percent of Americans drink enough water - which is eight 8-ounce glasses a day. She recommends drinking a full glass first thing in the morning to kick-start our brains. She explains that dehydration can make us feel sluggish and tired when we first wake up. Downing some water right away can counteract that.

I've been aware of the importance of drinking plenty of water, but I have to admit I haven't been drinking it when I first wake up. Mosconi has me convinced this would be a good thing to add to my routine.

So today I am focusing on ways to keep the water flowing in my life. I'm committing to an early morning glass - then seven more throughout the day. I'm eager to see if I'll notice increased energy.

Loren Eiseley (1907–1977), American anthropologist and natural science writer

OCTOBER 9

A Day to Focus on Gratitude

*When gratitude becomes an
essential foundation in our lives,
miracles start to appear everywhere.*

–Emmanuel Dagher

In her book, *What I Know for Sure,* Oprah Winfrey writes, "Gratitude can transform any situation. It alters your vibration, moving you from negative energy to positive. It's the quickest, easiest, most powerful way to effect change in your life—this I know for sure."

I know it, too. I feel the lift from negative to positive when I begin to intentionally concentrate on gratitude in a tough situation. I've also experienced the miracles that Emmanuel Dagher references.

That "miracle" feeling wells up when gratitude transports the ordinary to the extraordinary...

When gratitude changes the ordinary display of art on my refrigerator door to an extraordinary exhibition of love from three miraculous granddaughters...

When gratitude transforms an ordinary balcony view at sunset to a miraculous show of nature's artistry, connecting my heart with all who also marvel...

When gratitude shifts music from an ordinary listening experience to a soaring, heart-opening auditory miracle.

Today is a good day to focus on being grateful. I look forward to enjoying many miraculous moments. I wish many for you.

Emmanuel Dagher, American author and teacher

OCTOBER 10
Plant the Trees

*No one can reap the fruit
before planting the trees.*

—Luis Inacio Lula da Silva

I remember when my daughter had the lead in her high school play. She worked very, very hard, memorizing lines, attending practices, creating costumes and delivering multiple performances. At the end of the final evening, she looked at me with shining eyes and said, "I think this feeling is what people are trying to find by taking drugs. But you know what? It could never be as good as this, because they'd know they didn't create it themselves. I don't think there are shortcuts to this kind of happiness."

I often think about that conversation. It reminds me that some things are fabulous only because I've put in the time and effort. When I'm in the middle of an intense project that starts to feel hard, I ask myself if it's going to be worth it in the long run. If the answer is yes, then it helps me carry on. If the answer is no, then I remind myself I don't have to finish everything I begin, if it's not worthwhile.

Today I'm asking myself what "fruit" I'm hoping to reap and what "trees" I'll need to plant first. I'm happy to put in effort on worthwhile work. And I'm willing to stop doing things that aren't healthy for me.

Luis Inacio Lula da Silva, 35th president of Brazil

OCTOBER 11

How to Be on My Own Side

*I learned a long time ago, the wisest thing
I can do is be on my own side.*

—Maya Angelou

Today I am pondering what "being on my own side" feels like. Here's what I think:

- It feels like relief when I tell myself, "That's ok, sweetheart. You blew that one, but tomorrow's another day. I love you anyway."
- It feels like comfort when I make myself a cup of hibiscus tea before bed and stir in an extra spoon of honey.
- It feels like nurture when I remind myself to bring a cozy sweater when I go out because the forecast predicts a cold front coming through.
- It feels like delight when I stop at a bakery on my way home and buy myself a favorite cookie.

Today I'm focusing on being on my side all day long. I wonder what new ways I'll find to support myself.

Maya Angelou (1928–2014), American writer, poet and civil rights activist

OCTOBER 12
Grow Some Green

Spending time in green space or bringing nature into your everyday life can benefit both your mental and physical wellbeing. For example, doing things like growing food or flowers, exercising outdoors or being around animals can have lots of positive effects.

—From the article "Nature and mental health," on *Mind.org.uk*

On a windowsill in my kitchen there's a small pot that holds a chocolate mint plant. A couple of months ago it had a basil plant. I realize I haven't been paying much attention to this little pot. Once in a while I'll pick a mint leaf for some tea, but that's about it.

Today I'm deciding to put more thought into creating a windowsill garden. There's actually room for three pots. In addition to the mint, maybe I'll plant chives and sage. Or maybe some rosemary. I might even bring back the basil. Part of the fun will be visiting a nursery to make choices.

Today I'm focusing on the benefits of becoming an indoor herb gardener. It's an enjoyable and easy way to nurture my general well-being. Want to join me?

OCTOBER 13
The Gift of Music

> *Music is about as physical as it gets;*
> *your essential rhythm is your heartbeat;*
> *your essential sound, the breath. We're walking*
> *temples of noise, and when you add tender*
> *hearts to this mix, it somehow lets us meet in*
> *places we couldn't get to any other way.*
>
> —Anne Lamott,
> *Small Victories*

My sister-in-law is an organist. My husband and I had the great pleasure of being able to see her perform in a concert the other day. While the audience was appreciative, I wondered if they realized the hours and hours of practice it had taken to create such a splendid performance. It got me thinking about the incredible gifts that have been offered to humanity by composers and artists over the centuries; those people who give so much of themselves to create and make music for others' enjoyment.

Music certainly does connect me to something essential within myself. I'm realizing how many of my memories are associated with a certain song or musical piece. I'm also realizing how often I forget to listen to the fuller range of music that is available to me. If I'm intentional in my listening choices, I experience a transporting connection to the depth of human expression.

Today I am remembering to be grateful for the gift of music in my life, delighting in its elemental richness.

OCTOBER 14
Don't Set Myself on Fire

*You are not required to set yourself
on fire to keep other people warm.*

−Joan Crawford

Joan Crawford said it right, but there was a time in my life when I didn't realize this. If I cared about someone and they were sad, I thought it was my duty to do anything - everything - to try to cheer them up. "Nothing's too hard for friends or family," I used to tell myself. It never occurred to me that spending some time being sad might be a necessary part of my friend's life journey; that it might lead to beneficial learning for them. At any rate, I was very mistaken that "nothing was too hard for a friend." In my quest to be the "fixer," plenty was not only too hard, but downright unhealthy.

A caring therapist gave me this image: I'm standing next to a pit of quicksand. My friend is beginning to sink in the pit. "Here," I say, holding out a sturdy branch, "Grab hold and pull yourself out." "No, no," my friend replies. "That's too hard. You jump in here and pull me out."

Of course, once I jump in the pit myself, I've lost my footing on solid ground. The only outcome will be that both my friend and I sink in the quicksand. The only rational response is to stay out of the pit. I've now learned to offer help to people in a healthier way. I remind myself that I don't know what is best for everyone in my life in every situation. I can offer to be a loving presence, but it is not my job to "fix" anything.

Today I am remembering the importance of taking good care of myself while caring for others.

OCTOBER 15
Smile More

There is fear when frowning.
There is love when smiling.

—Maxime Lagacé

"Perhaps the most compelling reason to smile is that it may lengthen your overall lifespan. One study found that genuine, intense smiling is associated with longer life." So begins an article on the *VeryWellMind* website, "10 Big Benefits of Smiling," by Mark Stibich, PhD, medically reviewed by Rachel Goldman, PhD.

Here's more: "Believe it or not, smiling can reduce stress even if you don't feel like smiling or even if you fake it with a smile that isn't genuine. When you are stressed, try intentionally putting a smile on your face. It may help improve your mood and ability to manage the stress you are experiencing."

It's interesting to find out that my body reacts to a smile by reducing stress. It's one more reason to smile more often. There's also the fact that smiling is good for my immune system, and that the "contagion" power in smiling can raise the positive energy in a group.

I have to admit that I've sometimes seen myself in photographs and was startled that I looked rather glum. I knew I had actually been quite happy, but my face didn't show it. Smiling, in the past, was not my "default" face setting.

Today I am paying attention to how much I smile. I intend to do it a lot - to help myself feel happier and less stressed, and to help raise positive feelings in people around me. I hope you'll try this, too.

Maxime Lagacé, Canadian professional ice hockey goaltender

OCTOBER 16

Cultivate My Strength

You have power over your mind - not outside events. Realize this, and you will find strength.

—Marcus Aurelius,
Meditations

Today instead of picking a quality card at random (see January 3), I am choosing to cultivate the quality of "Strength." As Roman Emperor and philosopher Marcus Aurelius declared two thousand years ago, our strength comes from realizing we can control our thinking, but not events outside ourselves.

Turning on the news these days can be disconcerting. I admit there are times I feel helpless. Cultivating the strength inside me means remembering the power I have to choose my attitude. I can choose discouragement or positive vision. Choosing vision means focusing on what I'm FOR, not what I'm against.

I am FOR all the magical moments life holds;
I am FOR times of loving connections;
I am FOR people who come to work and do their best each day;
I am FOR children who have not yet learned to be ashamed of themselves in any way;
I am FOR all the people in the world who care as much for others as themselves.

Today my strength comes from holding a vision based on the best of humanity.

Marcus Aurelius (161 AD–180 AD), Roman emperor and philosopher

OCTOBER 17

Open My Heart to Animals

*Until one has loved an animal, a part
of one's soul remains unawakened.*

—Anatole France

After my fifteen-year-old cat died and I later moved from my large home into a smaller townhouse, I assumed my years of having an animal in my life were over. I kept reading how healthy it is to commune with animals, but it never occurred to me that I could still make that happen if I no longer had a pet at my place.

Surprisingly though, I learned I still could. When I started paying attention I found animals of many kinds all around. The trees by our home are filled with a variety of birds. By putting a blue jay feeder on our balcony, we get to "visit" with colorful friends most evenings. Scattering whole peanuts on the lawn under our balcony means we also get to enjoy the scampering of squirrels.

Our next door neighbor has a delightful dog named Karma that we're quite fond of, and down the block we've become friends with a chubby cat named Oliver (and his cat parent, too).

Now we also have the sweetest, most child-friendly dog in our life. She lives rather far away with our son Matt, daughter-in-law Chris, and our two granddaughters, but she comes to visit us from time to time and certainly brings us joy.

Today I am thinking about the many ways I have to connect with animals. I am savoring each one and looking for more. I encourage you to do the same.

Anatole France (1844–1924), French poet, journalist, and novelist

OCTOBER 18

Write a Letter to My Younger Self

Earn your own respect. It takes ages, it's a constant and worthy battle and it's by far the hardest to win.

—Joanna Cannon,
Three Things I'd Tell My Younger Self

The premise of Joanna Cannon's book, quoted above, is to figure out what we know now that our younger selves did not, and what we would tell them if we could. I've been pondering that proposition. If I could write a letter that could go back in time and reach my younger self, this is what I think I'd say to her:

"Please don't worry so much. Worry never 'protects' you. Trust the process of life. There's so much that's beautiful and breathtaking. You'll have times that hurt, but if you let yourself feel your emotions, they will pass through you, and you will handle them.

And if you pay attention, there will be lessons in most everything, even the sad times. So please pay attention. There are so, so many good lessons to learn.

One more thing: Your relationship with yourself is the foundation for every other worthwhile relationship. I urge you to make it a great one."

I'm sending love to my younger self and doing my best today to live up to what I've learned from experience.

Joanna Cannon, British author

OCTOBER 19

Write a Letter to My Future Self

*A vision is not just a picture of what could be;
it is an appeal to our better selves, a call
to become something more.*

—Rosabeth Moss Kanter

Since I tried the exercise of writing a letter to my younger self yesterday, today I thought I'd take a go at writing one to future me. I've decided I don't want to be too prescriptive. Instead of urging certain outcomes, what I really want to do is encourage a way of being. So, here I go:

"I hope you have learned to take nothing for granted. I hope you are savoring each day to its fullest, living a life of appreciation, filled with moments of both calm and exuberance. My greatest wish for you, though, is that you have come to experience yourself as the presence of love. I hope you know how to fully give and receive love – in all its glorious forms. And I hope you are living a life of service, following the calling of your heart."

Today I am beginning down the path to find that future self.

OCTOBER 20
Let Poetry Add Richness to Life

Poetry is finer and more philosophical than history; for poetry expresses the universal, and history only the particular.

—Aristotle

Susan Hooper, in her *Psychology Today* article "Why Poetry Matters Now—And Why It's Gaining Readers," writes that more people are enjoying poetry now than they have in years. She explains, "Once confined largely to the rarefied realm of college English departments, poetry has come down from the ivory tower and burst out into the streets…A 2018 National Endowment for the Arts study found that nationwide interest in poetry rose between 2012 and 2017—for the first time in the history of the NEA's survey…18–24-year-olds who read poetry more than doubled, placing this age group above all others when it comes to poetry-reading rates.'"

Hooper's article reminds me of the richness poetry adds to my life when I remember to enjoy it. One of my favorite poets is Mary Oliver. I've often found the right poem at just the right time in her beautiful collection of wise musings. And there are so many others. Amanda Gorman, the first US National Youth Poet Laureate, has touched the hearts of people around the world, and I am one of them. Hers is a poetry of hope. Joy Harjo, the first Native American to become United States Poet Laureate, is another favorite, inviting me into a world I don't know. Teaching me.

A book of poems by Rumi, the 13th century Persian mystic, sits on my bedside table, a gift from my friend Scott, connecting me to wisdom that has stood the test of time. And then…Maya Angelou, and Rainer Maria Rilke and Langston Hughes and Fortesa Latifi…and…and…They all feel like old friends. Today I am promising myself to visit them more often.

Aristotle (384–322 BC), Greek philosopher and polymath

OCTOBER 21
Acknowledge My Efforts

> *She was part of a group that helped tilt the world just a tiny bit the right way. Yes, she, one tiny person, was part of it. Hardly noticeable, true, but "hardly" was more than nothing. "Hardly" made all the difference in the world in how she saw herself.*
>
> —Ray Smith,
> *The Magnolia That Bloomed Unseen*

I hope today that every single person who is working in early care and education in any way, will stop for a moment and acknowledge the importance and dignity of their work. I've seen firsthand the power it has to change lives for the better. And then I hope that every other person in all other endeavors will stop for a moment and acknowledge the value of their work.

It is a sad reality that we humans don't often allow ourselves to feel good about daily steps and effort. And let's be clear: imperfect effort counts. Each day that we show up and do our part, however small we judge it to be, we help make life work for all of us. How much better might we all feel if we celebrated those connections more often? How much more content might we feel if we gave ourselves more credit, and gave each other more recognition?

Today I am celebrating all the ways in which I "help tilt the world just a tiny bit the right way." I do it even when I forget to realize it, and you do, too.

OCTOBER 22
Walk After Eating

Trying out new ways of using your body in handling various situations breaks you free from old ways of thinking and being.

—Mirka Knaster

"Just 2 Minutes of Walking After a Meal Is Surprisingly Good for You," proclaims an article in the *New York Times*. This is new information to me. According to the article by Rachel Fairbank, "just a few minutes of light-intensity walking after a meal were enough to significantly improve blood sugar levels compared to say, sitting at a desk, or plopping down on a couch."

I had always thought that if I couldn't take a long walk, it wouldn't be worth doing. It's good to know that just a few minutes can do a world of good. This opens up possibilities for a two-minute walk after lunch, even if I've eaten in front of my computer, or a quick walk around my home after dinner, even if it's freezing outside.

Today I am making a commitment to some kind of walking after every meal. Knowing that just two minutes will help me makes this seem very possible.

Mirka Knaster, European-American author

OCTOBER 23

Raise My Vibrational Energy?

If you want to find the secrets of the universe, think in terms of energy, frequency and vibration.

—Nikola Tesla

Marney A. White, PhD, MS and Rebecca Joy Stanborough, wrote an article on *healthline.com* called "What is Vibrational Energy?" They answer the article's question this way:

"Vibrational energy experts claim that certain emotions and thought patterns, such as joy, peace, and acceptance, create high frequency vibrations, while other feelings and mindsets (such as anger, despair, and fear) vibrate at a lower rate.

There isn't much scientific evidence to support this correlation. But there is plenty of evidence linking positive emotions and thinking patterns to better health and greater goal achievement."

White and Stanborough explain that until more research has been found specifically related to vibrational energy, there is still plenty of research showing the health benefits of the things energy practitioners believe raise vibration. These include meditation, gratitude, generosity, acceptance and deep breathing.

So, today I can be assured that when I meditate or focus on feelings of acceptance or gratitude or practice generosity, I am certainly doing my health a favor.

Nikola Tesla (1856–1943), Serbian-American inventor, electrical and mechanical engineer

OCTOBER 24

Find Inspiration in Lives from the Past

I just love biography, and I'm fascinated by people who have shifted our destinies or our points of view.

—Richard Attenborough

During the worst of the pandemic, I benefited greatly from reading a biography of Eleanor Roosevelt and all she overcame during flu epidemics and polio and wars. Later, I read her own book, *You Learn By Living*, and found myself coming back to it often. I reread Viktor Frankl's *Man's Search for Meaning*, and studied Mary Catherine Bateson's *Composing a Life* where she tells the stories of five remarkable women. I realized that these books weren't just for times of stress. There was so much I could learn from inspiring figures at any time.

I decided then to reread my husband John Rosenow's book, *Living Long and Living Well*. John wrote something that has stayed with me. He described characteristics that the people in his book had in common:
- "They stayed engaged, focused on the future, and created strong connections with people.
- They maintained healthy habits, mostly.
- They persevered through setbacks, including serious health issues, seeing them as episodes to move through rather than reasons to be disengaged from life.
- They expressed the courage of their convictions.
- They mentored young people, passing along their wisdom...No matter what the reality of our lives, those are choices available to most of us."

Today I am reminding myself that admirable people from the past weren't super humans, but simply those who did their best and didn't give up. I am grateful for their examples.

Richard Attenborough (1923–2014), English actor and filmmaker

OCTOBER 25

Revisit Happy Memories

It takes one thought, one second, one moment or positive memory to act as a catalyst for the light to gradually seep in again.

—Fearne Cotton

Some days are just harder than others. One strategy that works to pick me up when I'm feeling sad, or overloaded, is to take a minute and scroll through photographs on my phone. Those pictures transport me back to happy memories and never fail to raise my spirits. I have a section of favorites that I love to revisit often.

Even without photos, I can call up memories that will cheer me. I remember the births of my children and grandchildren. I think about heartwarming times spent teaching preschoolers. Trips to the mountains with friends, or summer days at the seashore as a child bring me smiles.

It's a simple strategy but such a powerful one. Today I am remembering with gratitude how memory can be such a wonderful tool to lift me up on down days.

Fearne Cotton, English broadcaster and author

OCTOBER 26

Listen with My Heart

Being listened to and heard is one of the greatest desires of the human heart. And those who learn to listen are the most loved and respected.

–Richard Carlson,
Don't Sweat the Small Stuff

One of the most valuable skills I ever learned was to stop trying to "fix" people's problems, and simply start listening to them with an open heart. This practice has become a part of my life in all situations — with work colleagues, personal friends, family members, and sometimes with the person waiting next to me in line at the post office.

A key to this heart-centered approach is to see the other person as a valuable human being who has all the resources inside themselves to be able to solve their own problem. They aren't "broken." My job is to view them through the eyes of love and believe in their inner strength. This keeps me from trying to offer advice or "teach" them something I think they need to learn. It's amazing what can happen when a person feels truly heard and understood. I am careful, as I listen, to reflect back what I'm hearing so the person knows I care, and so I can check if my perceptions are accurate. I might say, "I think you said you feel like no one is taking you seriously. Am I understanding you correctly?"

Many times I've experienced a moment when the person I'm listening to is able to find a solution to their problem, all on their own. In that case I can very enthusiastically acknowledge them for their wisdom. Even if no solution is found during our conversation, I have communicated my faith in their ability to find one eventually.

Today I am enthusiastically offering others the gift of heart-centered listening, gratefully experiencing loving connections.

Richard Carlson (1961–2006), American author, psychotherapist, motivational speaker

OCTOBER 27

Self-Reflection

The journey into self-love and self-acceptance must begin with self-examination... until you take the journey of self-reflection, it is almost impossible to grow or learn in life.

—Iyanla Vanzant

I am a much happier person if I build regular times of self-reflection into my life. When I was teaching, my own self-reflective practice happened daily. And as an early childhood administrator, I built paid meeting times into our weekly schedule so teaching teams could spend valuable hours sharing, assessing and reflecting together.

But self-reflection is certainly not just for educators. I believe it's part of a fulfilling and meaningful life. It's an important part of how I'm able to learn and grow from my mistakes. After the initial disappointment or hurt has passed through me, then I can journal or meditate about the incident. I must meet myself with self-love and total acceptance before I'm able to reflect honestly. If I am able to say, "I realize now that I didn't listen well in that meeting and cut people off," without feeling the arrows of self-criticism coming my way, then the reflection will be valuable. The minute I start "beating myself up," I have moved from self-reflection to self-rejection. That is something to be avoided at all costs.

Today I am remembering to give myself opportunities where I can reflect on my life in an atmosphere of total acceptance and love.

Iyanla Vanzant, American author, lawyer, television personality

OCTOBER 28

Let the Sunshine In

*Sunshine is delicious, rain is refreshing,
wind braces us up, snow is exhilarating;
there is really no such thing as bad weather,
only different kinds of good weather.*

—John Ruskin

An article in *Medical News Today*, called "What to know about the health benefits of sunlight," by Cynthia Cobb and Danielle Dresden explains why we all need to be sure we're spending enough time in the sun, "Of all the health benefits of sunlight, initiating the process of producing vitamin D in the body may be the best known. When UVB rays hit human skin, they interact with the 7-DHC protein there to produce vitamin D3. People can get vitamin D from their diet and supplements, but sunlight is an important source of this essential nutrient. Vitamin D is necessary for key biological processes to take place in the body. Its benefits include:

- supporting healthy bones
- managing calcium levels
- reducing inflammation
- supporting the immune system and glucose metabolism

Researchers...suggest that exposure to sunlight triggers the skin to release stores of nitrogen oxides, which cause arteries to dilate, lowering blood pressure."

The authors explain that since we've all been cautioned about overexposure to sunlight, we may have taken things too far. Getting enough sun exposure is equally as important. If we work in windowless spaces, all the more reason to get out into the sun at least once a day.

So, today, and every day, I'll be looking for my moment in the sun.

John Ruskin (1819–1900), English writer and philosopher

OCTOBER 29
Pay Attention to Synchronicities

> *When you stop existing and you start*
> *truly living, each moment of the day comes*
> *alive with wonder and synchronicity.*
>
> —Steve Maraboli,
> *Life, the Truth, and Being Free*

Once, when I was perusing a marvelous bookstore while on vacation, I came across an exceptionally lovely volume of poetry. I was so drawn to it, and longed to buy it, but convinced myself I didn't need to spend money on any more books right then. To my surprise I arrived home to find that same book of poetry waiting for me in my mailbox, a gift from a treasured friend. That moment of synchronicity got my attention.

I devoured the poems with anticipation, more attuned to their meaning than I might have been without the synchronistic event. Through that small treasure trove of wisdom, I found so many answers to questions I was wrestling with at the time. With gratitude, I vowed that from then on I would be on the lookout for gifts that came to me as synchronicities. And I have been.

I pay attention now when I'm thinking about someone I haven't seen for a while and they call a few minutes later. I stay open to new opportunities when one person tells me about an idea and later that week someone else brings up the same idea. I am less a believer in coincidence than I used to be and much more in harmony with the possibility of synchronicity. I don't have to understand how it works. But it would be a shame to miss any assistance available to me.

Today I am gratefully open to the possibility of synchronicities, and I am paying attention.

Steve Maraboli, author, speaker, behavioral science academic

OCTOBER 30

Reset After a Difficult Time

How great it is when we come to know that times of disappointment can be followed by times of fulfillment; that sorrow can be followed by joy; that guilt over falling short of our ideals can be replaced by pride in doing all that we can.

—Fred Rogers,
*The World According to Mr. Rogers:
Important Things to Remember*

Sometimes, despite my best intentions, and what I thought was careful planning, life hits me with a series of challenges all at once. When I'm in the middle of it all, I've learned that sometimes I just have to tough it out until it's over. But once I'm back on more solid ground again, it's important to "reset," as I like to think of it. If I don't acknowledge that things have been difficult, those feelings can become buried and blocked. Then I cause myself to carry the difficulty with me longer than necessary. So, the first part of a reset is saying, "Wow, that was a hard patch."

The next part is asking myself what I need. More sleep? Dinner out? A nice glass of wine and some dark chocolate? Time to write in my journal? A funny movie? It's important to consider only choices that I can actually do for myself. That overworked part of me just might say it needs a trip to the beach, or some other extravagant wish. If that's not in the cards right now, I have to gently and kindly acknowledge the desire, and then focus on what is possible at the moment. Once I've decided what I'm wanting and can realistically have, it's important to do it as soon as possible. Otherwise the already discouraged part of me feels even more let down. When I'm going out to dinner or watching the fun movie, I remind myself that this reset time is designed to help me feel better. That kind of self-care can keep me from experiencing the damage of burnout.

Today I commit to making renewing times happen as soon as possible after difficult ones.

Fred Rogers (1928–2003), American television host, author, minister, known professionally as Mr. Rogers

OCTOBER 31

Halloween Thoughts

*If you fall in love with the imagination,
you understand that it is a free spirit. It will
go anywhere, and it can do anything.*

—Alice Walker

According to the *History Channel* website, "Halloween, celebrated annually on October 31, is one of the world's oldest holidays. Although it's derived from ancient festivals and religious rituals, Halloween is still widely celebrated today in a number of countries around the globe. In countries such as Ireland, Canada and the United States, traditions include costume parties, trick-or-treating, pranks and games. Versions of the holiday are celebrated elsewhere, too. In Mexico and other Latin American countries, Día de los Muertos—the Day of the Dead—honors deceased loved ones and ancestors. In England, Guy Fawkes Day, which falls on November 5, is commemorated with bonfires and fireworks."

As a child, Halloween was a time I could let my imagination run wild, pretending to be characters from my favorite books or movies. I wasn't interested in scary costumes like my friends were. For me it was thrilling to spend time "becoming" someone new. Those happy memories motivate me to connect more with imagination during the entire year. Certainly I want to support it with children; I love playing imaginative games with my granddaughters. And throughout my career I've advocated for the type of education that helps children's imaginations flourish. Now I'm asking myself how I can cultivate my own imaginative pursuits more. I think it begins with curiosity. What would I like to learn more about?

Today I'm inviting my imagination to be the free spirit Alice Walker calls it. I'm open to new ideas and I'm ready to go where they might take me.

Alice Walker, American writer, poet, and social activist

November

*The thinnest yellow light of November
is more warming and exhilarating
than any wine they tell of.*

—Henry David Thoreau

Henry David Thoreau (1817–1862), American naturalist and essayist

NOVEMBER 1
A Month of Thankfulness

The thankful receiver bears a plentiful harvest.

—William Blake

I have decided to make November a month of thankfulness for myself and not confine my gratitude to just one day. In the US, Thanksgiving Day is always celebrated on the fourth Thursday of November. In Canada it's the second Monday of October. Seventeen other countries around the world, from Japan to Liberia, celebrate a day of thanks sometime throughout the year. It's a good idea. Without a specific time to focus on the importance of being grateful, it would be too easy to get stuck in a cycle of petty complaining, always wanting more. We humans tend to take our good fortune for granted. So focusing for a full month on the bounty in my life seems like a wise move.

I know how easy it is to forget the newest blessing and go on to wanting the next. My husband and I focused on finding just the right place to live when we moved from our house of 30 years. When we finally found it, we were elated...for a little while. Soon, it was just normal. It became shockingly easy to take it for granted. And so it is with most of our abundance in life.

Today I am thankful for so many gifts that would be easy to forget. Here's a sampling: accessible food and water; heat and cooling when I need them; people to love; a body that mostly still works; dazzling trees and mischievous birds outside my window; the generosity of people who write books for me to enjoy; music that transports; and interesting weather. Simple yet profound. I am setting an intention to keep my sincere thanksgiving going all month.

William Blake (1757–1827), English poet

NOVEMBER 2
Keep It Simple, Sweetheart

Out of clutter, find simplicity.

—Albert Einstein

How easy is it to let clutter grow unchecked? For me, far too easy. Even after a productive purging of my living quarters, I turn around a few weeks later and am dismayed to see how much of the messiness has made its way back. There are the stacks of unopened mail and the birthday cards displayed on the side table long past their time, and too many books left around, and the cozy throw blankets we got out to snuggle with on a cold night, but never returned to their rightful places, and the big platter we took down for a party which belongs on the high shelf I need a step stool to reach. Each item, I know, is a sign of a full life, but they have become too much of a good thing, as William Shakespeare would say.

What I'm realizing is that I've forgotten my intention to put away just a bit of clutter each morning or at night right before bed. If I fall into the trap of, "I'll clean up when I have more time," soon the sheer volume of things to deal with becomes overwhelming. And Albert Einstein is right. Once clutter is disposed of, I feel a sense of simplicity again that is so calming and pleasant.

So today I am reminding myself to simply put away a little clutter each day. It's a gift I can give myself toward more peaceful living.

Albert Einstein (1879–1955), German-born theoretical physicist

NOVEMBER 3
Do Not Be Defeated

*You may encounter many defeats,
but you must not be defeated. In fact,
it may be necessary to encounter the defeats,
so you can know who you are, what you can
rise from, how you can still come out of it.*

—Maya Angelou

I suspect no one much likes the word "defeat." I think I'd prefer "challenge," or "setback," or "opportunity for growth." And yet, some things in life may need to be thought of as defeats. In business we try things that don't work. In our personal lives we enter into marriages that weren't meant to last the long term. People we love die tragically and hopes we've held must be let go.

If Maya Angelou is right, perhaps the defeats are indeed necessary so we learn to know our internal strength and what we are able to do when we must. I look back to the hardest times in my life and realize they introduced me to my indestructible center. We all have one, but don't always realize how strong it really is until we need it. I am grateful to know mine is always there.

Today I am remembering that defeats do not ever have to defeat me. I wish you that unshakable understanding as well.

Maya Angelou (1928–2014), American writer, poet and civil rights activist

NOVEMBER 4
Take Energy Breaks

Rest when you're weary. Refresh and renew yourself, your body, your mind, your spirit. Then get back to work.

—Ralph Marston

Jim Loehr and Tony Schwartz, in their book, *The Power of Full Engagement*, explain the reasons why people need to take energy breaks on a regular basis throughout the day:

"In the early 1950's, researchers Eugene Aserinsky and Nathan Kleitman discovered that sleep occurs in smaller cycles of 90-120-minute segments...In the 1970's, further research showed that a version of this same 90-120-minute cycle – ultradian rhythms – operates in our waking lives...These ultradian rhythms help to account for the ebb and flow of our energy throughout the day....Somewhere between 90 and 120 minutes, the body begins to crave a period of rest and recovery. Signals include a desire to yawn and stretch, hunger pangs, increased tension, difficulty concentrating...a higher incidence of mistakes. We are capable of overriding these natural cycles, but only by summoning the fight-or-flight response and flooding our bodies with stress hormones that are designed to help us handle emergencies."

The authors describe the long-term cost of this constant barrage of stress hormones. I can summarize it this way: it's not good. The better choice is to build in recovery times – energy breaks – every hour-and-a-half to three hours. These breaks can be a walk around the block, a snack, a quick period of stretching, or a short meditation. Even just a trip to the restroom helps.

Today I am paying attention to my body's need for these breaks. I am promising myself I will not go more than three hours without giving myself a chance to renew my energy.

Ralph Marston (1907–1967), American professional football player and writer

NOVEMBER 5
Treasure True Friendship

Friendships multiply joy and divide grief.
—Thomas Fuller

The older I've gotten, the more I realize that to live a happy life it only takes a few close relationships, if they are truly authentic ones. Those are the people I call first to help me multiply my joy, and the ones I reach out to immediately when I need help dividing grief. They have seen me at my worst and love me anyway. They are genuinely happy for my happiness. I sincerely hope I am all that for them as well.

It's a silly misunderstanding of the ego to think we must be perfect to be worthy of good friends. Our true friends, which can certainly include family members, know that perfection is impossible and only ask for authenticity. Today I am giving thanks for those kinds of friendships and the life-enhancing gifts that they are.

Thomas Fuller (1608–1661), English historian and writer

NOVEMBER 6
Beauty Emergencies

We live in a wonderful world that is full of beauty, charm and adventure. There is no end to the adventures that we can have if only we seek them with our eyes open.

—Jawaharlal Nehru

Maggie Smith, in her book, *Keep Moving*, writes about a morning she looked out her bathroom window and was stopped in her tracks. "I couldn't believe the sky I saw – magenta, aqua, purple. I shouted to the kids, 'Hurry, look out back!' My son, who was downstairs, went straight to the back door to see the sunrise. But my daughter came running into the upstairs bathroom. 'What's wrong?' she asked. 'Nothing's wrong. Just a beauty emergency. Look at the sky.' Because she is my child, she knows what a beauty emergency is: one of those things you have to look at now, before it's gone."

I want to have more beauty emergencies in my life. Recently when my nine-year-old granddaughter was visiting, she and her sister were having a snack on our balcony when Lyla burst inside saying, "Nana, I need your phone - now!" I gave it to her quickly, trusting the urgency in her voice, and a minute later she came back with a spectacular photo of a sunset, its transitory beauty captured for us all to enjoy.

Today I am on the lookout for fleeting moments of beauty – the butterfly there for just an instant; the last day the leaves will look like fire, right before they drop for the year; the breathtaking pictures the sky makes at beginnings and endings of days; the way snow swirls as it's falling; the waves crashing on rocks so their spray gushes in the air and catches sunlight sparkles; the shine left on the pavement just after it rains.

I hope I have at least one beauty emergency today.

Jawaharlal Nehru (1889–1964), former Prime Minister of India, author

NOVEMBER 7

Release Shame

> *We live in a world where most people still subscribe to the belief that shame is a good tool for keeping people in line. Not only is this wrong, but it's dangerous. Shame is highly correlated with addiction, violence, aggression, depression, eating disorders, and bullying.*
>
> —Brené Brown

My parents came from a generation that said, "Shame on you." It was said to them and they said it to their children. I'm certain they didn't mean to cause harm, but using shame as a disciplinary tool is dangerous. I have struggled with feelings of shame throughout my life, and despite my best efforts, I'm certain I've passed along some of those feelings to my children.

Here's the good news. We adults are becoming more aware of the need to stop shaming. When I began working with preschoolers, my much-older cooperating teacher would often say to a child, "We don't run inside. You should know better." It wasn't meant to be cruel, but the unintentional effect was to give the child this shaming message: "Everyone else knows not to run. What's wrong with you? Why don't you know better?" Fortunately, many of us throughout the field began reflecting on how our words affected children. Many positive changes have occurred to move our messages from shaming to respect. This is definitely a healthy step forward.

Now if we could only make that change in our internal self-talk. If I listen carefully, how often do I say to myself, "You should have known better?" More than I would like. Today I am listening carefully for any old shaming messages that might still be hanging around. If I hear them, I promise to substitute ones that are more loving and self-supportive.

Brené Brown, American professor and author

NOVEMBER 8
More Laughter, Less Worry

Laughter serves as a blocking agent.
Like a bulletproof vest, it may help protect
you against the ravages of negative emotions
that can assault you in disease.

—Norman Cousins

Sometimes we've just got to laugh - even when things don't feel great. Actually, that's the time we *most* need to laugh. In 1986, in *The Washington Post*, Don Colburn wrote an article called, "Normans Cousins, Still Laughing." It was a profile of Cousins, the longtime editor of the *Saturday Review*, who had overcome a serious disease. As Colburn described, "Cousins wrote an article titled 'Anatomy of an Illness' in *The New England Journal of Medicine*. Cousins' article chronicled his remarkable recovery from a severe and life-threatening disease of the connective tissue called degenerative collagen illness. He was hospitalized in 1964 with severe pain, high fever and near-paralysis of the legs, neck and back. 'Being unable to move my body was all the evidence I needed that the specialists were dealing with real concerns,' he wrote. 'But deep down, I knew I had a good chance and relished the idea of bucking the odds.'...

The key to his recovery, he said, was a powerful drug called laughter. 'I made the joyous discovery that 10 minutes of genuine belly laughter had an anesthetic effect.'...Flat on his back in a New York hospital, Cousins persuaded the nurses to read him excerpts from the humor columns of E.B. White and Max Eastman and show him 'Candid Camera' reruns and old Marx Brothers movies." Cousins didn't think that laughter alone was a substitute for medical treatment, but he did believe it was a great supplement.

Since then, much has been written about laughter's role in healing. Today my goal is to laugh more and worry less.

Norman Cousins (1915–1990), American journalist, author and professor

NOVEMBER 9
Check In on Self Talk

There is no inspiration without being armed with the ability of self-talk.

—Mwanandeke Kindembo

It's time again to pay attention to how I've been talking to myself. In the US, it can often start to feel hectic in November, with preparations beginning for Thanksgiving and whatever other holidays we might be celebrating. I want to be alert to any negative self-talk that starts popping up, such as "why aren't you farther ahead in your holiday planning?" Now is the time I need my self-talk to bring me inspiration, not serve as ammunition against me.

Years ago at one of the first staff retreats I held as a new early care and education program director, I began our time together by asking each person to share a quality that they especially appreciated about themselves. I didn't realize how hard this would be for people, but it makes sense that it was. Most of us were programmed as children to "not get too big for our britches" or "not blow our own horns." When I saw everyone's reluctance to participate, I asked, "Would it be easier to tell me something about yourself you're working on making better?" Everyone nodded that it would be much easier to talk about that.

What ensued from that moment was a heart-to-heart conversation about what it means if we dismiss our positive qualities and only admit to our "faults." I wondered aloud how we would be able to help children embrace their worth if we feel shaky about our own. It was the first of many such conversations, and it began a healing journey for all of us to learn to talk to ourselves as kindly as we wish to talk with children.

So today is a good time to remind myself to be kind in my self-talk. I hope you'll check in with yourself, too.

Mwanandeke Kindembo, Congolese author and engineer

NOVEMBER 10
Take Action When Situations Need Change

*If you do not change direction,
you may end up where you are heading.*

—Lao Tzu

There are times in life when it is not healthy to end up where we are heading. Being in any kind of abusive situation is a time when change is called for to keep ourselves safe – physically and/or psychologically. Finding the courage to leave an abusive marriage or a psychologically abusive work situation is vital.

It's important to understand that the skill of acceptance (see July 11) does not mean approval. I can accept the fact that I am in an unhealthy situation, and also know I must take action to make changes. Without acceptance, we often find ourselves in denial, and that is one of the most dangerous places to be.

Even when we are not the ones in the unhealthy situation, there are times we feel compelled to take action on behalf of others. Opportunities abound to work for change to make life better for refugees, for children experiencing hunger, for those facing racism or oppression of any kind. We can lend our time as a volunteer, donate money, write advocacy emails; any or all of the above.

What does not work is unthinkingly heading down unhealthy paths, abdicating our responsibility for changing direction. Today I am asking myself if there are paths I wish to change. And then I am taking action.

NOVEMBER 11
Creative Eating

It seems to me that our three basic needs, for food and security and love, are so entwined that we cannot think of one without the other.

—M.F.K. Fisher

I never used to think of cooking as a pleasurable endeavor. I've learned to think differently, mostly by watching my son and son-in-law so thoroughly enjoy their time in the kitchen. They've also introduced me to the joys of creative eating, as have my daughter and daughter-in-law as we plan together for interesting meals on our shared vacations. I do think M.F.K. Fisher is right: eating thoughtfully chosen and prepared food with people we love feels safe and joyful. And remembering that those moments are a privilege many do not have only increases the gratitude I feel.

Today I am planning for some creative cooking and eating. I think I'll make a roasted tomato soup and use one of the spice mixes my son-in-law has gifted me, or maybe some of the homemade spice blend my son has shared. I'll serve it with an apple pie made from fruit harvested at local farms. Maybe I'll even add some vanilla bean ice cream. The key will be to remain fully present as I cook and eat, savoring and appreciating each step.

There were periods in my life when I didn't feel I had the time to do much cooking. There still are days now when I feel the same. Whether or not I cook, though, I can always remember to be grateful when I eat. That opportunity is before me daily, reminding me of my connection to the land, to people who grow my food, and to loved ones who share meals with me.

I wonder what interesting food you might cook or eat today.

M.F.K. Fisher (1908–1992), American food writer

NOVEMBER 12
World Kindness Day

*What wisdom can you find that
is greater than kindness?*

—Jean-Jacques Rousseau

According to the website, National Days, "World Kindness Day is an international holiday that was formed in 1998 to promote kindness throughout the world and is observed annually on November 13...in many countries including the United States, Canada, Japan, Australia and the U.A.E....to diffuse this crucial quality that brings people of every kind together."

I know. There's a special day for everything it seems, but I figured a focus on kindness was something I want to support. *The Power of Kindness*, by Piero Ferrucci, is a beautifully touching book that's helped me better understand the complexities of what we call kindness. Ferrucci tells a story about his son that helped him realize that sometimes kindness means honestly addressing a problem instead of trying to find the easy way out. He writes, "Some time ago, my son Emilio was going back to school after vacation. He did not like the idea at all and was filled with anxiety...I tried to lift his spirits, to distract him, convince him it was not as bad as it seemed, but in vain. Then I hit upon the idea of offering him something that is almost taboo in our family: French fries at a fast-food place. Usually anything that is prohibited appeals to Emilio, especially junk food. I thought I had the ace up my sleeve. But no. Emilio's reply ought to be chiseled in stone: 'Dad, you don't solve problems with french fries.' Touché. You don't pretend problems do not exist, and you can't solve them with ephemeral distractions... Offering French fries to my son in order to console and distract him from his anxiety was by no means a kind act."

Today I am pondering all that it means to be kind, approaching this day with reflection.

Jean-Jacques Rousseau (1712–1778), Swiss philosopher

NOVEMBER 13

Get Along With Others

Alone we can do so little;
together we can do so much.

–Helen Keller

"Success is not just about how creative or smart or driven you are, but how well you are able to connect with, contribute to, and benefit from the ecosystem of people around you," wrote researcher Shawn Achor in his book, *Big Potential: How Transforming the Pursuit of Success Raises Our Achievement, Happiness and Well-Being.*

"[S]cientifically in the modern world, the biggest impediment to your success and realizing your potential is not lack of productivity, hard work, or intelligence; it is the way in which we pursue it. The pursuit of potential must not be a lonely road. The conclusion of a decade of research is clear: It's not faster alone; it's better together."

Achor's research is decisive: people who are able to develop and maintain good working relationships with colleagues are not only the most successful in the workplace — they are also the happiest. Approaching others through the tools of non-judgment, acceptance and assuming best intentions can help us forge healthy working relationships. The caveat to this is the ability to recognize if we are ever in a truly unhealthy environment (see November 11), and to remove ourselves from that toxic situation.

Today I am recognizing the importance of working well with other people. I am doing my part to approach others with unconditional positive regard and a willingness to listen with my heart. Today I do my best to contribute to the well-being of all of us.

Helen Keller (1880–1968), American author and disability rights advocate

NOVEMBER 14
Change the Mental Subject

> *People tend to dwell more on negative things than on good things. So the mind then becomes obsessed with negative things, with judgments, guilt and anxiety produced by thoughts about the future and so on.*
>
> —Eckhart Tolle

I have to be careful with myself so I don't fall into the habit of dwelling on negativity and worry. It's all too easy to begin obsessing, as Eckhart Tolle says, until I find myself engaging in negative future fantasies or all kinds of self-criticism. If I didn't stop myself it would be easy to endlessly revisit past mistakes, running them over and over in my mind until I'm mired in guilt.

It's at times like those I have to be firm with myself about changing the mental subject. If I've considered what there was to learn from my mistake, if I've made any amends that were possible, if I've engaged in compassionate self-forgiveness, then it's time to close the book on the subject. This takes discipline and insistence, but it's vital for well-being.

One of the best ways I've learned to do this mental "channel changing" is to say, "Stop focusing so much on yourself and think about something you can do for someone else." It reminds me that obsessing about mistakes is really a selfish pursuit.

Today if I find myself engaging in obsessive thinking, I plan to change my mental focus toward an action step I can take to bring a bit of cheer to another person.

Eckhart Tolle, German-born author and teacher

NOVEMBER 15

Release Jealousy

*Don't blow off another's candle for it
won't make yours shine brighter.*

—Jaachynma N.E. Agu

I don't believe that anyone who is a student in this earth school gets to escape feelings of jealousy. In *The Book of Joy*, the Dalai Lama, Desmond Tutu and Douglas Abrams write this about envy, "'It is not that you wake up in the morning and you say, Now I'm going to be envious. It just rises spontaneously,' the Archbishop began, once again arguing for the naturalness of our emotions and for self-compassion. 'I mean you get up, and you're trying to be a good person and that guy goes past yet again, for the third time this week, in his Mercedes-Benz...You have been trying not to feel jealous...but the feeling just comes up.'"

Jealousy may be a natural human emotion, but the book cautions that, "According to the happiness research, 'upward comparisons' are particularly corrosive to our well-being. Envy doesn't leave room for joy." The Dalai Lama provides this perspective: "Often envy comes because we are too focused on our material possessions and not on our true inner values. Most important is to develop a sense of concern for others' well-being. If you have genuine kindness and compassion, then when someone gets something or has more success, you are able to rejoice in their good fortune."

I agree with both wise thinkers. Today, if I start to experience jealousy, I can remind myself that it's a perfectly normal feeling. Then I can remember that there are more important things in life than material possessions and that I want to be a person who celebrates others' good fortune. Then I can take a moment to give thanks for all the blessings in my life, knowing there are people who would trade places with me in a second.

Jaachynma N.E. Agu, Nigerian author

NOVEMBER 16

HOW I Do Is More Important than WHAT I Do

I asked a wise man, "Tell me sir, in which field could I make a great career?" He said with a smile, "Be a good human being. There is a huge opportunity in this area and very little competition."

—Jalāl al-Dīn Muḥammad Rūmī

Here I am again, reminding myself that it is more important to focus on HOW I am in the world, than WHAT I do. That means that the mindset I bring to my work, or any endeavor, is every bit as important as the actions I take. In fact, grounding myself in loving energy will also influence my actions. I am sure of it.

I can remember times when I found myself feeling worry and negativity about a project I was working on. It seemed like no matter what I did, I was slogging through quicksand and running into roadblocks. What I learned to do in times like those was to shift my thoughts away from the specifics of what I was involved in, and begin to focus on who I want to be in the world. I would remember that I want to be a grateful person, so I would go down my mental list of reasons I have for gratitude. I would think about my intention to show up in the world as a loving presence, so I would choose a few action steps I could take right then to share love with others. I might place a call to thank someone for a kindness, or send an encouraging email to a person I knew needed support.

Almost always, after I spent time reminding myself about HOW I want to be, the WHAT to do in whatever I was working on seemed to be easier to figure out. I've never found any good to come from a continued focus on worry or frustration. Moving into a space that allows me to reconnect with my core being has consistently been helpful. That is how I am choosing to be today.

Jalāl al-Dīn Muḥammad Rūmī (1207–1273), Persian poet

NOVEMBER 17

Find a Time to "Just Be"

I am a human being, not a human doing.

−Kurt Vonnegut, Jr.

Today I plan to find a time when I can just "be" — when I can leave behind feelings of needing to "accomplish" anything, and simply enjoy life.

What might that look like? Perhaps I'll sit outside and watch the bird feeder. Maybe I'll listen to music in my comfy padded chair. It could be that I'll have a glass wine while enjoying a leisurely conversation with someone I love.

Whatever it looks like, I plan to savor the "beingness" of that time. I hope you can find some moments like that for yourself as well.

Kurt Vonnegut, Jr. (1922–2007), American author

NOVEMBER 18
Discover the New in the Familiar

The real voyage of discovery consists not in seeking new landscapes, but in having new eyes.

—Marcel Proust

"When you visit a familiar place, it's never stagnant. There's always change, and every new day brings a tilt, another view, something that previously escaped you," wrote Dara McAnulty, in his wonderful book, *Diary of a Young Naturalist*. His outlook on the world, seen through his orientation as a teenager with autism, helped him note and record valuable insights in fresh new ways. I loved "visiting" places with him because he continually saw them through the "new eyes" Proust speaks of.

McAnulty's work inspires me to visit my familiar places with the expectation of discovering them anew. Tonight I'll take a walk to a pond near my home and look for something that's changed about it since the last time I visited. I'm certain there are myriad changes happening always, but my "old eyes" don't always notice. I suspect developing a new way of looking will bring much more enjoyment to an old familiar walk.

Marcel Proust (1871–1992), French novelist

NOVEMBER 19
What If There's Nothing to Fix?

> *We all deserve to live fully, to be seen and accepted by others, to love ourselves unconditionally and feel a sense of belonging without conditions.*
>
> —Suzanne Jones,
> There is Nothing to Fix:
> Becoming Whole Through
> Radical Self-Acceptance

What if just for today I practiced radical self-acceptance? What if I were very clear with myself that I am just wonderful the way I am? What if I told myself there is NOTHING I need to do today?

I've offered many tools and skills in this book that I find helpful, and I hope you find some of them useful, too. But make no mistake: I am not offering them to you – or to myself for that matter – because we are broken and need to be fixed. Far from it. I am simply sharing ideas that I've found fun, supportive, and most of all, encouraging.

I love encouraging myself. I do not love "fixing" myself because I'm exactly fine just as I am right now. I wanted to remind myself – and you – about that today.

Suzanne Jones, American author and trauma recovery expert

NOVEMBER 20

World Children's Day

It is the responsibility of every adult...to make sure that children hear what we have learned from the lessons of life and to hear over and over that we love them and that they are not alone.

—Marian Wright Edelman

Yes, it's yet another specially designated day, but I had to include this one since my whole career has focused on efforts to secure children's well-being. According to the United Nations website, "World Children's Day was first established in 1954...and is celebrated on 20 November each year to promote international togetherness, awareness among children worldwide, and improving children's welfare."

I firmly believe, as Marian Wright Edelman does, that it is the responsibility of every adult, not just parents or teachers, to ensure the welfare of the world's children. In his book *Big Potential*, researcher Shawn Achor writes this: "When Maasai warriors of Kenya, some of the fiercest and most intelligent fighters in history, greet each other, they do not say 'How are you?' as we do in Western cultures. They say, 'How are the children?' The proper answer, even for those without children, is 'All the children are well.' That's because, according to their social script, things can't be good for one individual unless everyone in the community is thriving. The science in this book proves they are right. We can't just worry about what is good for us; we need to worry about whether everyone around us is thriving."

And that includes the world's children. Today, and every day, I am continuing to do what I can to safeguard a better world for every child. Let's all join together in redoubling our efforts so that someday we may be able to say, "All the children are well," and really mean it.

Marian Wright Edelman, American activist for civil rights and children's rights and founder of the Children's Defense Fund

NOVEMBER 21
Get Inspired by Movies

For me, filmmaking combines everything. That's the reason I've made cinema my life's work. In films, painting and literature, theatre and music come together.

—Akira Kurosawa

Sometimes nothing can change a low mood for me like watching an inspiring movie. The other day as I perused Netflix, I came across a film called "Crip Camp." Here's how it's described: "A groundbreaking summer camp for teens with disabilities proves so inspiring that a group of its alumni join the radical disability rights movement to advocate for historic legislation changes." Much of the film centers on Judith Ellen "Judy" Heumann, an American disability rights activist, and her indefatigable fight to finally enact legislation that would make life better for those with disabilities.

Watching the movie reminded me of how many people have been and still are working on behalf of a better world for all of us. Sometimes it doesn't feel like that. When you start to get discouraged, I urge you to watch "Crip Camp," or other films like it.

I am continuing to be on the lookout for movies that connect me with the best of humanity.

Akira Kurosawa (1910–1998), Japanese filmmaker

NOVEMBER 22
The Four Agreements
First Agreement –
Be Impeccable with Your Word

Integrity is doing the right thing when nobody's watching, and doing as you say you would do.

—Roy T. Bennett,
The Light in the Heart

I have reread more than once Don Miguel Ruiz's best-selling book, *The Four Agreements*. Today, and for the three days following, I am going to be highlighting the wisdom contained in each "agreement."

The premise of Ruiz's book is that there is a code of conduct found in ancient Toltec wisdom that can help us lead happier lives. The Toltec culture was prominent from 950–1150 in Mexico.

The first of Ruiz's four agreements is "be impeccable with your word." This reminds me to be mindful of what I say to others, being careful not to casually agree to commitments unless I am certain I can keep them. I know how bad it feels whenever I break promises to anyone, myself included.

Today I am considering carefully before I enter into commitments. I am speaking my truth in all situations.

NOVEMBER 23
Second Agreement – Don't Take Anything Personally

*Nothing others do is because of you.
What others say and do is a projection of
their own reality, their own dream. When you
are immune to the opinions and actions of others,
you won't be the victim of needless suffering.*

–Don Miguel Ruiz,
The Four Agreements

The second agreement reminds me, as Ruiz says above, that I need not base my feelings about myself on others' words or actions. While I do want to be open to constructive feedback (see October 6), I do not have to "suffer" if other people are projecting their own pain onto me.

I can recognize that when a person's feedback is filled with toxic, unwarranted criticism, then it is not constructive feedback, and merely a projection of issues the other person is dealing with. That's the time for me to set boundaries and not take anything personally.

Today I will remember that, to paraphrase Eleanor Roosevelt, no one can make me feel bad without my consent.

Don Miguel Ruiz, Mexican writer

NOVEMBER 24

Third Agreement – Don't Make Assumptions

Assumptions are dangerous things to make, and like all dangerous things to make – bombs, for instance, or strawberry shortcake – if you make even the tiniest mistake you can find yourself in terrible trouble. Making assumptions simply means believing things are a certain way with little or no evidence that shows you are correct, and you can see at once how this can lead to terrible trouble.

–Lemony Snicket, pen name of Daniel Handler,
The Austere Academy (A Series of Unfortunate Events, #5)

Don Miguel Ruiz (see November 22) believes that the best way to keep ourselves from making assumptions is to ask questions that ensure good, clear communication. He explains that sometimes when we are afraid to have honest conversations, the assumptions made lead to far worse situations than a stressful conversation would have been.

In the Harvard Business Review book, *On Communication*, an article by Holly Weeks asks the question, "Since stressful conversations are so common – and so painful – why don't we work harder to improve them?" One strategy she recommends is to prepare for uncomfortable conversations by rehearsing them with a neutral friend. She also advocates setting intentions at the beginning of conversations to help both parties focus on a positive outcome. Asking uncomfortable questions of people can be prefaced by an explanation, such as, "I don't want to assume anything, so it would really help me if we could talk openly about some questions I have."

Today I am being careful not to make assumptions about any situation. I am making a commitment to have honest conversations that help everyone deal with facts.

Lemony Snicket, pen name of Daniel Handler, American author

NOVEMBER 25
Fourth Agreement – Always Do Your Best

A person who tries has an advantage over the person who wishes.

—Utibe Samuel Mbom

Don Miguel Ruiz (see November 22) believes that doing one's best varies from situation to situation. When we're home sick in bed, our best will be very different from when we're healthy and full of energy. That seems obvious, but yet we often judge ourselves against the very best day we've ever had, feeling like we are falling short if each day isn't as productive or exceptional.

Today I am allowing myself realistic expectations of what doing my best means. Perhaps a way to assess my efforts is to ask, "Did I try?" If the answer is yes, then I know I've taken the first important step.

Utibe Samuel Mbom, Nigerian author, model, entrepreneur

NOVEMBER 26

People Can Rise to My Belief in Them

Assume the best intent in others around you. You will often be right, and even when you're not, people can rise to your view of them. Not always, but enough that I believe it's worth it.

—Sallie Krawcheck

This is a principle I wholeheartedly believe in, whether in a work setting, or with children, or honestly, just with myself. Sometimes I need to remember who I truly am so I can rise to that level.

What I sincerely believe about everyone — myself included — is that our true selves are so much more majestic than we let people see. At our core, I do believe we each have an unshakable loving essence. Pierre Tiellard de Chardin, a French philosopher, teacher and writer, was famous for saying, "We are not human beings having a spiritual experience. We are spiritual beings having a human experience."

Thinking of all of us that way changes the equation of life. Today as I go about my daily round, it is my intention to look at each person through the eyes of love. I can't wait to see how it changes my interactions.

Sallie Krawcheck, American entrepreneur, CEO and co-founder of Ellevest

NOVEMBER 27
Make Friends with Fear and Anger

> *If you try to get rid of fear and anger*
> *without knowing their meaning, they will*
> *grow stronger and return. We are all broken,*
> *we human creatures, and to pretend*
> *we're not is to inhibit healing.*
>
> —Madeleine L'Engle,
> *The Irrational Season*

I have been doing a lot of thinking about Madeleine L'Engle's words. As a child, her book, *A Wrinkle in Time*, affected me deeply. The story acknowledged the most fearful parts of life, but ultimately provided reassurance that love is stronger than fear. Her writing influenced how I view life. So, I've been asking myself how her assertion that "we are all broken," squares with my belief that we do not need to "fix" ourselves. This is what I've decided: What if brokenness is not something to be fixed, but something to be accepted as a necessary part of life? Could it be that figuring out how to deal with fear and anger is one of the life lessons we are all in this earth school to learn? If, as Michael Singer asserts in his book, *The Untethered Soul*, the best way to deal with fear and anger is to fully embrace them, feel them and let them flow through us, then perhaps an important part of that process is also learning from our emotions.

As counterintuitive as it sounds, it helps me to think of fear and anger as friends that have come for my benefit. Journaling with those emotions can be insightful and healing. When I literally ask them to write to me about what they are here to teach, I discover opportunities to grow in new ways. There are times when I'm in the grip of strong emotion that it does feel like a part of me has broken open. But perhaps what has really happened is that I've been opened up to new insights. It's another opportunity to connect with my internal strength. Today, if I experience intense emotions, I'll remember the gift of learning and growth they are bringing.

Madeleine L'Engle (1918–2007), American writer

NOVEMBER 28

Practical Love

*Do not waste time bothering whether you
'love' your neighbor; act as if you did.*

—C.S. Lewis

There have been many times in my life when I experienced the love of family and friends through their practical actions. People have brought me meals and sent good books to read when I was sick. I've left work at the end of the day to find that caring colleagues had cleared my car of the snow that had fallen throughout the day. My children and their spouses spent hours investigating places to stay and things to do so we could bring our whole family together for a fun and affordable vacation. One time when I was feeling discouragement about the state of the world, a friend made a donation in my name to a cause I cared about.

Through each of those practical actions I experienced love and care in a profound way. Today I am looking for my own opportunities to spread practical love. I can't wait to see what I'll come up with.

C.S. Lewis (1898–1963), British writer and theologian

NOVEMBER 29
True Humility

A humble person is more likely to be self-confident...a person with real humility knows how much they are loved.

—Cornelius Plantinga Jr.

Brazilian writer Paulo Coelho says, "Let us be absolutely clear about one thing: we must not confuse humility with false modesty or servility." The message from both Coelho and Cornelius Pantinga is that true humility comes from a healthy sense of self.

True humility never means feeling unworthy. Ron and Mary Hulnick, in their book, *Remembering the Light Within*, write, "Unworthiness is simply a case of mistaken identity. It's a case of attempted identity theft by your ego." True humility means not being controlled by the ego's mistaken feelings of lack or its desperate attempt to "prove" its worthiness.

True humility is the courage to be authentic and imperfect, with no need to try to "earn" love or acceptance. Today I am grateful to know I have nothing to prove. I can laugh at my imperfections and know I am worthy of love and belonging just as I am, right now, right here.

Cornelius Plantinga Jr., American theologian

NOVEMBER 30
Celebrate the Cracks

Our brokenness has no other beauty but the beauty that comes from the compassion that surrounds it.

—Henri Nouwen

In 1992 Leonard Cohen released the album "The Future" which included the song "Anthem" containing these lines:

"Forget your perfect offering.
There is a crack, a crack, in everything.
That's how the light gets in."

Rachel Naomi Remen, in her book, *Kitchen Table Wisdom*, where she writes about insights gained during her work with cancer patients, offers this:

"Wounding and healing are not opposites. They're part of the same thing. It is our wounds that enable us to be compassionate with the wounds of others. It is our limitations that make us kind to the limitations of other people. It is our loneliness that helps us to find other people...I think I have served people perfectly with parts of myself I used to be ashamed of."

It's a paradox of life, and one I've written about often in these pages, that it's our brokenness that ultimately leads to our wholeness, if we let it. No one escapes wounding in this life. If we allow our hurts and "cracks" to make us bitter and hateful and closed off to others, then we've missed the gifts available to us in pain. If, on the other hand, we use our wounds to help us become more empathetic and compassionate, then our "cracks" can indeed become openings for light.

Today I am grateful for the opportunities my wounds have brought to me.

Henri Nouwen (1932—1996), Dutch priest, professor, writer

December

December is a bewitching month.
The grey of cold teases
To explode into something worthwhile,
Into a dream of cold,
a starlight shower you can taste,
a cold that does not chill.

—Joseph Coelho

Joseph Coelho, English poet, playwright, author

DECEMBER 1

Many Ways to Celebrate

It is time for parents to teach young people early on that in diversity there is beauty and there is strength.

—Maya Angelou

The month of December is like a beautiful tapestry filled with religious and cultural celebrations of all kinds. St. Nicholas Day, Hanukkah, Winter Solstice, Christmas, Boxing Day, Kwanzaa, New Year's Eve: In my circle of friends and family I know people who celebrate each of these holidays (but no one I know celebrates them all).

I'm fortunate that this wide circle supports each other and no one asserts that their way of celebrating is better than anyone else's. In fact, there is admiration for the gorgeous range of traditions, food, clothing, greetings, games, and most importantly of all, expressions of faith and love.

Throughout this month I look forward to appreciating each of these heartfelt festivities, while also fully enjoying the ways I personally celebrate. What a gift it is that our world contains such an abundance of choices and meaning.

Maya Angelou (1928–2014), American writer, poet and civil rights activist

DECEMBER 2
Food for My Mind

The mind's health depends on what it feeds on. Avoid thoughts and conversations that kill your soul.

—Bangambiki Habyarimana

"Watch Ted Lasso," my daughter-in-law advised, "I really think you'll like it. It's the kind of show you look for." She knows me well. I want to spend my television or movie time with programs that give me a lift, that help me believe in the best of humanity.

Bangambiki Habyaraimana has put into words why I've always felt like this. I actually do believe my mind's health depends on what I feed it, and too much dark or violent programming is like feeding it poison. The same holds true for spending too much time with negativity on social media.

I'm guessing that each one of us must decide for ourselves what it is that destroys our souls or nourishes them. It may be different for every person, but I hope we are each honest with ourselves. Our mind's health is dependent on our protecting it from disastrous influences.

Today, and every day, I am paying attention to what I feed my mind. I choose to make it a healthy diet.

Bangambiki Habyarimana, Rwandan writer and blogger

DECEMBER 3
No Holiday Perfectionism

Perfectionism is self-abuse of the highest order.

—Anne Wilson Schaef

During any holiday, perfectionism can rear its ugly head again, even if it mostly behaves itself during the rest of the year. It has taken me a long while to believe that holiday time is not a test of whether I am a good mother, a good grandmother, a good friend, a good extended family member, a good colleague...choose one (or more). I now know I really do not need to prove myself by finding the "perfect" gifts or planning the "perfect" meals or arranging the "perfect" activities.

This year I am going to release myself from the grip of the holiday "perfects" and remind myself I am enough just as I am. I prepare for holiday festivities with calm and care and gratitude. Today I start this journey by reminding myself to relax and enjoy the ride.

Anne Wilson Schaef (1934—2020), American clinical psychologist and author

DECEMBER 4

Don't Miss It

You have to understand that it is your attempt to get special experiences from life that makes you miss the actual experience of life.

—Michael Singer,
*The Untethered Soul:
The Journey Beyond Yourself*

Wanting to be "special" is a desire of the ego. My authentic self knows that everything life offers can be seen as a gift. I don't need to try to make exceptional experiences happen. Being grateful for what I have and not wishing it away by longing for something "better" helps me enjoy life.

All lives have times of difficulty. Reading history confirms that. It also teaches that the people who found the most joy in life were the ones who looked for it in all circumstances. In his book, *Living Long and Living Well*, my husband John Rosenow tells the story of Nelson Mandela, who, after being imprisoned for 27 years for his work on behalf of apartheid, went on to become the first black African elected president of the Union of South Africa at age 76.

It would have been easy for Mandela to become bitter in prison. Instead, he chose to read whatever books he could get his hands on and recite Shakespeare and other poetry from memory. He cultivated relationships with fellow prisoners and guards, and enjoyed nature while on work detail near the ocean and by tending a small prison garden. Perhaps most importantly, he continually worked on his internal growth, cultivating equanimity, forgiveness, gratitude and humor. He changed from an angry "firebrand revolutionary" to an advocate for unity and non-racism. As John wrote, "Few people indeed would respond to 27 years in prison as did Nelson Mandela." And yet, each of us has the daily choice to respond to life by appreciating every day as a gift, instead of longing for "special" experiences.

Michael Singer, American author, motivational speaker, former software developer

DECEMBER 5
Help My Ego Release Fear

When you observe the ego in yourself, you are beginning to go beyond it. Don't take the ego too seriously. When you detect ego behavior in yourself, smile. At times you may even laugh.

—Eckhart Tolle

Gerald G. Jamplosky, MD, in his book, *Love is Letting Go of Fear*, writes:

"Our ego's laws are based on the belief that our happiness depends on how much money we have in the bank and how many possessions we own. Its voice of fear bombards us with an attitude of greed, thinking of ourselves first, and getting as much as we can and holding on to it. The fear that is the nucleus of our egos gives us an insatiable desire and hunger to consume more, more and an unending consumption of more. Our ego's cardinal rule is that nothing is ever enough."

When I find myself caught up in feelings of lack, I know that my ego has taken control. Instead of berating those feelings, I try to do what Eckhart Tolle recommends: laugh. "There goes my ego again," I remind myself, shaking my head with a bemused smile, "believing the misunderstanding that possessions determine happiness."

And then I do a "true abundance" check to remind my ego that all is well. I go down my list of what really matters: loving relationships; my strong unshakable center that grounds me in all situations; opportunities to serve others and make a useful contribution in the world; beauty from nature, music, literature...The list could be quite a long one, but usually after the first few items my ego has calmed down and lets the rational, authentic me take over again.

Today I am reminding myself that the fears of the ego are false. I trust the abundance of my life.

Eckhart Tolle, German-born author and teacher

DECEMBER 6
Spread Some Cheer

Once again, we come to the holiday season, a deeply religious time that each of us observes, in his own way, by going to the mall of his choice.

–Dave Barry

The Dave Barry quote is tongue-in-cheek, but there's more than a little sad truth in it. When buying things takes up the majority of my holiday energy, I know I've gotten off track. It's all too easy to get caught up in the feeling that we can buy our way to happiness, even if we keep holiday perfectionism at bay (see December 3). In my experience, too much focus on *things* keeps me from experiencing genuine love and connection. To counteract the holiday consumerism creep, today I am resolving to spread cheer to colleagues, friends and families in ways that aren't about spending a lot of money. People often experience a higher level of stress this time of the month, so I am hoping a dose of good cheer will be a welcome antidote.

Here are a few ideas on my list:
- Write a cheery note and leave it on a colleague's desk;
- Send an email to a family member, telling them what I especially appreciate about them;
- Pick up a holiday-themed warm beverage from a drive-through and deliver it to an overwhelmed young parent who is quarantining at home with sick children;
- Send an email to someone who has served as a mentor in my life, thanking them for their influence and support;
- Find an irreverently funny holiday-themed meme and pass it on to someone I think will find it as amusing as I do.

I wonder what would be on your list.

Dave Barry, American author and columnist

DECEMBER 7
Stop Apologizing So Much

If a project falls behind, skip the excuses ("I'm so sorry I don't have this to you yet") and exchange it: "Thank you for your patience as we navigate this project, you will have it by Friday of next week." Take your power back by owning your situation, cutting out the sob story, and giving a simple thank you.

—Heather Murphy

One of the best pieces of advice I received from an older mentor was to stop saying "I'm sorry" so much. What she taught me was to do as Heather Murphy advises in the quote above: Replace "I'm sorry" with "Thank you." Instead of "I'm sorry I'm late," say "Thank you for waiting for me." Instead of "I'm sorry to have to ask," use "Thank you for helping me out." "I'm sorry I can't come to the party" becomes "Thank you for the invitation." It's a subtle shift that keeps us from continually feeling as if we've done something wrong.

Of course there are times a sincere apology is in order, but more often than not saying "I'm sorry" simply has become a habit that keeps us feeling small and too much beholden to others.

Today I am doing myself a favor and remembering that often a sincere "thank you" is a much better option than an apology.

Heather Murphy, Canadian business consultant

DECEMBER 8
Accept Gratitude Graciously

Acceptance is an art - an art which most never bother to cultivate. We think that we have to learn how to give, but we forget about accepting things, which can be much harder than giving.

—Alexander McCall Smith

Bestselling author, Anne Lamott, in her book, *Small Victories*, writes this: "At the age of sixty, I finally realized that I had been raised not to say, 'You're welcome,' and I began to wonder how this habit had reinforced my sense of separation."

She was taught as a child, she explained, to minimize how much she had given or how much time and hard work something had taken. If thanked, she learned to respond with, "Don't mention it," or "It's nothing." But as an adult, her thinking has changed. "If generosity is nothing," she asks, "then what is anything? Now I make myself accept gratitude. I look people in the eye gently and say, 'You're really welcome.'"

As Alexander McCall Smith says, learning to accept from others is something that needs to be cultivated. I can relate to Anne Lamott. For years I was a master deflector of compliments. Finally one day a friend looked at me sternly and asked, "Would you please just say 'thank you?'" From that day on I realized that it was much kinder to accept a sincerely offered compliment than it was to brush it away from some false sense of modesty.

Today I am remembering to graciously accept the gift of other people's gratitude.

Alexander McCall Smith, British writer

DECEMBER 9

Connect with Trees

*I wish we could translate the language of trees —
hear their voices, know their stories.*

—Dara McAnulty,
Diary of a Young Naturalist

There are those who might dismiss Dara McAnulty as a "tree hugger" or overly sentimental about the natural world. But I think he's on to something. Often when I've been feeling sad, time spent under a tree can help. I do feel a sense of communion — one living being to another. Naturalist Lyanda Lynn Haupt, in her book, *Rooted: Life at the Crossroads of Science, Nature and Spirit*, reaffirms that this feeling is based on scientific evidence. She reports that, "Multiple studies appear in the most respected journals, including *Science, Nature* and *The Journal of the National Academy of Sciences*, detailing evidence that: trees are able to communicate with one another, both through the motions of their branches, spreading chemical messages above ground, and through a web of intertwined roots and fungal mycelia below ground." And, "humans are more creative, physically hale, and less depressed after walking in a forest."

Haupt also reports that average North Americans spend about 93 percent of their waking hours indoors or in cars, and another 7 percent walking between buildings and cars. "Regular — or *any* — experience of deep wilderness is missing from most of our modern lives. Without such contact, our radiant mental and physical intelligences are being diminished." I am one of the average North Americans who very rarely visit deep wilderness. I hope to find ways to do so more often. In the meantime, I can enjoy walking trails that take me near more plants and trees than I can find in my neighborhood. And even in winter, simply standing by a tree in my front yard allows me to connect with its living energy. Today I am setting the intention to find more ways to savor the gifts that trees provide.

DECEMBER 10
Make Friends with Myself

*Friendship with oneself is all important,
because without it one cannot be friends
with anyone else in the world.*

—Eleanor Roosevelt

Until I read the Eleanor Roosevelt quote above I had never really thought that I could have a friendship with myself. I've thought of self-support and self-compassion and self-forgiveness, but not friendship. It's a new idea. It seems like it might open up interesting possibilities.

At some level I've always related to myself like a supportive parent I think, focusing on childhood hurts that needed healing, or bucking myself up when current times felt hard. Thinking of myself as a friend feels like more fun. I could take myself on adventures, laugh at life's absurdities and discover new ways to be of service in the world. Friends can enjoy life together. It's actually rather amazing how good this shift in perception feels.

Today I am ready to begin a whole new way of being with myself. I can't wait to see where it takes me.

Eleanor Roosevelt (1884–1962), former First Lady of the United States, author and activist

DECEMBER 11
What Have I Learned from Failure?

> *Life isn't perfect, any failures you have are actually learning moments. They teach us how to grow and evolve.*
>
> –Phillipa Soo

As this calendar year is nearing its close, I'm asking myself what my failures have taught me these last twelve months; how I've grown and evolved. I'm not sure how I feel about the word failure. During the time I served as CEO of Dimensions Foundation, I urged our team to focus more on the phrase "opportunities for growth" than on failure. "Failure" can seem like such a finite word – over and done – no going forward. Calling it an "opportunity for growth" encourages looking for the learning in any setback. That was my reasoning, anyway.

But perhaps I need to come to terms with the word failure, just as with the word defeat (see November 3). It may be that accepting failure and defeat as a part of life opens MORE doors to learning, not fewer. Maybe sugar coating failure with happy words sends the message that there is something wrong with failing.

I have certainly had moments of failure this year. There have been times when I've absolutely failed at keeping my patience, staying in non-judgment, or being kind to myself or others. Now, the question is, how do I work with those failures? Do I beat myself up for falling short or do I let my stumbles help me grow and evolve? Will my failures help me feel more empathy for my fellow travelers in this world who also fall short of their ideal behavior? I believe all of us in this earth school are doing the best we can with the tools we have. Perhaps the most we can ask of ourselves is to be able to say, "I'll try again tomorrow."

DECEMBER 12
Easy Does It

Smile, breathe and go slowly.

—Thich Nhat Hanh

Thich Nhat Hanh's words offer wise advice for what can be a month filled with much activity. Sometimes remembering to take it easy, to "go slowly," is very necessary. There are probably many obligations we have entered into right now — some willingly and perhaps some reluctantly. Not every day offers opportunities for slowing down, but we must find ways to do so.

Right this minute, in the middle of my writing, I am taking a break so I can just sit still, smile and breathe deeply. Once more: smile; breathe. Just those few moments remind me that life does not have to feel like an emergency. No matter what is happening around us, we can give ourselves the gift of a few minutes of calm.

Today and for the rest of this month I'm going to treat myself well by creating an "easy does it" moment sometime each day. I hope you'll join me.

Thich Nhat Hanh (1926–2022), Vietnamese Buddhist monk, peace activist, author and teacher

DECEMBER 13

Create a New Tradition

Tradition is a guide and not a jailer.

—W. Somerset Maugham

During this month when many are observing holidays, some of us may be bumping into family traditions that no longer feel like they fit. When that happens, it's good to remember W. Somerset Maugham's advice that tradition should not be a jailer. It really is okay to revise a tradition – or even replace it.

As my family continued to grow, when children married and then grandchildren arrived, what once worked for us at holiday time needed to be reworked. I made the decision that no tradition was more important than people's feelings. Creating celebrations that invited everyone in and made things as easy as possible for complicated schedules, was most important to me. Now our holiday gatherings shift and change each year as life shifts and changes.

But here's our new tradition: We will always find a way to share love with each other. That's all that matters. The HOW is way less important than the WHAT.

This month I release myself from the tyranny that can come from too-rigid traditions. I wish you the same.

DECEMBER 14

Watch the Lights

This is the season when people of all faiths and cultures are pushing back against the planetary darkness. We string bulbs, ignite bonfires, and light candles.

—Anita Diamant

Light-filled holidays abound this month. Rabbi Rafael Goldstein says, "Hanukkah celebrates the rays of hope and light." Dr. Maulana Karenga, creator of Kwanzaa, explains that lighting seven candles is for seven principles that are "the best of African thought and practice." The Christmas custom of decorating trees with lights symbolizes Christians' belief in Christ as the light of the world. One of the oldest holidays, Winter Solstice, uses light as the center of its observance.

I have a story about light. It was the first Christmas after John and I married. My children and their new stepfather connected as if they'd known each other forever, and perhaps they had on some level. John waited a long time to marry; waiting to find us he says now. I was cautious about another marriage, waiting to see if I could trust enough to try again. When the marriage finally happened, all of us felt as if we'd weathered a tough patch, and we were grateful. But there was still a feeling that it might be too good to be true. We each still held our breath at times. And then, our first Christmas Eve. We found a real tree, carefully added decorations, darkened the room and plugged in the tree lights. That's when the miracle happened. We each felt it. There was a glow, a comfort and a knowing of safety that can only be described as "The light was with us." It was a moment of marvel and magic. We each stopped holding our breath and began our lifetime of breathing easier.

Today I wish a miracle of light for all of us, we people who muck around in darkness much of the time. Erasmus said, "Give light, and the darkness will disappear of itself." Let it be so.

Anita Diamant, American author

DECEMBER 15
Find the Source of Self-Respect

> *Character — the willingness to accept responsibility for one's own life — is the source from which self-respect springs.*
>
> —Joan Didion,
> On Self-Respect

After almost a year of writing words of encouragement, I am realizing that there is great satisfaction in accepting responsibility for my own life. I believe that is one of the most important earth school lessons. I am not in control of life, but neither am I powerless. I am able to choose my response in every situation once I have dealt in a healthy way with my emotions. And, I know that whatever happens TO me will eventually be FOR me if I look for the gift in it.

Psychology professor, Martin Seligman, in his book, *Authentic Happiness*, asks the question, "What is the good life?" He answers it this way, based on his research work: "The good life is using your signature strengths every day to produce authentic happiness and abundant gratification." To put this definition into practice means we must each identify our signature strengths and how we can use them every day. Seligman identifies his strength as a love for learning and says he puts it to daily use by teaching college students. That may be true, but I am guessing college teaching is not the only way he uses his special strength. I would think that a person who loves learning might serve as a motivator for many people in all aspects of his life.

If one of my strengths is to be an encourager, then one way I use it is by writing this book. But I hope that's not the only way. Perhaps a signature strength can be thought of as a way of being. Maybe taking responsibility for our lives means identifying our unique strengths and incorporating them into all we do. That sounds like a blueprint for authentic success.

DECEMBER 16

Routines Can Be Joyful

Have regular hours for work and play; make each day both useful and pleasant, and prove that you understand the worth of time by employing it well. Then youth will bring few regrets, and life will become a beautiful success.

–Louisa May Alcott,
Little Women

I haven't always thought of myself as a person who likes routines, but over the years I have come to understand the value of having some things I can count on. How much routine a person wants in life is another personality preference characteristic, but I do believe all human beings benefit from a few things that happen on a regular basis. If we have a job where someone else sets the hours, then that routine is decided for us. But the routines I'm thinking of that feel the most joyful are the ones we choose for ourselves.

Here are some of my favorite routines:
- I begin my mornings with a hot beverage (almost always coffee), and then do the three things that center me for the day (see August 1);
- My husband and I end almost every day with Evening Appreciations (see September 5);
- I try to take a walk in nature each day if at all possible;
- Once a month my husband and I pick an organization or cause we believe in and send a donation.

Each of these regular practices add joy to my life. I am grateful for their comforting presence. I wonder what routines in your life bring you joy?

Louisa May Alcott (1832–1888), American novelist and poet

DECEMBER 17

Be Useful

This is the true joy in life, being used for a purpose recognized by yourself as a mighty one. Being a force of nature instead of a feverish, selfish little clod of ailments and grievances, complaining that the world will not devote itself to making you happy.

—George Bernard Shaw

Eleanor Roosevelt, in her book, *You Learn by Living*, wrote, "Someone once asked me what I regarded as the three most important requirements for happiness. My answer was: 'A feeling that you have been honest with yourself and those around you; a feeling that you have done the best you could both in your personal life and in your work; and the ability to love others.' But there is another basic requirement and I can't understand now how I forgot it at the time: that is the feeling that you are, in some way, useful."

The George Bernard Shaw quote helps me keep looking for ways to add to the greater good. At the end of my mother's life she entered a hospice facility. Each day I visited I was greeted by an older man who would smile and offer a cheery wish: "I hope your day is bright." Once I told him he was a burst of sunshine in a sad place. "Oh I hope so," he said. "This is now my mission in life. I can't much see to read or write, but I can offer what comfort I can for as long as I have left." His words brought me to tears. Instead of bemoaning his fate, he used his last days to be of service.

Today I am thinking of all the ways we humans can be useful. Certainly our work is one. But beyond that, we always have the chance to lift each other up. I intend to do more of that.

George Bernard Shaw (1856–1950), Irish playwright

DECEMBER 18

Overcome Pessimism

Optimistic young adults stay healthier throughout middle age and, ultimately, live longer than pessimists.

—Angela Duckworth

One thing I've learned about life is that if I had listened to every pessimistic prediction that came my way, I would not have tried any of the things I've done. I think back forty years ago to when I first became director of an early care and education program. These were some of the pessimistic predictions I heard: "Forty percent of your staff will leave each year; Dealing with parents will be a nightmare; No one will respect your work."

My first decision as director was to reject that pessimism. And because I did, I began reaching out to community members, forming an advisory board, finding my courage, asking for help from university professors and business people I didn't know, making the case that quality for our youngest citizens is everyone's business. Board members wrote grants in support of program needs, taught me how to do so myself, and soon important initiatives were underway.

I vowed that all staff would feel valued, and promised myself to do everything in my power to give them the working conditions they deserved. We set a goal to get pay and benefits as close to public school range as possible. At meetings, we practiced talking about our work with pride, remembering Eleanor Roosevelt's words, "No one can make you feel inferior without your consent." We created respectful and mutually supportive partnerships with families. None of the dire predictions came true because we simply would not accept them. Today I am remembering that I do not have to let pessimism keep me from moving forward in authentic, heartfelt ways. I can replace pessimism with trust in my inner knowing.

Angela Duckworth, American psychology professor and science author

DECEMBER 19

Music Makes Things Better

*Music produces a kind of pleasure which
human nature cannot do without.*

—Confucius,
The Book of Rites

I feel so much better when I surround myself with music. Even though I know this, it's only been recently that I've realized I can use music to make unpleasant tasks a whole lot easier.

Here's an example: I dislike cleaning my kitchen when I'm doing the serious things like scouring the oven or scrubbing out the refrigerator. In the past I've often procrastinated about these chores — a long time. The other day I created a game for myself to kick start my work. I decided to play some of my favorite holiday music for twenty minutes to see how much I could get done if I worked really hard during that time.

Not only did the challenge get me going and motivate me to use some real elbow grease, I also realized how much nicer it was to work with fun music playing. I ended up doing another twenty minutes and sanitizing my garbage cans as well. It was a win. Why I haven't thought of that strategy years ago, I don't know, but I gladly pass it on to you today.

From now on, I intend to look for ways that music can make everything a little better.

Confucius (551–479 BC), Chinese philosopher

DECEMBER 20
Arc of the Moral Universe

*The arc of the moral universe is long,
but it bends toward justice.*

—Martin Luther King Jr.

Martin Luther King Jr. used the famous quote above in his speeches, acknowledging the originator of the words as theologian Theodore Parker, who published sermons that were widely read in his time, many of them against slavery. Martin Luther King Jr. read and analyzed a number of great thinkers as he studied to receive his PhD in systematic theology from Boston University in 1955. Many of these thoughts became part of Dr. King's most famous speeches.

The political realities of our world today can often feel gloomy and disheartening. It's hard to witness the hateful rhetoric and extreme divisions. When I find myself feeling most discouraged, I remember that over the long reach of history, the arc of the universe has indeed bent toward justice. I think this happens, though, not by inevitability, but because of the efforts of people who take action based on unconditional positive regard for others. I do not believe that selfish efforts will ultimately prevail. And I believe there are enough of us who are prepared to work hard on behalf of justice that the arc of the universe will indeed continue to bend that way.

Martin Luther King Jr. (1929–1968), American minister and civil rights activist, quoting American theologian Theodore Parker (1810–1860)

DECEMBER 21

Do for Others without Losing Myself

*One of the great ironies of life is this:
He or she who serves almost always benefits
more than he or she who is served.*

—Gordon B. Hinckley,
Standing for Something

Booker T. Washington, American author and presidential advisor to Abraham Lincoln, wrote, "those who are happiest are those who do the most for others." I believe that to be true, with one caveat: while doing for others, we must also do for ourselves.

Service to others is indeed gratifying. Gordon B. Hinckley is right. Caring for other people and working for causes we believe to be important can bring great satisfaction. But martyrdom is not noble; it is unhealthy and dangerous.

Today is a great time to remember that as I provide help for others I must also be a good friend to myself. I will not overwork to the point of exhaustion, or forget to feed myself nourishing meals, or think that other people's needs are more important than my own.

I am finding a healthy balance between service and self-care.

Gordon B. Hinckley (1910–2008), American religious leader and author

DECEMBER 22
Be Beautiful

To be beautiful means to be yourself.
You don't need to be accepted by others.
You need to accept yourself.

—Thich Nhat Hanh

Believing ourselves to be genuinely beautiful is not about outer appearance or gender. It's about recognizing the majesty of our core being, our authentic self and inner guide. Thich Nhat Hanh is right. To see ourselves as truly beautiful, it takes complete self-acceptance.

Over the course of this past year, I've written much about self-acceptance, about letting go of judgment and not expecting perfection of ourselves. I am a work in progress when it comes to these ideas. I suspect we all are. That may be one of the greatest lessons we are here to learn in this earth school, to one day be able to see ourselves as we truly are – nothing but beautiful.

I send loving wishes to you on this journey. I'll be right there beside you.

Thich Nhat Hanh (1926–2022), Vietnamese Buddhist monk, peace activist, author and teacher

DECEMBER 23
Miracles Abound

*There are only two ways to live your life.
One is as though nothing is a miracle. The other
is as though everything is a miracle.*

—Albert Einstein

Abraham Maslow was an American psychologist best known for creating Maslow's hierarchy of needs, a theory of psychological health which describes how human needs must be fulfilled as a matter of priority, beginning with the most basic and leading eventually to self-actualization. He believed when humans were able to reach their highest potential, they would be able to understand the miracle of life. He wrote: "The sacred is in the ordinary…it is to be found in one's neighbors, friends and family, in one's own backyard…To be looking elsewhere is to me a sure sign of ignorance that everything is miraculous."

Today I am taking to heart the wisdom of Einstein and Maslow, choosing to live my life as though everything is a miracle. That way of thinking means it's not as easy to dismiss anything as unimportant. Certainly, it calls us to see the miracle in every human being. That means we have the inconvenient and difficult task of caring about the well-being of everyone. If each person is a miracle, then it is harder to dismiss them because we don't agree with their politics, or turn our backs on them because they live far away from us.

At times it feels overwhelming to live in a world filled with miraculous people who all need our love and concern. Today if I feel the weight of that crushing task, I'll remind myself of the words of nineteenth century American author, historian and minister, Edward Everett Hale (see June 3) who wrote: "I am only one but I am one. I cannot do everything, but I can do something. And I will not let what I cannot do interfere with what I can do."

Albert Einstein (1879–1955), German-born theoretical physicist

DECEMBER 24

Hope

*Nothing can be done without
hope and confidence.*

—Helen Keller

As I began this year of writing, I described my desire to bring hope to myself – and to you. Sharing the tools and learning I've developed over my lifetime has reminded me of the power of optimism and trust. Writing about serious subjects has reminded me of the need for humor. We must take our work in this world seriously, but not ourselves.

As I looked for appropriate quotes for each daily entry in this book, the words of people from many nations and walks of life and periods of history confirmed my unshakable belief that love is stronger than any negative force brought against it. I will have to trust that it's done the same for you. Because Helen Keller is right. If we lose hope, then all else is lost.

As many celebrate Christmas Eve today, American poet Emily Dickinson's words seem most appropriate:

"Hope is the thing with feathers –
That perches in the soul –
And sings the tune without the words –
And never stops – at all."

Helen Keller (1880–1968), American author and disability rights advocate

DECEMBER 25
Heal the World through Joy

Once upon a time, when women were birds, there was a simple understanding that to sing at dawn and to sing at dusk was to heal the world through joy. The birds still remember what we have forgotten, that the world is meant to be celebrated.

—Terry Tempest Williams,
When Women Were Birds

On a day when many around the world are observing the Christmas holiday, I urge us all to remember the power of joy. I believe, as Terry Tempest Williams does, that our world must be celebrated. And there are countless gifts to celebrate. I've written about many of them in these pages over the past year. And you know many more in your own hearts.

If you ever feel discouraged, I want to remind you of bells ringing, forsythia bursting, breath freezing, waves rolling, babies sighing, new books opening, coffee brewing, work on behalf of justice, the lilt of rain...Oh, and the taste of laughter and touch of heart song and the gulp of one moment of pure love. Each of these alone is worth any hardship the world can send our way.

Let's always remember the great privilege of being alive in this astounding, bewildering, difficult, and astonishingly beautiful world.

I don't think it's naïve or simplistic to believe that together we can heal our world by sharing our joy. It may be the only thing that will.

Terry Tempest Williams, American writer and conservationist

DECEMBER 26

Begin Each Day Anew

Many of us are inclined toward self-pity, not allowing for the balance of life's natural tragedies. We will face good and bad times – and they will pass. With certainty they will pass.

–Karen Casey,
Each Day a New Beginning

Each entry in this book represents a new day – a chance to begin again. Nothing that has happened to us in the past need control our future. Life is a continual cycle of ups and downs, but if we cooperate with the natural flow, we will be ok. I often remind myself of one of Abraham Lincoln's favorite phrases, "This too shall pass."

We have an opportunity to learn something from each day, but we need not take the heartaches and difficulties with us in order to keep the lesson. As we allow the full range of our emotions to be with us in all situations, we give our feelings permission to be present, to be heard, to teach us what we need to learn, and then to flow though us.

As we near the end of this calendar year and approach the beginning of a new one, I am promising myself to leave each day's concerns behind so I can begin anew in the morning. Jiddu Krishnamurti, the nineteenth century born Indian philosopher, speaker and author wrote, "Your eyes are blinded with your worries, you cannot see the beauty of the sunset."

Let's don't let that be us. Let's promise each other to release our worries at the end of each day. When I enjoy the beauty of each evening's sunset, I will be thinking of you.

Karen Casey, American author

DECEMBER 27
My Word is My Law

*Your mind believes what you tell it,
so tell it positive things.*

—Jennifer Milius

Because our mind takes quite literally the words it hears us say, paying attention to the way we talk is extremely important. So, instead of saying, "I'm not good at exercising," it would be much better to tell ourselves, "I'm in the process of learning to exercise more often." Telling other people, "I'm always late," not only cements that description of us in our own minds, but in theirs as well. It would be much more helpful to say, "I'm working on being on time."

For any of us who have children or work with children, this is an important skill to teach them. It's also extremely helpful to talk with them about what we want, instead of what we don't want. Asking children to "walk" instead of saying "don't run," helps their minds focus on the positive action we want them to take.

Today, and every day, I am paying attention to how I talk to and about myself, and to the children in my life. I am in the process of learning to speak in ways that affirm positive actions.

Jennifer Milius, American author

DECEMBER 28
Find the Beauty of Change

*In every change, in every falling leaf,
there is some pain, some beauty.
And that's the way new leaves grow.*

—Amit Ray

A couple I know who are in their early seventies have mightily resisted retirement and feel bitter about any changes in their careers at all. They rail against the signs of aging and complain about fluctuations in their relationships with their grown children. It's as if they want time to stand still forever. To me, this is fighting against a process that is natural and beautiful. It's a process with some pain, yes, but with much, much more beauty.

Nothing stays the same. That is not the way of nature and we are part of nature. To resist life's inevitable progression is to cause ourselves needless suffering. This is true whether we are twenty-one or ninety-one.

It's a paradox of life that in order for new things to grow in us, some things must die. To fight against those figurative deaths is folly. That kind of resistance keeps us from discovering the beauty of new growth.

Today I am embracing the sometimes tender feelings that come with change, remembering that letting go of the old is opening the door to lovely new beginnings.

Amit Ray, Indian author

DECEMBER 29

Learn to Crave the Things I Already Have

Being happy is something that each of us determines, it is not something that we find outside of ourself, it is within us and our choice.

—Catherine Pulsifer

Throughout this book, I have written many words about the power of acceptance, gratitude and personal choice. Catherine Pulsifer's writing speaks to me of the wisdom of choosing to be happy with my life just as it is now. That doesn't mean I'm not open to change; it simply means that I can be content and grateful for what I have in my life right this moment.

A good friend told me that he has learned to "crave the things he already has." I love that phrase. I put it to work often. Here's an example: I think to myself, "Wouldn't it be wonderful to live somewhere with a balcony that overlooks a view?" Then I give thanks for the fact that I already do.

I don't entertain thoughts like, "Wouldn't it be nice to live somewhere larger?" That's counterproductive and ungrateful. Instead I focus on the things in my life I already have that bring me joy. I like to imagine that when I complain, the universe looks at me and says, "Well, she doesn't appreciate what she has. Why give her any more?" And when I am grateful, the universe says, "Oh look at how much she's enjoying that. Let's give her more."

Today I am grateful for all that is part of my life. I am learning to crave the blessings I already have.

DECEMBER 30
Courage is the Heart of Encouragement

Strength is nothing without courage.

—West African proverb

The origin of the word "encouragement" is from the French *encoragier*– *en* meaning "in" and *corage* meaning "courage." So to feel encouraged is to connect with our courage. I hope over this past year I have helped you do that. I know there were many times as I wrote that I reminded myself to not give in to discouragement, but to remember the courageous core me. Often I found that reminder in the words of wise writers and thinkers throughout history.

In a clever little book, *The Tao of Pooh*, author Benjamin Hoff uses the characters from the A.A. Milne *Winnie the Pooh* collection to explain the wise philosophy of Taoism. It's a delightful approach I found surprisingly helpful. My son, a college professor who studies complex philosophical ideas, gave me the book. It's a gift that made a complicated philosophy accessible. In one passage, the author pretends to be having a conversation with Pooh as they study a painting called "the vinegar of life." The author asks, "In the painting why is Lao-tse smiling? [Lao-tse, often written Lao-Tzu, is the father of Taoism.] After all, that vinegar that represents life must certainly have an unpleasant taste, as the expressions on the faces of the other two men indicate. But, through working in harmony with life's circumstances, Taoist understanding changes what others may perceive as negative into something positive. Life itself, when understood and utilized for what it is, is sweet."

Much of what I've written over the past year has reminded me to find the sweetness in life's challenges. That takes courage, but I believe we have great courage, you and I. Let's let that courage be our encourager.

DECEMBER 31
Trust Myself

*Just trust yourself, then you
will know how to live.*

—Johann Wolfgang von Goethe

It has been a year of encouraging myself — and you, I hope. These pages will continue to be here for us, but now the ideas in them have also become part of who we are. Unconditional love has been the melody; hope the counterpoint.

We each have a core of inner wisdom that is always with us. Sometimes it is more accessible and other times more elusive, but it remains strong and unshakable, even if we lose touch with it for a moment.

My last encouragement for this year is to keep trusting myself and my authentic inner voice. With love and best wishes on this New Year's Eve, I urge you to do the same.

Johann Wolfgang von Goethe (1749–1832),
German poet, playwright, novelist, scientist

References

Achor, Shawn, *Big Potential: How Transforming the Pursuit of Success Raises Our Achievement, Happiness and Well-Being*. New York, NY: Currency, 2018.

Alcala, Elizabeth, "The Psychological Benefits of Watching Movies." *The Acronym*. December 8, 2020. https://sites.imsa.edu/acronym/2020/12/08/the-psychological-benefits-of-watching-movies/

Association for Psychological Science, "Repeated Exposure to Media Images of Traumatic Events May Be Harmful to Mental and Physical Health." *Association for Psychological Science*. September 4, 2012. https://www.psychologicalscience.org/news/releases/repeated-exposure-to-media-images-of-traumatic-events-may-be-harmful-to-mental-and-physical-health.html

Bateson, Mary Catherine, *Composing a Further Life: The Age of Active Wisdom*. New York, NY: Random House, 2011.

Bateson, Mary Catherine, *Composing a Life: Life as a Work in Progress – The Improvisations of Five Extraordinary Women*. New York, NY: Penguin Group, 1990.

Beattie, Melody, *Codependent No More: How to Stop Controlling Others and Start Caring for Yourself*. Center City, MN: Hazelden Publishing, 1986.

Blanchard, Sam, "Quality of Friends – NOT Quantity – Is the Key to Being Happy and Large Networks on Social Media Are No Match for Closeness in Real Life, Study Finds." *Daily Mail*. November 18, 2019. https://www.dailymail.co.uk/health/article-7698953/Quality-friends-NOT-quantity-key-happy-study-finds.html

Brooks, David, "How to Survive the Blitz." *The Atlantic*. March 29, 2020. https://www.theatlantic.com/ideas/archive/2020/03/virus-and-blitz/608965/

Brown, Brené, *Dare to Lead: Brave Work. Tough Conversations. Whole Hearts*. New York, NY: Random House, 2018.

Brown, Brené, *Daring Greatly: How the Courage to Be Vulnerable Transforms the Way We Live, Love, Parent, and Lead*. New York, NY: Avery Publishing, 2015.

Brown, Brené, *I Thought It Was Just Me (But It Isn't): Making the Journey from "What Will People Think?" to "I Am Enough."* New York, NY: Penguin Random House, 2008.

Brown, Brené, *Rising Strong: How the Ability to Reset Transforms the Way We Live, Love, Parent, and Lead*. New York, NY: Random House, 2017.

Bruno, Holly Elissa, *Happiness is Running through the Streets to Find You: Translating Trauma's Harsh Legacy into Healing*. Lincoln, NE: Exchange Press, 2020.

Cameron, Julia, *The Artist's Way, 25th Edition: A Spiritual Path to Higher Creativity*. New York, NY: Penguin Group, 2016.

Cannon, Joanna, *Three Things I'd Tell My Younger Self*. Glasgow, Scotland: The Borough Press, 2018.

Carlson, Richard, *Don't Sweat the Small Stuff and It's All Small Stuff: Simple Ways to Keep the Little Things from Taking Over Your Life*. New York, NY: Hachette Book Group, 1997.

Carnegie, Dale, *How to Stop Worrying and Start Living*. New York, NY: Pocket Books, 1985.

Cherry, Kendra, "What is Toxic Positivity?" *VeryWellMind*. Updated September 28, 2022. https://www.verywellmind.com/what-is-toxic-positivity-5093958

Christensen, Jan, *Magnificent Mind: Uncover Your Psychological Well Being So You Can Live in Heaven While on Earth*. Victoria, British Columbia: Tellwell Talent, 2020.

Cobb, Cynthia and Danielle Dresden, "What to Know About the Health Benefits of Sunlight." *MedicalNewsToday*. November 3, 2020. https://www.medicalnewstoday.com/articles/benefits-of-sunlight

Colburn, Dan, "Norman Cousins, Still Laughing." *Washington Post*. October 21, 1986. https://www.washingtonpost.com/archive/lifestyle/wellness/1986/10/21/norman-cousins-still-laughing/e17f23cb-3e8c-4f58-b907-2dcd00326e22/

Collins, Lily, *Unfiltered: No Shame, No Regrets, Just Me*. New York, NY: Harper Collins, 2018.

Dalai Lama, Desmond Tutu, and Douglas Abrams, *The Book of Joy: Lasting Happiness in a Changing World*. New York, NY: Penguin Random House, 2016.

Dalton-Smith, Saundra, "The 7 Types of Rest that Every Person Needs." *Ideas. Ted.Com*. January 6, 2021. https://ideas.ted.com/the-7-types-of-rest-that-every-person-needs/

Daniels, Joan and Nancy Burke, "Eating Rainbows." Rogel Cancer Center, University of Michigan Delagran, Louise, "How Does Nature Impact Our Wellbeing?" Earl E. Bakken Center for Spirituality and Healing, University of Minnesota. https://www.takingcharge.csh.umn.edu/how-does-nature-impact-our-wellbeing

Delagran, Louise, "How Does Nature Impact Our Wellbeing?" Earl E. Bakken Center for Spirituality and Healing, University of Minnesota. https://www.takingcharge.csh.umn.edu/how-does-nature-impact-our-wellbeing

Dembling, Sophia, "Hurtful Misconceptions Across the Introvert-Extrovert Divide." *Psychology Today*. August 13, 2012. https://www.psychologytoday.com/us/blog/the-introverts-corner/201208/hurtful-misconceptions-across-the-introvert-extrovert-divide

Dweck, Carol, Mindset: *The New Psychology of Success*. New York, NY: Ballantine Books, 2007.

Dyer, Wayne, *The Power of Intention: Learning to Co-Create Your World Your Way*. Carlsbad, CA: Hay House, 2004.

Eisenberger, Naomi and George Kohlrieser, "Lead with Your Heart, Not Just Your Head." *Harvard Business Review*. November 16, 2012. https://hbr.org/2012/11/are-you-getting-personal-as-a

Exploring Your Mind Staff. "5 Benefits of Mandalas." *ExploringYourMind*. April 15, 2020. https://exploringyourmind.com/5-benefits-of-mandalas/

Fairbank, Rachel, "Just 2 Minutes of Walking After a Meal Is Surprisingly Good for You." *New York Times*. August 4, 2022. https://www.nytimes.com/2022/08/04/well/move/walking-after-eating-blood-sugar.html

Ferruci, Piero, *The Power of Kindness: The Unexpected Benefits of Leading a Compassionate Life*. New York, NY: Penguin Group, 2006.

Frankl, Viktor, *Man's Search for Meaning*. Boston, MA: Beacon Press, 2006.

Garboden Murray, Carol, *Illuminating Care: The Pedagogy and Practice of Care in Early Childhood Communities*. Lincoln, NE: Exchange Press, 2021.

Gilbert, Elizabeth, *Eat, Pray, Love: One Woman's Search for Everything Across Italy, India and Indonesia*. New York, NY: Riverhead Books, 2007.

Gillihan, Seth, "5 Reasons We Worry, and 5 Ways to Worry Less." *Psychology Today*. October 7, 2016. https://www.psychologytoday.com/us/blog/think-act-be/201610/5-reasons-we-worry-and-5-ways-worry-less

Goodall, Jane, *Harvest for Hope: A Guide to Mindful Eating*. New York, NY: Grand Central Publishing, 2006.

Goodall, Jane, *The Book of Hope: A Survival Guide for Trying Times*. New York, NY: Celadon Books, 2021.

Grazer, Brian and Charles Fishman, *A Curious Mind: The Secret to a Bigger Life*. New York, NY: Simon & Schuster, 2015.

Greenlee, Gina, *Postcards and Pearls: Life Lessons from Solo Moments on the Road*. Chula Vista, CA: Aventine Press, 2008.

Haelle, Tara, "Your Surge Capacity is Depleted – It's Why You Feel Awful." *Elemental*. April 17, 2020. https://elemental.medium.com/your-surge-capacity-is-depleted-it-s-why-you-feel-awful-de285d542f4c

Happify Staff. "Reasons You Need at Least 8 Hugs a Day." *Happify*. https://www.happify.com/hd/8-reasons-why-you-need-at-least-8-hugs-a-day/

Harris, Dan, *10 % Happier: How I Tamed the Voice in My Head, Reduced Stress Without Losing My Edge, and Found Self-Help That Actually Works – A True Story*. New York, NY: HarperCollins Publishers, 2014.

Harvard Business Review, *On Communication*. Boston, MA: Harvard Business Review Press, 2013.

Haupt, Lyanda Lynn, *Rooted: Life at the Crossroads of Science, Nature, and Spirit*. New York, NY: Hachette Book Group, 2021.

Helgoe, Laurie, *Introvert Power: Why Your Inner Life is Your Hidden Strength*. Naperville, IL: Sourcebooks, Inc., 2013.

Hillman, James, *The Soul's Code: In Search of Character and Calling*. New York, NY: Grand Central Publishing, 1996.

Hoff, Benjamin, *The Tao of Pooh*. New York, NY: Penguin Group, 1982.

Holden, Robert, *Authentic Success: Essential Lessons and Practices from the World's Leading Coaching Program on Success Intelligence*. Carlsbad, CA: Hay House, 2011.

Hooper, Susan, "Why Poetry Matters Now – and Why It's Gaining Readers." *Psychology Today*. January 30, 2021. https://www.psychologytoday.com/us/blog/detours-and-tangents/202101/why-poetry-matters-now-and-why-it-s-gaining-readers

Houston, Jean, *A Mythic Life: Learning to Live Our Greater Story*. New York, NY: HarperCollins Publishers, 1996.

Huffington, Arianna, *The Sleep Revolution: Transforming Your Life, One Night at a Time*. New York, NY: Harmony Books, 2017.

Huffington, Arianna, *Thrive: The Third Metric to Redefining Success and Creating a Life of Well-Being, Wisdom, and Wonder*. New York, NY: Harmony Books, 2015.

Hulnick, Mary and Ron, *Remembering the Light Within: A Course in Soul-Centered Living*. Carlsbad, CA: Hay House, 2017.

Inskeep, Steve with Michael Pollan, "'In Defense of Food' Author Offers Advice for Health." *NPR*. January 1, 2008. https://www.npr.org/2008/01/01/17725932/in-defense-of-food-author-offers-advice-for-health.

Jampolsky, Gerald, *Love is Letting Go of Fear: Third Edition*. New York, NY: Celestial Arts, Random House, 2011.

Jantz, Gregory, "The Power of Positive Self-Talk." *Psychology Today*. May 16, 2016. https://www.psychologytoday.com/us/blog/hope-relationships/201605/the-power-positive-self-talk

Javier, Najooka, "Watching Movies Has Psychological Benefits, And Here Is All We Know About It." *The Bridge Chronicle*. October 12, 2021. https://www.thebridgechronicle.com/lifestyle/living/watching-movies-has-psychological-benefits-and-here-is-all-we-know-about-it.

Johns Hopkins Medicine, "Keep Your Brain Young with Music." https://www.hopkinsmedicine.org/health/wellness-and-prevention/keep-your-brain-young-with-music

Joseph, Stephen, "How to See Challenges as Opportunities." *Psychology Today*. November 5, 2016. https://www.psychologytoday.com/us/blog/what-doesnt-kill-us/201611/how-see-challenges-opportunities

Kabat-Zinn, Jon, *Wherever You Go, There You Are: Mindfulness Meditation in Everyday Life*. New York, NY: Hachette Book Group, 2005.

Kaufman, Scott Barry, "The Pressing Need to Quiet Our Egos." *Scientific American*. May 21, 2018. https://blogs.scientificamerican.com/beautiful-minds/the-pressing-need-for-everyone-to-quiet-their-egos/#:~:text=The%20goal%20of%20the%20quiet,for%20the%20esteem%20from%20others

Keltner, Dacher, "The Power of Kindness." *Mindful*. February 8, 2017. https://www.mindful.org/the-power-of-kindness/

Kingsolver, Barbara, *Animal, Vegetable, Miracle: A Year of Food Life*. New York, NY: Harper Perennial, 2017.

Kondo, Marie, *The Life-Changing Magic of Tidying Up: The Japanese Art of Decluttering and Organizing*. Berkeley, CA: Ten Speed Press, 2014.

Lamott, Anne, *Small Victories: Spotting Improbable Moments of Grace*. New York, NY: Penguin Group, 2014.

Lee, Ingrid Fetell, *Joyful: The Surprising Power of Ordinary Things to Create Extraordinary Happiness*. New York, NY: Hachette Book Group, 2018.

Leech, Joe, "10 Reasons to Get More Sleep." *Healthline*. January 6, 2022. https://www.healthline.com/nutrition/10-reasons-why-good-sleep-is-important

L'Engle, Madeleine, *The Irrational Season*. San Francisco, CA: Harper One, 1984.

Levine, Stephen, *A Year to Live: How to Live This Year as If It Were Your Last*. New York, NY: Bell Tower Publishing, 1998.

Lindbergh, Anne Morrow, *Gift from the Sea*. White Plains, NY: Peter Pauper Press, 2002.

Loehr, Jim and Tony Schwartz, *The Power of Full Engagement*. New York, NY: Simon & Schuster, 2003.

Maathai, Wangari, *Unbowed: A Memoir*. New York, NY: Anchor Books, 2007.

Martin, William, *The Parent's Tao Te Ching: Ancient Advice for Modern Parents*. Boston, MA: Da Capo Lifelong Books, 1999.

Mayo Clinic Staff. "Stress Relief from Laughter? It's No Joke." July 29, 2021. https://www.mayoclinic.org/healthy-lifestyle/stress-management/in-depth/stress-relief/art-20044456

McAnulty, Dara, *Diary of a Young Naturalist*. Minneapolis, MN: Milkweed Editions, 2020.

McCrae, James, "9 Reasons Why It's Okay to Be Weird." *Huffpost*. October 15, 2015. https://www.huffpost.com/entry/okay-to-be-weird_b_8234080

Mental Health Foundation United Kingdom Staff, "How Connecting with Nature Benefits Our Mental Health." Mental Health Awareness Week, 2021. https://www.mentalhealth.org.uk/sites/default/files/2022-06/MHAW21-Nature-research-report.pdf

Meyers, Karen, *The Truth about Death and Dying*. New York, NY: Facts on File, Inc., 2009.

Milne, A.A., *The House at Pooh Corner: Reissue Edition*. London, United Kingdom: Puffin Books, 1992.

Mind Staff, "Nature and Mental Health." *Mind*. https://www.mind.org.uk/information-support/tips-for-everyday-living/nature-and-mental-health/how-nature-benefits-mental-health/

Miranda, Lin-Manuel and Jonny Sun, *Gmorning, Gnight!: Little Pep Talks for Me & You*. New York, NY: Random House, 2018.

Moniuszko, Sara, "Have You Heard of Grounding or Earthing? What Is It and Why Is It Getting Attention?" *USA Today*. August 10, 2022. https://www.usatoday.com/story/life/health-wellness/2022/08/10/earthing-grounding-what-to-know/10264397002/

Mosconi, Lisa, *Brain Food: The Surprising Science of Eating for Cognitive Power*. New York, NY: Penguin Random House, 2018.

Nhat Hanh, Thich, *The Heart of the Buddha's Teaching: Transforming Suffering into Peace, Joy and Liberation*. New York, NY: Harmony Books, 1999.

Nhat Hanh, Thich, *The Pocket Thich Nhat Hanh*. Boulder, CO: Shambala Publications, 2012.

Nosrat, Samin, *Salt Fat Acid Heat*. New York, NY: Simon & Schuster, 2017.

Okumura, Kaki, "The Very Serious Benefits of Being Silly." *Forge*. January 19, 2021. https://forge.medium.com/i-had-to-up-my-goofiness-to-save-me-from-myself-6ebad23109d0

Pausch, Randy, *The Last Lecture*. Westport, CT: Hyperion Press, 2008.

Pipher, Mary, *Cultivating Joy*. Exchange Magazine. September/October 2021

Remen, Rachel Naomi, *Kitchen Table Wisdom: Stories That Heal*. New York, NY: Riverhead Books, 1996.

Rogers, Fred, *The World According to Mister Rogers: Important Things to Remember*. New York, NY: Hyperion, 2003.

Roosevelt, Eleanor, *You Learn by Living: Eleven Keys for a More Fulfilling Life.* New York, NY: Harper & Row, 1960.

Rosenow, John, *Living Long & Living Well: Inspiring Stories of Creating and Contributing During the Wisdom Years.* Lincoln, NE: Wisdom Oak Press, 2014.

Rosenow, Nancy, *Heart-Centered Teaching Inspired by Nature: Using Nature's Wisdom to Bring More Joy and Effectiveness to Our Work with Children.* Lincoln, NE: Dimensions Educational Research Foundation, 2012.

Rubin, Gretchen, *The Happiness Project: Or, Why I Spent a Year Trying to Sing in the Morning, Clean My Closets, Fight Right, Read Aristotle and Generally Have More Fun.* New York, NY: HarperCollins Publishers, 2009.

Ruiz, Don Miguel, *The Four Agreements: A Practical Guide to Personal Freedom (A Toltec Wisdom Book).* San Rafael, CA: Amber-Allen Publishing, 1997.

Ruiz, Don Miguel, *The Mastery of Love.* San Rafael, CA: Amber-Allen Publishing, 1999.

Santi, Jenny, "The Secret to Happiness is Helping Others." *Time Collection.* https://time.com/collection/guide-to-happiness/4070299/secret-to-happiness/

Schiffman, Richard, "Laughter May Be Effective Medicine for These Trying Times." *The New York Times.* October 1, 2020. https://www.nytimes.com/2020/10/01/well/mind/laughter-may-be-effective-medicine-for-these-trying-times.html

Schonert-Reichl, Kimberly and Shelly Hymel, "Educating the Heart as Well as the Mind: Social and Emotional Learning for School and Life Success." ERIC. 2007. https://eric.ed.gov/?id=EJ771005

Seligman, Martin, *Authentic Happiness: Using the New Positive Psychology to Realize Your Potential for Lasting Fulfillment.* New York, NY: Simon & Schuster, 2002.

Seppala, Emma, Christina Bradley, and Michael Goldstein, "Research: Why Breathing Is So Effective at Reducing Stress." *Harvard Business Review.* September 29, 2020. https://hbr.org/2020/09/research-why-breathing-is-so-effective-at-reducing-stress

Singer, Michael A., *The Untethered Soul: The Journey Beyond Yourself.* Oakland, CA: New Harbinger Publications and Noetic Books, 2007.

Smith, Maggie, *Keep Moving: Notes on Loss, Creativity, and Change.* New York, NY: Simon & Schuster, 2020.

Solly, Meilan, "British Doctors May Soon Prescribe Art, Music, Dance, Singing Lessons." *Smithsonian.* November 8, 2018. https://www.smithsonianmag.com/smart-news/british-doctors-may-soon-prescribe-art-music-dance-singing-lessons-180970750/

Stanborough, Rebecca Joy, "Benefits of Reading Books: How It Can Positively Affect Your Life." *Healthline.* October 15, 2019. https://www.healthline.com/health/benefits-of-reading-books

Stanborough, Rebecca Joy, "What is Vibrational Energy?" *Healthline.* November 14, 2020. https://www.healthline.com/health/vibrational-energy

Stibich, Mark, "10 Big Benefits of Smiling." *VeryWellMind.* September 10, 2022. https://www.verywellmind.com/top-reasons-to-smile-every-day-2223755

Terrones, Nick, *A Can of Worms: Fearless Conversations with Toddlers.* Lincoln, NE: Exchange Press, 2021.

Van der Kolk, Bessel, *The Body Keeps the Score: Brain, Mind and Body in the Healing of Trauma.* New York, NY: Penguin Group, 2015.

Ware, Bronnie, *Top Five Regrets of the Dying: A Life Transformed by the Dearly Departing.* Carlsbad, CA: Hay House, 2019.

Wenner, Melinda, "The Serious Need for Play." *Scientific American Mind.* February 1, 2009. https://www.scientificamerican.com/article/the-serious-need-for-play/

Weston, Phoebe, "Look Up, Look Down: Experts Urge Us to Take a Closer Look at the Concrete Jungle." *The Guardian.* April 30, 2020. https://www.theguardian.com/environment/2020/apr/30/an-opportunity-to-experts-urge-us-to-take-a-closer-look-at-nature-aoe

Williams, Terry Tempest, *When Women Were Birds.* London, United Kingdom: Picador Books, 2013.

Winfrey, Oprah, *What I Know for Sure.* New York, NY: Flatiron Books, 2014.

Wycklendt, Megan, "Six Reasons You'd Be Happier If You Stopped Saying 'Busy.'" *Washington Post.* March, 17, 2015. https://www.washingtonpost.com/news/inspired-life/wp/2015/03/17/six-reasons-why-you-shouldnt-use-the-b-word-so-much/

Yenigun, Sami, "Play Doesn't End With Childhood: Why Adults Need Recess Too." *NPREd.* August 6, 2014. https://www.npr.org/sections/ed/2014/08/06/336360521/play-doesnt-end-with-childhood-why-adults-need-recess-too

About the Author

Nancy Rosenow is founder and retired CEO of Dimensions Educational Research Foundation, home of Exchange Press, Nature Explore, Dimensions Education Programs, and administrative partner for the World Forum Foundation on Early Care and Education. She has been an early childhood educator, program director and workshop facilitator, and has written books and articles for various publications. She lives in Lincoln, NE with her husband John and has two children, two children-in-law and three grandchildren.

www.ingramcontent.com/pod-product-compliance
Lightning Source LLC
Chambersburg PA
CBHW050100170426
43198CB00014B/2404